INDIA-VIETNAM STRATEGIC PARTNERSHIP

Exploring Vistas for Expanded Cooperation

INDIA-VIETNAM STRATEGIC PARTNERSHIP

Exploring Vistas for Expanded Cooperation

Edited by

VIJAY SAKHUJA

India-Vietnam Strategic Partnership: Exploring Vistas for Expanded Cooperation
   Vijay Sakhuja (Ed)

ISBN 978-81-8274-549-0

First Published in 2011

Published by
PENTAGON PRESS
206, Peacock Lane, Shahpur Jat,
New Delhi-110049
Phones: 011-64706243, 26491568
Telefax: 011-26490600
email: rajan@pentagonpress.in
website: www.pentagonpress.in

Printed at Avantika Printers Private Limited.

Contents

Preface

India has had a long tradition of close ties with Vietnam. The friendly and cooperative relationship between India and Vietnam cannot be over-emphasised. Throughout the past 60 years of our independence, India and Vietnam have consistently supported each other on core areas of national interest.

Vietnam's achievements are remarkable and India has always taken pride in acclaiming them. In recent times, Vietnam's transformation including its 'doi moi' – economic reforms have been greatly admired. Vietnam as a rapidly expanding economy with GDP growth rate of over 8 percent is already making a mark in terms of exports, FDI, joint ventures, etc. Militarily and strategically, it is an important player in the Asia-Pacific and as a leading member of ASEAN, it is deeply engaged in issues of security and peace in the region as well as economic integration within ASEAN and with its partners.

In 2010, Vietnam hosted the ASEAN-India Summit as well as the East Asia Summit. India attaches great importance to its relationship with Vietnam and countries of ASEAN as well as East Asia. As India progresses in its Look East Policy, its engagement with Southeast and East Asia is a major step in closer relations and economic integration and Vietnam's support in the ASEAN-driven institutions, therefore, becomes crucial.

The situation in the Asia-Pacific continues to be volatile with a number of recent incidents. In this regard China's stance on the contentious issue of South China Sea islands in which Vietnam is also one of the claimants assumes importance. It is also noteworthy that the US, the preponderant power in the Asia-Pacific, is showing renewed interest after a perceived neglect of the region for nearly eight years. On the backdrop of these developments, the

Vietnamese perspective on issues of security and stability as well as economic outlook is particularly important.

The India-Vietnam bilateral relationship has been marked by high level exchanges all throughout. On a number of political issues, there has been close consultation. India is thankful for Vietnam's support for India's Permanent Membership in the United Nations. Both sides enjoy excellent defence cooperation. On the economic side, the two-way bilateral trade has now crossed 2.5 billion US dollars, though it is still heavily in India's favour. India, therefore, needs to find ways and means to rectify the situation. There are also a number of Indian investments in Vietnam. It will be desirable if proposals of major Indian investments which are pending fructify soon. India was the first country to explore opportunities in the natural gas fields in Vietnam. Overall, the level of trade or investment is very small, certainly not commensurate with the political understanding and friendship that exist between the two.

It is important that close friends sit together and evaluate what needs to be done or rectify the state of bilateral relations so that the friendship is sustained and strengthened. India believes that Vietnam attaches the same kind of high priority that India attaches to Vietnam. It is in this context that India and Vietnam need to do a stock-taking of our relationship so that newer vistas of cooperation can be explored. This volume will hopefully help Indian and Vietnamese policy makers, practitioners, academicians and general public to understand each other better for enhancing bilateral relations.

Ambassador Sudhir T. Devare
Director General
Indian Council of World Affairs

Introduction

The long history of cultural contacts dating back to ancient times and the close ties of friendship between India and Vietnam led by Prime Minister Nehru and President Ho Chi Minh have acted as catalyst for sustained friendly and cordial relations between the two sides. India enthusiastically welcomed the unification of Vietnam in 1976 and during the Cold War, both sides maintained diplomatic and political contacts. However, there was nominal bilateral trade and minimal security cooperation despite their close relations with the Soviet Union.

At the end of the Cold War, Vietnam lost its strategic guarantor i.e. Soviet Union and it began to adapt to the new security environment, took steps to normalize its relations with the neighbours, opened its economy and subsequently joined the ASEAN in 1995. India too responded to the post-Cold War environment and announced the Look East Policy which heralded a new era of politico-economic engagements with Southeast Asian countries. These developments enabled both India and Vietnam to further shore up their earlier ties.

In 2007, India and Vietnam signed the New Strategic Partnership that envisages bilateral political and economic engagements, security and defence cooperation, scientific and technological capacity building and enhanced cultural contacts. Further, the two sides also committed themselves to diversifying and deepening relationship and work closely in regional and multilateral forums to address the rapidly changing international environment.

As part of its Look East Policy, India acknowledges Vietnam's position and role in the ASEAN. India remains committed to the ASEAN principles of friendship and cooperation, supports the ASEAN Regional Forum (ARF), acknowledges the viability of the East Asian Summit (EAS) and accepts other ASEAN initiatives such as the ASEAN Defence Ministers' Meeting + 8.

Since the signing of the New Strategic Partnership, India and Vietnam have deepened their relationship and expanded their economic interactions in several sectors through cooperation between Chambers of Commerce and Industry, constituting Joint Business Council, and other initiatives for economic development. These engagements have paved the way for exchange of information on trade opportunities and business investments. There has also been some progress in sharing knowledge in the field of biotechnology, health and agriculture. India has expressed its interest to improve connectivity with Vietnam through road, aviation and shipping links.

The defence and security relations between India and Vietnam too have made significant progress and cover several facets including high level visits, military training and joint exercises. These foster military to military contacts aimed at capacity building to address issues of common concerns such as terrorism, piracy, sea-lane security, environmental pollution and other non-traditional security threats.

At another level, India and Vietnam must contend with a rising China. Interestingly, India and Vietnam, in the past, engaged in border war with China. Further, Vietnam has territorial disputes in the South China Sea and India too is concerned about the Chinese military modernisation and also its military and nuclear cooperation with some of the South Asian countries.

In geostrategic terms, India and Vietnam are maritime states and are highly dependent on sea based commerce for their economic vitality. Their geographic location bestows on them the responsibility to protect international shipping routes in the Indian Ocean and the South China Sea. The ongoing developments in the South China Sea involving China, some ASEAN countries that have territorial claims in the region and the US, are of concern to India. This is so because nearly 55 percent of Indian trade passes through the region and its safety and security is critical for India's economic prosperity. By virtue of its eastbound trade, India is a stakeholder in the evolving security developments in East Asia.

This edited volume emerges as a result of a conference in New Delhi at which papers were presented highlighting the conformation of the cognition that India and Vietnam must strengthen their strategic partnership and explore newer vistas for enhanced cooperation. The conference was built around four broad themes and the paper presenters attempted to address a number of issues including (a) The evolving politico-diplomatic order in the Asia Pacific region and the role of multilateral institutions such as the EAS; (b) the current status of India-Vietnam bilateral trade and opportunities for expanding economic relations; (c) vistas for broadening Indo-Vietnamese defence cooperation; and (d) contemporary developments in South China Sea and its impact on India and Vietnam.

The Contributors

Ambassador S.T. Devare is Director General, Indian Council of World Affairs, New Delhi.

Prof. Y. Yagama Reddy is a faculty member at the Centre for Southeast Asian & Pacific Studies, Sri Venkateswara University, Tirupati.

Dr. Nguyen Huy Hoang is Director of the Department of Economic, Political and International Studies, Institute for Southeast Asian Studies, Vietnam Academy of Social Sciences.

Mr. Shantanu Srivastava is Managing Director & CEO, Ishan International Pvt. Ltd. and Managing Director, Norvis Holdings (S) Pte. Ltd.

Dr. Saroj K. Mohanty is Professor/Senior Fellow at the Research and Information System for Developing Countries (RIS), New Delhi.

Dr. Tran Truong Thuy is Research Fellow and Director of the Program for South China Sea Studies at the Diplomatic Academy of Vietnam (DAV).

Dr. Vijay Sakhuja, is Director (Research), Indian Council of World Affairs, New Delhi.

Prof. K. Raja Reddy is a senior teacher and former Director of the Centre for Southeast Asian and Pacific Studies, Sri Venkateswara University, Tirupati.

Dr. Pankaj Jha is Associate Fellow at Institute for Defence and Strategic Studies (IDSA), New Delhi.

Dr. Binoda Kumar Mishra is a Fellow at Maulana Abul Kalam Azad Institute of Asian Studies (MAKAIAS), Kolkata.

P.V. Rao has served as Professor of Political Science and Director, Centre for Indian Ocean Studies, Osmania University.

Dr. Tridib Chakraborti is Professor in the Department of International Relations, Jadavpur University, Kolkata.

1

Emerging India: Need for Action Oriented Inclusive Approach in the Context of Asia-Pacific Multilateralism

Y. Yagama Reddy

While speaking eloquently of the "deeper urge of the mind and spirit of Asia which has persisted in spite of the isolationism which grew up during the years of European domination",[1] Jawaharlal Nehru explained the Asian identity in a nutshell that "we are of Asia and the people of Asia are nearer and closer to us than others". Underlining the need for regionalism and institutionalization of cooperation and mutual understanding, he further noted: "we have many problems in common, especially in the Pacific and in the southeastern region of Asia, and we have to cooperate together to find solutions".[2]

Thus, the phrases such as "One Asia", "Asian Century", "Asian Community", "Asian Identity" and "Asian-ness", which have gained momentum in recent years, are not altogether new. Jawaharlal Nehru was thus far ahead of the present day propositions of the Asian Solidarity, given the fact that he envisioned Asia as an integrated whole and stressed Asian solidarity as a precondition in order for Asia to lend its legitimate weight to world politics.[3] Other leading Asian nationalists, like Indonesia's Sukarno, Vietnam's Ho Chi Minh and Burma's Aung San, had also seen regionalism as an important instrument in advancing decolonization. To the nationalist leaders, Asia seemed to be a reasonable basis to develop cooperation in the post-colonial context. Pan-Asianism was essentially a top-down construction, with India and Indonesia playing a leading role in it. Following its debut at a multilateral forum when it was invited to the Paris Peace Conference in 1919 as one of the victorious powers of World War I, Japan subscribed to the framework of an inclusive and multilateral approach to regionalism.[4]

India, which was considered as a leader of pan-Asian efforts, was looked upon to garner greater economic and political weight in Asia in view of its physical connectivity to large parts of Asia, its wherewithal for enhancing economic cooperation in South Asia and its institutional synergies for deepening defence and security cooperation in Asia.[5] India's emerging influence in East and Southeast Asia owes much to its geography, economic, and historical ties. India's geographic position, military strength, and natural resources impressed so much the British India's Viceroy, Lord Curzon, as to proclaim that the master of India would become the greatest power on the Asian continent.[6] However, India's engagement in the past with much of Asia, including Southeast and East Asia, was built on an idealistic conception of Asian brotherhood, based on shared experiences of colonialism and cultural ties. Meanwhile, the Non-Aligned Movement (NAM), which was launched at Belgrade in 1961, soon absorbed most of India's multilateral diplomatic attention. From the 1960s onwards, however, India's preoccupation with conflicts in the sub-continent precluded its involvement in Asian regionalism; and about the same time the Cold War cleavages had induced India to develop apathy towards multilateralism.

ASEAN: the Forerunner of Multilateralism in Asia

The Cold War, though frustrated the early post-war efforts for an Asian regional group, shaped an alternative approach to regional order. Southeast Asian countries drew towards each other to seek greater strength in self-reliance. They were convinced that together in the Association of Southeast Asian Nations (ASEAN), they could better overcome their problems. ASEAN members felt the need for a larger institutional framework within the "Asia Pacific" to address problems pertaining to security and the economic interdependence between Southeast Asia and Northeast Asia. Thailand's Prime Minister Khoman described ASEAN as the "first indigenous Asian organization" to be "initiated within the community of nations of the area to help themselves".[7] ASEAN has thus taken the lead in building up an East

Asian community, a model community into which countries in other regions might coalesce for a variety of reasons.[8] In the initial stages, ASEAN's lack of resolve in shaping the direction of Asian multilateralism had, however, made the non-ASEAN members little worried. Exposure to regional and international opinions paved the way for engagement; and, as Singapore Prime Minister Goh Chok Tong once observed, no country could remain immune from the pressure of world opinion.

There have been some interesting concepts elaborated like 'new world order', 'clash of civilizations', 'security community', 'international society', and 'regional integration', with varying interpretations on which there is little consensus. With the shift of the centre of gravity from the Atlantic to the Asia-Pacific and the relative decline of the US power, several countries are able to negate the US objectives in this region; and the emerging multilateralism is seen as a way to oppose American preeminence in the region. Some other strategic analysts also are critical of the existing alliances as being subordinate to the American interests.[9] There is some substance in this criticism, given the fact that the US bilateral security alliances (with Japan, South Korea, Thailand and the Philippines) remain strong; consequently, the regional security system what is viewed as an 'instrument of strategic insurance' makes its bilateral features in the Asia-Pacific strengthened.[10] It is in this context that the multilateral cooperation in Asia Pacific security marks a departure from a long tradition of bilateral security relations.

Asia-Pacific is diverse, complex and geographically too expansive. Yet, the Asian region, stretching from the Persian Gulf in the west, through the Himalayas and related mountain chains extending as far east as Greater Khingan Range (in eastern Russia), and further down to Australia in the South, portrays a degree of semblance in its physiographic (expansive mountainous topography skirted by the coastal plains) and its consequent drainage pattern formed by several rivers flowing into the Indian and Pacific oceans. This spatial realm forms an isosceles triangular in its shape, the equal sides of which are invariably formed by a long stretch of coastline from the Persian Gulf down up to South East Cape (Australia) and then to the Sea of Okhotsk (north of Japan), and the other side from the Persian Gulf to Greater Khingan Range is formed by the mountain chains that insulated this entire realm from the overland European influence for over centuries until the discovery of sea routes. This territory is popular in its regional character composed of West Asia (to a larger extent), South Asia, East Asia, Southeast

Asia and Australia. Besides geographical determinism that makes this part of Asia-Pacific region as an entity *per se*, historical momentum, political evolution and economic dynamism have conferred on this region a preponderant strategic significance, as evidently understood from all the geopolitical postulations advanced from the dawn of 20th century. If Halford Mackinder delineated this part of Asia-Pacific as the Inner (Marginal) Crescent and the Insular (Outer) Crescent in his Heartland theory, Nicholas Spykman projected it as 'Rimland', capable of exercising control over the Eurasian Heartland. As a logical corollary, this part of the Asia-Pacific had become the theatre for Cold War equations manifested in the Korean War, Indochina War, Australia, New Zealand, United States Security Treaty (ANZUS) and Southeast Asia Treaty Organization (SEATO).

For all its being a political laboratory for experimentation of Cold War ideologies, post-Cold War globalization has visualized the Asia-Pacific region as a key driver for technological innovation. Accounting for almost one-third of global GDP,[11] Asia-Pacific emerges to the position of leading global liberalization through its 'open regionalism' that subscribes to regionalism-oriented-multilateralism.[12] Having its focus on functional, action-oriented and inclusive multilateralism, this approach seeks to bring countries in the region together as equal partners to address challenges through voluntary and coordinated actions. The development of East Asian regionalism – giving allowance to the diversities, differences and historical antagonisms – has ensured the much needed regional cooperation in East Asia in a steadfast manner and thereby peace and security in the complex and dynamic region of Asia-Pacific.

Proliferated Multilateral Organizations and Ambivalence

Multilateral institutions, seen as mechanisms for a cohesive regional integration, have come into existence. Unfortunately, East Asia and the Asia-Pacific, though having the potential to contribute greatly to any future East Asian Community, have overlapping memberships. Mention may be made of pan-Pacific multilateral bodies – like the Asia Pacific Economic Community (APEC), a multilateral economic body, and the ASEAN Regional Forum (ARF), a multilateral security body – which have included not only the countries geographically lying in East Asia but several other extra-regional states. These regional organizations and institutions are also identified with the stigma of being "either too weak to be effective in conflict resolution/

management or are susceptible to manipulation by major players". In effect, as testified by Dr. Mohan Malik, Professor in Asian Geopolitics & Security Studies at the Asia-Pacific Center for Security Studies, Honolulu, all these regional organizations remain mute spectators to intra-state and regional conflicts.[13] Besides sluggishness coupled with firm resistance to reform, the proliferation of multilateral organizations in the Asia Pacific demonstrates a deep and growing ambivalence about who exactly comprises "the region". There is sharp disagreement over whether multilateralism should be East Asian or trans-Pacific in character. Sharp rise of nationalistic sentiment in the region in recent years – particularly in China, South Korea, and Japan – tends to impinge on the prospects of realizing East Asian community.[14] This prompted the strategic analysts Brian L. Job and Erin Williams to observe that "Asia Pacific multilateralism is in need of institutional innovation".[15]

East Asia Summit typifying pan-Asian Multilateralism

ASEAN-based multilateral institutions, like ARF, then ASEAN-plus-Three (APT) and East Asia Summit (EAS), through a series of ministerial conferences and multilateral dialogues over the last two decades since early 1990s, have projected "East Asian regionalism" onto the centre stage of global interest. One of the exciting developments today is the growing links between the ARF and other Asia Pacific multilateral forums. Other regional bodies, such as APEC and APT, which are viewed as competing against ARF, are rather complementary to the ARF. Although economic in orientation, APEC and APT help to reinforce the ARF process. In April 2005, the foreign ministers of the ten ASEAN member states signalled that the proposed EAS could develop into a more inclusive organization. Accordingly, the leaders' statement issued on 14 December 2005 (the 'Kuala Lumpur Declaration on the East Asia Summit') affirmed that "the EAS is intended to be an open, inclusive, transparent and outward-looking forum, with ASEAN as the driving force working in partnership with other participants of the East Asia Summit". EAS, which has consequently come to be known as ASEAN+6, is considered the first major step towards building an East Asian Community. Some viewed the EAS as an outgrowth of the East Asian Economic Caucus (EAEC), a concept put forward by Mahathir Mohammed, the former Prime Minister of Malaysia. But, Kishore Mahbubani, formerly a senior official in Singapore's Ministry of Foreign Affairs and Trade, looked upon the EAS as the real beginning of the Pacific century.[16] Australia has advanced the rationale for an Asia-Pacific Community that there is no existing institution that covers the whole region (including India) and includes the different issues such as economy, security and environment. Despite Chinese efforts to curtail India's influence, New Delhi came to be recognized as an Asia-Pacific power when it became the founder member of the EAS in 2005.

In the context of the EAS, Australia, New Zealand and India are seen by ASEAN as counterweights to China and Japan. Their participation will reassure Washington that the Summit will not become a bloc designed to exclude American influence from the Indo-Pacific region.[17] The US, which has its well-expressed concerns over China's aggressive territorial claims in the Pacific and Indian Ocean regions, suggested an international mechanism to solve the disputes over the South China Sea which is "pivotal" to regional stability.[18] Yet, the formidable challenge from China to the U.S. supremacy is economic, not military, in nature. Obvoiusly, Washington has shored up APEC modelled trans-Pacific multilateralism vis-à-vis an exclusive EAS type pan-Asian multilateralism; but its friends and allies have favoured pan-Asian multilateralism in the Asia-Pacific region as opposed to trans-Pacific multilateralism.[19] The US prefers institutions set in the wider Asia-Pacific context (ARF, APEC etc.) and primarily as complementary diplomatic instruments to its system of bilateral military alliances testifying to its unipolarity.[20] The 'web of interlocking bilateral relationships', as called by the former Malaysian Foreign Minister Tan Sri Gazhali Shyaffie, would lead to the multilateral level, within the framework of ASEAN.[21] Several American observers are also critical of the EAS and its earlier incarnation (APT) duplicating APEC's economic and ARF's security agendas and eventually undermining the trans-Pacific multilateralism.[22] About the same time, the loyal allies of the United States such as Japan, South Korea and Australia have opined the EAS as the magnetic force of a new geopolitical pole.[23]

Being wary of China's actions through the Shanghai Cooperation Organization (SCO) as challenging America's presence in the Central Asian region, the U.S. presence in the region is favoured to thwart any future bid by China to re-establish a China-led "East Asia Co-prosperity Sphere". Though Beijing considers "multilateralism as the panacea for the 21st century's security problems," its multilateral diplomacy clearly reveals China's preferences for a Sino-centric Asian order (unipolarity in Asia), as opposed to multipolarity at the global level, much to the detriment of the US.[24] China's objective of emerging as a "global great power that is second to none" or as the sole predominant power in the Asia-Pacific has also met with reaction from other regional states, particularly India, Japan, Vietnam and Indonesia.

Look East Policy – a Strategic Shift in India's Outlook of Multilateralism

India altered its perception of multilateral institutional mechanisms in the context of post-Cold War globalization and the consequential paradigm shift in the global power structure. India too has embarked on forging new partnerships with several countries cutting across the hitherto ideological parameters. India's vital role in the Asia-Pacific/East Asia rightfully emerges, as its emergent economic power rise and strategic capacity are leveraged in its diplomatic potential. The critical need for India's leveraging strategy of engagement with East Asia is vital as the region is replete with several traditional and non-traditional challenges that are ripe for regional competition and rivalry among states. India's "Look East" policy is more comprehensive with its "extended neighbourhood" encompassing not only the ASEAN, but also Northeast Asia, apart from Australia and New Zealand. The Indian Prime Minister Manmohan Singh hailed the "Look East" policy as "a strategic shift" in India's perspective to the extent of "intensifying the political dialogue, expanding trade and steadily enlarging people-to-people contacts between all the countries of the region".[25] This paradigm shift in India's geo-strategic and geo-economic perceptions provided new vistas of engagement in multilateralism.

While a host of factors including geography, economics, and historical ties are at the root of India's emerging influence in East and Southeast Asia, India's push toward the Pacific Ocean must be viewed through the prism of its northern neighbour. Indian perspectives tend to project China as a country with territorial ambitions. India's concerns also relate to Chinese encirclement of India, through what is loudly known as 'string of pearls strategy', in an attempt to establish a strategic presence in India's neighbourhood – port projects like Coco islands (Myanmar), Gwadar (Pakistan), Hambantota (Sri Lanka) and Chittagong (Bangladesh).[26] As China's influence in Southeast Asia has posed serious security concerns for India, India is looking towards ASEAN to carry forward a multilateral security order in the Asia-Pacific. About the same time, ASEAN, which had earlier entertained apprehensions over India's blue water navy and nuclear capabilities, looks at India's security needs as a factor emanating from the compulsions of the geopolitical position.[27] India, which does not have a historical legacy of invasion or domination in the region, is looked upon as an alternative by the ASEAN member countries to reduce their economic dependence on both China and Japan.[28] This is amply testified by the trade statistics. ASEAN exports (US$ 143.1 billion) in 1990 were twice larger than the China's exports (US$ 64.5 billion) and eight times larger than the India's exports. Even ten years later in 2000, ASEAN exports had been 70 per cent higher than China's exports. But in 2005, China's export earnings (US$ 763.2 billion) were 20 per cent larger than ASEAN's (US$ 626.9 billion). China's export expansion was phenomenal – an increase of 3.4 times in ASEAN and .5 times in India.[29]

India's Push toward Asia-Pacific

That India's presence in Southeast Asia is very much sought after is eloquently expressed by several distinguished commentators. For instance, Singapore's Foreign Minister noted, India's presence as being "a beneficial and beneficent one to all of us in South-east Asia"[30] and Singapore's Deputy Prime Minister observed "… a dynamic India would counterbalance the pull of the Chinese economy, and offer a more diversified basis for prosperity"….[31] Similarly, a Singapore diplomat stated that ASEAN countries "envisage India as a counter-balance to a possibly over dominant China in the future"….[32] Similar expressions have emerged from other quarters:

> "India can play in the security architecture of the wider Asia-Pacific region," Stephen Smith.[33]

India is to "become a psychological deterrent to China's increasing influence and gradual domination of this region", noted Meidyatama Suryodiningrat, the editor of the *Jakarta Post*.[34]

The inclusion of India, Australia and New Zealand is hailed as a partial balancer to the geopolitical weight of China within the grouping.[35]

Far beyond the perception that some countries in the Asia Pacific hoping for countering China are getting closer to India, India's role in East Asia goes much beyond "matching" or rivaling Beijing's forays in the region; instead, New Delhi has its own interests in that part of the world. India's role in the wider Asia-Pacific has been significant than the headway it has made with regional institutional mechanisms in the South Asia region.[36] Being apprehensive of India's great-power pretensions and distrustful of the "Look East" policy as being "counter-China" strategy unveiled by the Washington-

Tokyo-New Delhi grouping, Beijing has geared its diplomacy to confine India to the periphery of a future East Asia Community. China's military alliances and forward deployment of its naval assets in the Indian Ocean region impelled India to seeking access to the Vietnamese (Cam Ranh Bay), Taiwanese (Kaohsiung) and Japanese (Okinawa) ports for the forward deployment of Indian naval assets to protect India's shipping and trade routes and access to energy resources from the Russian Sakhalin province.[37] India is in a fundamentally competitive if not conflictual relationship with China in their joint quest for energy resources.

The two Asian powers, referred as "non-identical conjoined twins", continue to "suffer from a trust deficit and are increasingly concerned about each other's strategic intent", although leaders on both sides try to downplay the border sparring.[38] Though both consciously downplay their differences, "the two may never be friends, but will not go to war and will not queer the pitch beyond a point".[39] The maritime rivalry, likely to be intensified in the Indian and the Pacific Oceans ostensibly to safeguard their respective sea lanes of commerce and communication, will likely to intensify their mutual distrust and tensions.

The mounting economic and geopolitical stature of China and India lies at the base of their status as predominant powers in the region capable of wielding diplomatic clout in the context of multi-polarity. The phrases frequently used in the recent times, 'rise of China' and 'rise of India' do testify to their prominence as potential centres of political power and economic strength and as Asian giants giving credence to the concepts of Asian Century and New Asia.[40] The geoeconomic compulsions of the New Economic Order have added a maritime dimension to the Sino-Indian geopolitical rivalry protracted for the last 50 years.

Rationale behind India-Vietnam Strategic Partnership

China's emergence as a major strategic destabilizing entity occasioned a strategic naval dialogue between India and Vietnam for exchange of views on the options available to India and Vietnam to protect their maritime interests. India and Vietnam are both geostrategically important countries, vital to all major nations with a stake in the freedom of high seas. India and Vietnam share similarities based on history, geography and agrarian economy. Both had endured the colonial rule effectively at least for a century, say, the French in the case of Vietnam and the British in India. Independence had been won by the intense nationalist movements; and Vietnam was forced to embark on warfare against the French and then the United States to get its territory unified. The long coastline has warranted both these nations to equip with maritime capabilities in pursuit of defending their respective territorial sovereignty. Similarly, the vast expansive mountainous terrain becomes quite conducive to clandestine operations to the extent of threatening internal security. Like Ganges and Bramaputra rivers, Mekong has its origin in Tibet-Himalayan region of China; and thus both India and Vietnam are prone to river water disputes with China.

Sharing disputed borders with China, both have been subjected to military aggression by China. Russia, which had been a strategic ally of both India and Vietnam during the Cold War period, seemed to be quite soft on the Chinese neighbour who is engaged in building up military might and force projection capabilities. In the context of shared threat perception of India and Vietnam vis-à-vis China, building a bilateral strategic partnership based on the convergence of interests is the logical option.[41] As the bilateral ties between India and Vietnam have withstood post-Cold War strategic permutations, India needs to safeguard its commercial and strategic interests in Southeast Asia. India and Vietnam, as per the joint declaration made at the end of the state visit of the Prime Minister of the Socialist Republic of Vietnam H.E. Mr. Nguyen Tan Dung to India on July 4-6, 2007, resolved to establish a New Strategic Partnership encompassing bilateral relations in the political, economic, security, defence, cultural, scientific and technological dimensions and steer their cooperation in regional and multilateral fora.[42] There is need for India to conduct more bilateral naval exercises in the South China Sea along with Vietnam for theatre awareness. Though China stands guilty of strategically destabilizing both India and Vietnam's neighbourhood, India has been reluctant in pursuing its strategic objectives in a more pronounced manner.[43] For instance, India's reservations about the supply of variegated assortment of military hardware, including the locally designed surface-to-surface Prithvi missile to Vietnam, forced Hanoi to acquire defence hardware from India's traditional adversary, Pakistan.[44]

New Delhi's strategic partnerships with "China-wary" countries such as Japan, Vietnam, Indonesia, Taiwan and Mongolia are seen as logical diplomatic pursuit to counter Beijing's perceived encirclement of India. There is an imperative need for paying more attention to the China-specific dimensions of our strategic relations with the US, Japan, Vietnam and South

Korea. It is with the fear of becoming China's economic dependencies that many Southeast Asian countries are driven into courting Japan, India and Australia to leverage their strategic clout. Professor Mohan Malik, divided the responses of the Asian-Pacific states to China's rise into three categories.

(a) First-Tier – Balancing: India, Japan, Australia, Vietnam, Taiwan, Indonesia, and Mongolia are pursuing a clear balance-of-power vis-à-vis China by strengthening their security ties with the United States as well as with each other.

(b) Second-Tier – Balancing and Bandwagoning: South Korea, Thailand, the Philippines, Malaysia, Laos, East Timor and Singapore are both bandwagoning with and balancing (or hedging) against China.

(c) Third-Tier – Bandwagoning: North Korea, Pakistan, Burma, Russia, Cambodia, Bangladesh, Nepal, and some Central Asians countries and Iran are clearly bandwagoning with China – albeit, for entirely different motives.

China, whose 'geopolitical discomfort' is based on the assumption that the U.S., Japan, Australia and India would eventually form an informal quadrilateral alliance to contain China, has been pursuing 'exclusivist multilateral diplomacy' designed to erode U.S. hegemony through the establishment of regional organizations and institutions that exclude the United States (SCO, APT and EAS).[45] India's increasing role in the Asia-Pacific, with the firm support from the region's premier naval power, the United States, has facilitated India's enhanced relations with many Southeast Asian nations as well as Japan, South Korea and Australia, which have close ties with America.

Need for Action-oriented-inclusive Approach

It is rather difficult for the nations in the Asia-Pacific to ignore India's economic potentiality that would qualify India to emerge as an Asia-Pacific power, a status that would facilitate the evolution of a multipolar equation.[46] Given China's strategic presence in India's neighbourhood, it is imperative for India to evolve its mechanisms to defend its interests through its association in the Quadrilateral Initiative and the Japan's initiative "Asian Arc of Freedom".[47] New Delhi and Seoul's "long-term cooperative partnership", "Asia-Pacific alliance between India and Japan", "New Strategic Partnership" of India and Vietnam and India's "enhanced security" ties with Japan and Australia – all testify to India's "greater role in building the security architecture of the Asia-Pacific region".[48] Yet, India would prefer a multipolar power structure in the Asia-Pacific, since multipolarity allows independence and balancing among the major states, which is inhibiting the emergence of multiple poles of approximately equal power.[49] By endorsing the ASEAN Foreign Ministers decision towards the inclusion of the US and Russia as members of EAS, the Indian Defence Minister A.K. Antony, during his 3-day (3-5 September, 2010) visit to South Korea, asserted that India looks at the emerging architecture in East Asia as "open and inclusive" and considers itself as part of East Asia.[50] As the Asia-Pacific region evolves and Asia-Pacific century emerges, there has arisen the need for an approach to regional economic and security cooperation. The need for paying greater attention "to the entire Asia-Pacific region", has also been underscored by the Indian Prime Minister Manmohan Singh, who further added that India's attention "must seep into our defence and foreign policy planning as never before", by way of reciprocating the "palpable desire on the countries of this region to enhance cooperation with us".[51]

In the context India's Look East policy being acclaimed by the countries in its 'extended neighbourhood' encompassing the Asia-Pacific realm, India needs to harness the options and opportunities in the offing for realizing a multipolar power structure in the vibrant Asia-Pacific region. Towards this end, India needs to adopt an action-oriented and inclusive approach rather than a regionalism-oriented-multilateralism that could involve countries in the region as equal partners to address challenges through voluntary and coordinated actions.

NOTES

1. Amitav Acharya, *Regional Institutions and Security Order in Asia*, Centre for Peace and Development Studies, Goa: 2007.

2. For the text of Jawaharlal Nehru's speech at the Asian Relations Conference, see *Asian Relations: Report of the Proceedings and Documentation of the First Asian Relations Conference, New Delhi, March-April 1947*, Asia Relations Organization, New Delhi, 1948, p. 22. Also see S. Gopal (ed.), *Selected Works of Jawaharlal Nehru*, Second Series, Vol. II, Jawaharlal Nehru Memorial Fund, New Delhi, 1984, pp. 504-05.

3. Address by External Affairs Minister K. Natwar Singh at the seminar on *Europe and Asia: Perspectives on the Emerging International Order*, organized by the Observer Research Foundation, New Delhi, 19 November 2004, at http://www. meaindia.nic.in/ speech/ 2004/11/19ss02.htm

4. Hitoshi Tanaka and Adam P. Liff, *Japan's Foreign Policy and East Asian Regionalism*,

Council on Foreign Relations (CFR), New York and Washington, DC: December 2009. Also see Akiko Fukushima, "Japan's Emerging View of Security Multilateralism in Asia", *Security Multilateralism in Asia: Views from the United States and Japan*, Policy Papers, Institute on Global Conflict and Cooperation, University of California: Berkeley, 06-01-1999, at http://escholarship. org/uc/item/ 8cj4p21s

5. Rajendra K. Jain, "India, the European Union and Asian Regionalism", paper presented at the EUSA-AP Conference on *Multilateralism and Regionalism in Europe and Asia-Pacific,* Tokyo, 8-10 December 2005.

6. George N. Curzon, *The Place of India in the Empire,* J. Murray, London, 1909, p. 12.

7. Amitav Acharya, n.1.

8. Yeo Lay Hwee, "Realism and Reactive Regionalism: Where is East Asian Regionalism Heading?" *UNISCI Discussion Papers*, May 2005.

9. Douglas Paal, *Nesting the Alliances in the Emerging Context of Asia-Pacific Multilateral Processes: A U.S. Perspective,* July 1999, at http://iis-db.stanford. edu/ pubs/ 10077/ Paal.pdf

10. Kimie Hara, "Rethinking the 'Cold War' in the Asia-Pacific", *The Pacific Review*, Vol.12, No.4, 1999, pp. 515-536.

11. Kurt M. Campbell, "Statement Before the House Committee on Foreign Affairs Subcommittee on Asia, the Pacific, and the Global Environment", *Regional Overview of East Asia and the Pacific*, US Dept of State, Washington, DC, 3 March, 2010, at http://www.state.gov/p/ eap/rls/rm/2010/03/137754.htm

12. Cae-One Kim, "Multilateralism and Regionalism in a Globalizing World: A Perspective from Asia Pacific Region", Keynote Speech at the *Third EUSA Asia-Pacific International Conference,* 8-10 December 2005.

13. Mohan Malik, Testimony Before the US-China Economic and Security Review Commission on the *Strategies and Objectives of China's Foreign Affairs & Asian Reactions to China's Rise,* Washington, 18 March 2008.

14. Hitoshi Tanaka with Adam P. Liff, "The Strategic Rationale for East Community Building," in Jusuf Wanandi and Tadashi Yamamoto (eds.), *East Asia at a Crossroads*, Tokyo: Japan Center for International Exchange, 2008, pp. 90-104.

15. Brian L. Job and Erin Williams, 2008: "A Wake-Up Call for Regional Multilateralism?" 2008 Regional Security Outlook, The Council for Security Cooperation in the Asia Pacific (CSCAP), at www.cscap.org or www. cscap.ca

16. Kishore Mahbubani, "Rising Unity in East Test for Global Trade", *New Zealand Herald,* 19 November 2005.

17. Michael Richardson, "Australia-Southeast Asia relations and the East Asian Summit", *Australian Journal of International Affairs,* Vol. 59, No. 3, September 2005, pp. 351-365.

18. B. Raman, "Need for India-Vietnam Strategic Naval Dialogue", *Chennai Centre for China Studies Paper No.553,* 30 July 2010.

19. Mohan Malik, "The East Asia Community and the Role of External Powers: Ensuring Asian Multilateralism is not Shanghaied", *The Korean Journal of Defence Analysis*, XIX (4), Winter 2007, pp. 29-50.

20. Barry Desker, "New Security Dimensions in the Asia-Pacific", *Asia-Pacific Review*, Vol.15, No.1, 2008, pp. 56-75.
21. T. Soedjati Djiwandono, "The Strategic Dynamics of Post-Cold War Southeast Asia", in Denny Roy (ed.), *The New Security Agenda in the Asia-Pacific Region*, Macmillan Press Ltd., London: 1997.
22. Ralph Cossa, "East Asia Community-Building: Time for the United States to get on Board", *Policy Analysis Brief*, The Stanley Foundation, September 2007, pp.1–8.
23. "Meeting the Superpower: George Bush Should Treat Meeting China as an Opportunity, Not Just a Threat", *The Economist*, 19 November 2005.
24. Mohan Malik, n.19.
25. Harjit Singh, "Indo-ASEAN Summit – next phase in India's Look East Policy", (3 December 2007), *India News Line*, 10 April 2010.
26. D.S. Rajan, *India-China Connectivity: No Need to Over Hype*, Chennai Centre for China Studies, Paper No.526, 24 June 2010.
27. Mohit Anand, *India-Asean Relations: Analysing Regional Implications*, No.72, Institute of Peace and Conflict Studies, New Delhi, May 2009.
28. Amitav Acharya, "Will Asia's Past Be Its Future?" *International Security*, Vol. 28, No. 3, (2003/04), pp. 150-151.
29. "Merchandize Exports of ASEAN, China, and India", *ASEAN Secretariat: Studies Unit Brief*: Paper #10-2006, December 2006.
30. Amit Baruah, "India has Legitimate Interests in South East Asia: George Yeo," *The Hindu*, 24 January 2007.
31. Lee Hsien Loong, "The Future of Asian Economies," Speech delivered at the *Davos World Economic Forum*, 24 January 2003.
32. K. Kesavapany, "Dire Need for an Asian Renaissance," *Business Times* (Singapore), 28 March 2008.
33. Stephen Smith, *Australia and India: A New Partnership in the Asia Pacific Century*, Speech delivered at the Indian Council of World Affairs, New Delhi, 11 September 2008.
34. Meidyatama Suryodiningrat, "Is India Ready to be Part of Southeast Asia Again?" *Jakarta Post*, 18 June 2007.
35. Clarissa Oon, "West is Welcome in ASEAN plus 3," *Straits Times*, 1 November 2005.
36. Shankari Sundararaman, "Asia-Pacific Multilateralism and Role for India", Paper presented at the International Seminar on *India and East Asia: Prospects of Cooperation and Problems of Integration*, organized by the Centre for Southeast Asian & Pacific Studies, Sri Venkateswara University, Tirupati, 7-9 October 2009.
37. Mohan Malik, "Delhi and Beijing tread warily", *South Asia*, 14 February 2006, at http://www. atimes. com/atimes/ South_ Asia/HB14Df02.html.
38. Vijay, Sakhuja, "Maritime Multilateralism: China's Strategy for the Indian Ocean", *China Brief*, Vol. 9, Issue 22, 4 November 2009.
39. Mahendra Ved, "India, China need to cook up a win-win deal", *Newstraitstimes*, 19 April 2010.
40. Barleen Monarch and Zhitao Ding, "Asian Tigers, Hear Them Roar", *Beijing Review*, 7, 10-13 April 2005.

41. Subhash Kapila, "India-Vietnam Strategic Partnership: The Convergence of Interests", *South Asia Analysis Group Papers*, Paper no.177, 2.1.2001, at http://www.southasiaanalysis.org/ \papers2\paper177.htm

42. "Vietnam, India issue joint declaration on strategic partnership", *VietNamNetBridge,* 07/07/2007.

43. Pankaj Jha, "The India-Vietnam Partnership", *Institute of Peace & Conflict Studies*, #3006, 19 November 2009.

44. *IntelliBriefs*, 28 August 2007, "Despite India's Protests, Vietnam buys arms from Pakistan", at http://IntelliBriefs.blogspot.com/2007/08/despite-Indias-protests-Vietnam-buys.html.

45. Mohan Malik, note 13.

46. Sandy Gordon, "India and Asia-Pacific Security", in Gary Klintworth (ed.,), *Asia-Pacific Security: Less Uncertainty, New Opportunity*, Addison Wesley Longman Australia Pty Ltd., Melbourne, 1996, pp. 65-78.

47. R. Hariharan, "Asia's New Security Paradigm", *SAJOSPS*, July-December 2007.

48. Condoleezza Rice, "U.S.-India Civilian Nuclear Cooperation Agreement," 5 April 2006, *at http://www.state.gov/ secretary / rm / 2006/64146.htm*

49. *Walter C. Ladwig III,* "Delhi's Pacific Ambition: Naval Power, "Look East," and India's Emerging Influence in the Asia-Pacific", *Asian Security*, vol. 5, no. 2, 2009, pp. 87-113.

50. *The Hindu*, 4 September 2010.

51. "Asia-Pacific region needs greater attention, says Manmohan Singh", *The Hindu*, 14 September 2010.

2

Exploring Areas for Cooperation in Vietnam-India Economic Relations in the Context of ASEAN-India Free Trade Agreement

Nguyen Huy Hoang

Vietnam and India have always enjoyed traditionally close relations since their independence.[1] The two have shared similar experiences in struggle for liberation from foreign rules, and their fights for the national independence. India is one of the countries that supported and assisted Vietnam in its independence from France; oppose the US involvement in Vietnam War, and Vietnam's unification and early days of the post-war reconstruction in the late 1970s and during its comprehensive reforms since 1986. However, their economic relations have never been significant until the 1990s due to differences in domestic institutions, development paradigm and foreign policy preferences, which played an obstruction role in the process of development of bilateral economic relations between the two countries. The turning point for the economic relations was the years when the two countries carried out their own economic reforms towards market base and economic liberalization (Vietnam in 1986 and India in 1991). Since then, the economic relations between Vietnam and India have developed significantly as bilateral trade and investment between the two countries increased considerably, but not to their full potential as both government have expected.

In addition, with the process of India and East Asia integration, and some regional cooperation agreements recently signed between India and other parts or groupings of the region such as ASEAN-India Cooperation, ASEAN-India Free Trade Agreements and Ganga-Mekong Cooperation, the economic relations between Vietnam and India have more opportunities and priority to develop to their potential. In the context of regional cooperation in the form of multilateral relation is internationally widespread, bilateral cooperation is indeed really important between the two countries. On the background of this discussion, this paper sets to examine the current status of economic relations, identify the prospects of the possible areas for the future cooperation, and emphasize the challenges they are facing recently that could hamper the growth of the cooperation in the near future.

Current Status of Vietnam-India Economic Relations

In the context of the changing global economic situation with widespread regionalization and globalization as well as the regional cooperation, there are the potential prospects for enhancing bilateral economic relations between the two countries. Recently, Vietnam and India are among the fastest growing economies in the world with average economic growth rate at around 6 to 9% since 2000 and with their increasing shares in the global trade and Foreign Direct Investment (FDI) as well as enhancement of the industrial competitiveness in diversified sectors and growing knowledge intensive manufacturing sector in both the countries. In addition, there are many outstanding issues between the two countries that would enhance and foster the bilateral relations between them. Thus, in this new global economic context, the bilateral economic relations between Vietnam and India are expected to develop into new level of cooperation that is based on their existing traditional political relations.

Since the two countries officially established their diplomatic relations in 1972, many cooperation organs have been established. In addition, some important bilateral treaties and agreements related to economic relations have been signed, which contributed significantly to fostering the bilateral trade and investment between the two countries. These organs and agreements have huge impacts on the development of the mutual economic cooperation between the two countries. The economic ties between the countries entered into a new stage since the early 90s of the 20th Century, in which the bilateral trade and mutual investment have been considered as the core of the cooperation framework. To date, the established organisations, signed treaties and agreements since 1976 between the two countries are as follows:

(a) Agreement on Science and Technology signed in 1976 and renewed in 1996.

(b) Vietnam-India Joint Commission for Economic, Scientific and Technical Cooperation, established in December 1992, is a very important mechanism for the two countries to review and promote cooperation in all fields, including economic cooperation.

(c) Consular Agreement signed in September 1994.

(d) Avoidance of Double Taxation Agreement signed in September 1994. Agreements on aviation, tourism, and mining and geographical cooperation have also been signed.

(e) Bilateral Investment Promotion and Protection Agreement (BIPPA) signed in March 1997.

(f) Memorandum of Understanding (MoU) between the Indian Oil and Natural Gas Corporation Ltd (ONGC) and Petroleum Investment of Development Company (PIDC) of Vietnam signed in January 2001.

(g) MoU between Federation of Indian Chamber of Commerce and Industries (FICCI) and Vietnam Chamber of Commerce and Industries (VCCI) signed in 2001.

(h) Joint Declaration on the Framework of Comprehensive Cooperation signed in May 2003.

(i) MoU on Cooperation in the Field of Fisheries and Aquaculture signed in July 2007.

(j) Work Plan in the Field of Agriculture cooperation between the two countries signed in July 2007.

(k) MoU on Cooperation between Vietnam Steel Cooperation Essar Group signed in January 2007.

(l) MoU on Cooperation between Vietnam Steel Corporation and TATA Steel Ltd signed in July 2007.

(m) Vietnam-India Free Trade Agreement (VIFTA) in Goods is signed in October 2009 under the ASEAN-India Trade in Goods (AITIG)

Agreement which is within the framework of ASEAN-India Free Trade Agreement (AIFTA) signed in August 2009.

These treaties, agreements and cooperation organizations mentioned above illustrate that most of the cooperation frameworks came into operation in the 1990s. This proves that the bilateral economic cooperation between the two countries started to develop since the 1990s as discussed earlier in the section of the brief overview of the cooperation. Within only two decades, the two countries have done a lot to enhance the cooperation and to foster bilateral relations. These cooperation frameworks provided foundation and basis for the expectedly strong development of the economic ties between the two countries in the future, in the context of regional and global cooperation and integrations, and in the process of India's integration into East Asia.

Vietnam-India Bilateral Trade

Since the two countries started to sign various cooperation treaties and agreements in early 1990s, especially in the past 10 years, there has been a steady increase in the two-way trade turnovers between Vietnam and India. However, up to the 1990s, the bilateral trade volume between the two countries was really low due to differences in domestic institution, development choice and policies applied by each country in association with the low level of development existing in both the countries, especially in Vietnam, and the similarity in traded items in both Vietnam and India. Bilateral trade turnover during 1990s was only around US$ 80 million annually in average.[2] Turning point could be traced back to the first few years of the 21st Century, after more than ten years of the economic reforms implemented by respective countries took to effect, and the new reforms made in institutions and policies. Changes in institutions, growth path and policies drew closer economic relations between Vietnam and India. Since then, trade relation has been fostered, especially for the last eight years. Bilateral trade turnover between the two countries has been growing rapidly from US$ 72 million in 1995 to US$ 376 million in 2002 and crossed the mark of one billion USD (US$ 1.018 billion) in 2006. Despite the 2008 global financial and economic crisis, the trade volume was still very high, being stood at US$ 2.055 billion (Table 1). In the first six months of 2010, the trade volume between the two countries was US$ 1.3 billion, significantly higher than the same period last year.[3]

Table 1: Bilateral Total Trade volume between Vietnam and India at Current Prices

Year	2002	2003	2004	2005	2006	2007	2008	2009
Bilateral total trade volume (in US$ million)	376.63	489.22	670.77	696.55	1018.12	1536.63	2485.39	2055.63
Percentage change (%)	-	29.9	37.0	3.9	84.5	50.9	61.8	-17.3
Share in Vietnam's total trade volume (%)	1.03	1.08	1.15	1.01	1.20	1.38	1.73	1.62
Share in India's total trade volume (%)	0.39	0.32	0.32	0.33	0.33	0.37	0.47	0.49
Vietnam total trade growth (%)	16.7	24.6	28.7	18.7	22.4	31.4	28.8	-12.6

Source: *General Statistical Office of Vietnam (GSO); Ministry of Industry and Trade of Vietnam; International Merchandize Trade (various years): http://www.ficci.com; GSO of Vietnam; http://commerce.nic.in/pressrelease/pressrelease_year.asp?year1=2004.*

In the period from 1995 to 2001, the bilateral trade growth between the two countries increased by 20% per annum in average that help making a rapid increase in the total trade volume close to US$ 400 million in 2002 from the quite low level of just only 75 million US dollars in 1995.[4] In the last eight years (from 2002 to 2009), the bilateral trade growth made a huge momentum as the trade volume sharply increased from US$ 376 million to over 1 billion in 2006 and reached the high close to 2.5 billion USD in 2008 before witnessing a rather sharp decline in 2009 to 2.05 billion USD (−17.3%) due to the 2008 global financial crisis. During this period (2002-08), annual two-way trade growth was 44.46%. Closely looking at Table 1, we observe that the two-country bilateral trade grew rapidly in 2007, 2008 and 2009 with respective rate of growth per annum at 84.5%, 50.9% and 61.8%.

Despite the recent increase in the trade volume, the share of Vietnam's trade with India in Vietnam's total trade turnover remains small, even though the annual increase in percentage growth was significant (up to 84.5%). Over the period of seven years, from 2002 to 2008, the share in Vietnam's trade with India in its total trade has marginally increased from 1.03% in 2002 to 1.73% in 2008 before slightly declining to 1.62% in 2009 due to decline in both the Vietnam's trade with India in particular and its total trade in general caused by the 2008 global financial and economic crisis. It reveals that even though Vietnam-India trade volume is increasing, this is not in line with Vietnam's overall trade growth during the same period (from 16% to over 31%) (row 6 of Table 1). On the other side, during the period 2002-09, India's total trade volume with Vietnam constitutes from around 0.32 to 0.49% of its total trade.

Table 2: Balance of Bilateral Trade between Vietnam and India at Current Prices

Year	2002	2003	2004	2005	2006	2007	2008	2009
Vietnam's export to India (US$ million)	52.03	32.27	77.24	97.76	137.84	179.70	388.99	420.35
Growth rate of Vietnam's export (%)	-	-37.98	139.36	26.57	41.00	30.37	116.47	8.06
India's Export to Vietnam (US$ million)	324.60	456.95	593.53	598.79	880.28	1356.93	2094.40	1635.48
Growth rate of India's export (%)	-	40.77	29.89	0.89	47.01	54.15	54.35	-21.91
Trade deficit (Vietnam)	-272.57	-424.68	-516.29	-500.83	-742.44	-1177.2	-1705.4	-1215.1

Source: *International Merchandize Trade (various years): http://www.ficci.com; GSO of Vietnam; http://commerce.nic.in/pressrelease/pressrelease_year.asp?*

Table 2 presents the volume of Vietnam's export to and import from India, and its trade balance. The figures in the table suggest that the growth rate of the India's export to Vietnam is steadier and more stable than that of Vietnam's export to India as we can observe from Table 2 that the large amplitude in the growth rate of Vietnam's export to India as it declined by 37% in 2003 compared to 2002 before increasing by 139% in 2004 and again by 116.47% in 2008. A critical highlight of the bilateral trade between the two countries is the balance of trade which is always in favour of India not only in the period covered by this study but also since 1993. Before 1993, the bilateral trade was in favour of Vietnam as Vietnam export sustained at a level higher than its import from India. However, the balance of bilateral trade was in reducing trend (decreased from 40.8 million USD in 1990 to US$ 16 million in 1993).[5] As the data reveals, deficit in Vietnam's trade with India has been being increasing over the years, and the trend is quite steady (Figure 1). As data indicate, over the period from 2000 to 2009, particularly from 2002 to 2009, in average India's export to Vietnam was almost five to six times higher than Vietnam's export to India.

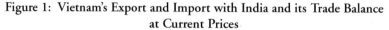

Figure 1: **Vietnam's Export and Import with India and its Trade Balance at Current Prices**

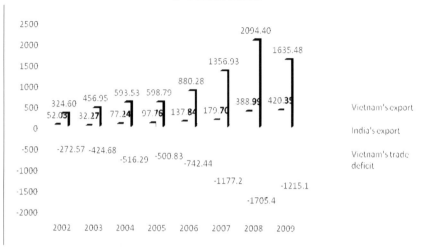

According to the 2006 data, the major items of Vietnam's export to India are coal, pepper, tea, coffee, cinnamon, rubber, computer hardware and electronic products with their respective share in Vietnam's total export to India are 14.69%; 7.96%; 5.94%; 5.61%; 5.14%; 5.01% and 4.98%. The main items of India's export to Vietnam and its share to the country's total export to Vietnam according to the 2006 data include animal feed ingredients (27.84%); ordinary metals (8.1%); plastic material (7.40%); pharmaceuticals (6.95%); machinery and equipment (5.5%); steel (5.04%), cotton (4.24%); medical ingredients (3.5%); chemical materials (3.23%); leather and textile materials (3.16%); and pesticides (2.92%).[6] However, there are changes in traded good and good structure between the two countries in recent years. In 2009, the main export items from Vietnam to India are mobile phones, computer hardware and software, electronic components, spare parts, coffee, ores and other natural minerals while cattle feed ingredients, pharmaceuticals, steels, spare parts, tobacco ingredients formed the major export items from India into Vietnam. Based on the structure of the bilateral trade we argue that the two countries just traded the goods with low valued added. High tech products seem to be absent or constitute a miniscule part in the list of the traded goods.[7]

As figures provided above revealed, the trade between Vietnam and India is still miniscule compared to their political and diplomatic relations as well as their economic potentials. India is not in the top-ten of merchandise trade partners of Vietnam despite the country is one of the economic powers in Asia and in the world. In addition, since 1993, the bilateral trade was always in favour of India. The reasons behind the less development of the trade between the two countries and the favourable balance of trade for India are the differences in institutions and policies applied in each country towards promoting mutual economic relations between the two countries. The import tariff applied by the Government of India is much higher than that applied by Vietnam, even though the two countries have signed several treaties and agreements related to trade and economic cooperation. Besides, the degree of trade liberalization and openness in each country also plays a vital role in the expansion of the bilateral trade. In addition, a study on the basket of traded good indicates that there is the similarity of the export items by both the countries. The main traded items in both the countries' list of exported goods are garment, tea, rice, cashew, footwear, pepper, marine products and computer software. However, for India's export, there is further scope for expansion of trade relation with Vietnam such as sophisticated electronic machinery and goods, and computer software. For Vietnam there is possibility of exporting crude oil and natural gas to India.

Vietnam-India Mutual Investment Cooperation

Mutual investment between Vietnam and India has made a momentum in recent years after India enhanced its efforts towards India-East Asian integration within its "Look-East Policy". Despite this, the FDI capital between the two countries is like a one way traffic. To date, there has not been any major investment from Vietnam in India. Vietnam's only investment project in India is the one by the FPT corporation worth US$ 150,000 invested in an Indian technology development and investment project. However, this project has been withdrawn from Indian market due to its ineffective operation caused by severe competition in the field of IT sector.

From India's side, with some adjustment and reform in Vietnam Foreign Investment Law as the country introduced favourable policies for foreign investors and implemented "One Door" mechanism, FDI increased sharply in the past 15 years. In addition, during the comprehensive reforms with its "Look-East Policy", Indian investors are going global, investing and venturing out in the world market. These reasons together have opened up significant opportunities for Indian investment for both tapping the growing domestic market and export in Vietnam. Vietnam's investment environment becomes more attractive with the implementation of 'one-stop-shop' policy licensing, the introduction of favourable conditions for investors by reducing land rent, granting exemption and reduction in import duties, preferential profit tax, etc.

With the changes made in Vietnam's policies towards attracting FDI, India's investment into Vietnam increased significantly in recent years. Up to 2006, India's FDI in Vietnam was US$ 580 million. There were significant changes in India's FDI to Vietnam in 2007 with Essar Group signing an MoU in January 2007 for setting up a hot rolling steel mill worth US$ 527 million in Ba Ria – Vung Tau and TATA Steel signing an MoU in July 2007 to set up a mega project on steel complex in Thach Khe – Ha Tinh with estimated investment capital worth up to US$ 3.5 billion from the TATA. If this project comes to operation, it would make India among top-10 investors in Vietnam and Vietnam becomes the biggest receiver of Indian FDI in ASEAN. Since December 2008, there are 30 projects from India invested in Vietnam with the registered capital up to US$ 185.45 million. Of the Indian companies invested earliest in Vietnam, the KEC for manufacturing components for transmission towers in Quang Ninh province and the Nagarjuna International Sugar Plant in Long AN province. The Oil & Natural Gas Commission of India was the first foreign company which signed a production sharing agreement with Petro Vietnam in 1988, a project through which natural gas reserve of over two trillion cubic feet have been discovered.

India's investment in Vietnam so far is mainly in sugar production, edible oil, pharmaceuticals, office furniture, plastic industries, rubber plantation, tea processing, mining, fertilizers and packaging. Recently, the investment from India concentrates more on heavy and technical industries such as steel industry and crude oil exploration. If the TATA mega project is approved by the government of Vietnam, it could draw more investment in service and complementary sectors. Thus, the recent changes in the investment direction reflect the quality of India's investment into Vietnam, tighten the two countries' economic relations as well as pushing the bilateral trade upward for future expansion.

In addition, Vietnam is one of the largest recipients of Indian aids through Lines of Credit extended by Department of Economic Affairs (DEA), Ministry of Finance of the Government of India. Since 1976, India has extended 14 Lines of Credit totaling Rs. 3,610 million rupees to Vietnam. In the 1980s,

Vietnam received relatively large amount of assistance, though these programmes were reduced during the 1990s. India announced another credit line of US$ 27 million to Vietnam an agreement which was signed in August 2004 between Exim Bank of India and Ministry of Finance of Vietnam. Most recent credit line of US$ 45 million is being implemented for Nam Chien Hydropower projects in Vietnam.

India has announced an aid of 100 million rupees to Vietnam for setting up of an Advanced Resource Centre in IT in Hanoi. Another grant of Rs. 122.07 million has also been given to Vietnam for assisting human resource development in the field of IT in six educational institutions in Vietnam. Implementation of both these projects is going on.

Prospect of areas for mutual cooperation and challenges in the economic relations between Vietnam and India

At present, with the tendency of globalization and regional integration and cooperation, the bilateral economic relations between Vietnam and India have more opportunities for enhancing the ties and promoting it to a higher level, given they have a traditionally good relation politically and diplomatically. Both the countries are in the cooperation framework of Mekong Ganga Cooperation, India-East Asian Integration and Pan-Asian Corridors and Gateways. Thus, there are prospects for the new areas of cooperation as well as challenges that both the countries are facing in the process of building up closer economic cooperation relation in the time ahead. In this section, we discuss about the prospects of the new areas of cooperation as well as challenges for the cooperation in years to come.

Prospects of areas for mutual cooperation in Vietnam-India economic relation

As discussed above, the current status of Vietnam-India bilateral trade relation has discovered the limitation of the relation as well as the obstruction that hamper the expansion of the bilateral trade in the past years.

As argued earlier, there are many areas where Vietnam and India can share experiences and benefit through bilateral cooperation. In fact, both Vietnam and India have large potential in natural resources, advantages in processing and manufacturing sectors that Indian companies can invest in Vietnam and vice versa, Vietnam investors can also invest in India. However, looking at the current economic and financial potentials as well as technical capability, Indian investors and companies have much larger capability than their counterparts from Vietnam's side. Thus, the potential sectors for future development in the bilateral ties are mostly identified for the Indian companies rather than for the Vietnam's investors. These sectors are as follows.

Prospects for Bilateral Trade

VIFTA signed in October 2009 would pave the way for fostering bilateral trade between the countries. In addition, with the process of India-East Asian integration is taking place, together with the role of the economic and transportation corridors to be built up in both Vietnam and India, the connectivity across Asia is foreseen in the near future. With the development of pan-Asia corridors and gateways within the process of India-East Asian and the framework of Mekong Ganga cooperation, the Vietnam-India connectivity will be facilitated and developed. Asian highways, Trans-Asian Railway could be a good example of the development of connectivity with Asia in general and between India and ASEAN, India and Vietnam in particular. The effect of the VIFTA together with these infrastructural developments would enhance bilateral trade between Vietnam in India.

Besides, with the process of economic liberalization are taking place in both the countries, the administration reform is a must, and domestic institution, growth paradigm as well and related foreign policies are on the process of adjustment in order to meet the requirement by the international and regional governing bodies. These processes could also facilitate the two countries' bilateral trade.

In addition, the issue of selecting goods and commodities for trade will also play an important role for expansion of the bilateral trade. According to the above arguments, there is similarity in the traded items by the two countries. Thus, both the countries should identify higher value-added and high-tech goods that pose each country's advantages for export. For example, India is capable of exporting automobiles, high-tech machineries and other high value added goods to Vietnam market, and Vietnam could also find out its advantages to produce and export its items to India.

Further, in the trade policy for the 2009-14 period, India considers Vietnam as one of the important destinations in its Look-East Policy. Apart from the traditional field of existing cooperation such as cooperation in telecommunication technology, agriculture, oil and gas sector, pharmaceuticals, etc, there will be prospect for the new areas of cooperation such as in steel sectors, automobile parts, and garments and textiles. In October 2009, India recognized Vietnam as a full market economy. All these conditions would push up bilateral trade between the two countries in years to come as both the countries plan to take measures to increase the bilateral trade volume to 5 billion USD by 2010 and by 2012.[8]

Prospects for Mutual Investment and Cooperation

Steel Industry and the Expansion of Service Sector

Given modern technology in steel industry that India posseses, TATA and Essar Group are the two famous groups doing business in the industry and are seeking investment license in Vietnam. In the case of TATA group, a mega project is being set up as a joint venture in the Thach Khe, Ha Tinh worth US$ 5 billion with TATA contributing 65% of the total project capital (around US$ 3.5 billion). The project would play an important role in addressing the problem of shortage of steel and meeting the demand of the material for the booming real estate sector and infrastructure construction in Vietnam.

Due to the increasing demand for steel in Vietnam's emerging market, the investment of TATA in Vietnam's steel industry would lift India into the list of top-ten countries investing in Vietnam, and it would play a vital role in fostering further cooperation between the two countries. With the mega project worth US$ 5 billion, the steel industry would be a potential area of cooperation between the two countries, because India can pass the rich experiences in steel sector to Vietnam. In addition, the mega joint-venture project would attract service and complementary sectors from India to invest in Vietnam. This would lead to the fact that a large number of experts and technical workers in the field need to be present in Vietnam for the business operation, and more Vietnamese engineers, technical workers and experts need to be trained in India. This would make the large number of people travelling between the two countries, paving way for the direct-air connectivity between Vietnam and India and to enhance the links and connectivity between the two countries that could pave way for the development of various cooperation in the future.

Pharmaceutical and Drug Sector

India is known for its development in pharmaceutical and drug production as its products are sold widely in many countries, especially in Asia, including Vietnam. Indian companies doing business in this field are having rich experiences. There is an Indian pharmaceutical company, Ranbaxy, which has invested to produce drug in Vietnam. In addition, there are 128 Indian drug companies, accounting for 25% of total foreign pharmaceutical companies, selling their products, but not participating in the process of drug manufacturing in Vietnam. Meanwhile, Vietnam imports major part of its pharmaceutical needs, including ingredients for drug production as well as finished pharmaceutical products, and the demand for drug is still growing. At present, pharmaceutical ingredients and drug are two main items Vietnam imports from India. Thus, there is still scope for further cooperation between the two countries in this sector. Vietnam can be a market for Indian drug and pharmaceutical products, enhancing India's export of these items to Vietnam. Further, India can be an expert to help Vietnam to develop and strengthen pharmaceutical industry. India's drug manufacturing companies can find opportunities to invest and produce drug in the Vietnam's market.

Oil and Gas Exploitation and Refineries

With its large deposit in natural oil and gas, Vietnam is one of the major oil and natural gas producers in Southeast Asia, but the country still imports oil products to meet its growing demand for energy and other supplies from oil. However, Vietnam still lacks technical know-how for oil exploitation and refineries. Thus, there are greater opportunities and potential for Indian companies to invest in this sector in Vietnam in order to exploit as well as to take part in the refinery process as India's companies have expertise in both the fields. To date, there are several Indian companies that have invested in the oil sector in Vietnam. In 1988, The Oil & Natural Gas Commission of India was the first foreign company to sign a production sharing agreement with Petro Vietnam. Then, ONGC Videsh and ESSAR group have invested in the oil sector in Vietnam. In 2007, Reliance Industry set up a unit for oil exploitation in Vietnam and became the third Indian company to invest in oil and gas exploitation in Vietnam.

Apart from having rich natural oil, Vietnam also has a gas reserve of hundred trillion cubic meters that would be a good opportunity for India's companies to set up joint venture with Vietnamese counterparts in exploring and exploiting oil and natural gas.

Transportation Sector

Transportation is an important factor in the process of economic development for a country which is in its beginning of development process. Presently, both Vietnam and India are facing degraded and less developed infrastructural system, and both the countries are building their transportation system to meet the challenges of the infrastructure development for economic growth.

For the railways, the system in Vietnam now is somehow outmoded and it needs to be improved. For this, India is having a more modern system, so Indian companies would recognize opportunities to develop its business in this sector in Vietnam and supply locomotives to railway transportation to Vietnam.

Besides, India and Vietnam could help each other in sharing experience to upgrade and expand its system of national highway, waterways and civil aviation system because both the countries are in the process of building inland road, water road and aviation system for development. Through this process, both the countries' companies would recognize the field for investing in other country. This would enhance cooperation between the countries.

Agriculture Sector

Vietnam and India are agricultural-based economies with their great potential in agriculture development and expansion. Each country has its own advantage and experiences. For example, Vietnam has more experience than India in increasing agricultural production and developing marine product and rice cultivation. Meanwhile, India has a strong advantage in cultivating soya and making various soya based products. Thus both the countries can share their experiences. In addition, two countries can cooperate to set up the institutions to conduct joint researches in agricultural sector. The benefits of the research outcome would foster the development of agricultural sector in both the countries.

Information Technology Sector

As we know, science and technology sector provides immense opportunities for economic growth of both the countries. Especially in the Information Technology sector, India and Vietnam can establish joint ventures in Vietnam as India's firms are more developed and have more experiences in this sector. Further, given India's expertise in these areas, it can train Vietnamese manpower to cater to the market needs of high-skilled labour.

Knowledge-based Industry Sector

India is more experienced in developing knowledge-based industry while Vietnam is a new comer in this field. Thus Vietnam could benefit from India's experience. India would invest in Vietnam in the field of education to pass the knowledge and know-how to Vietnam as it needs to develop human resources to meet the demand of economic development in the decades ahead.

Challenges Facing the Development of the Bilateral Economic Cooperation

Despite prospects for mutual cooperation in various fields between the two countries, and there are massive changes and adjustments made by both the countries during their economic reforms and liberalization process over the past two decades, there are still many challenges that could hamper the development of the economic relation cooperation between the two countries can be identified. First, as mentioned above, the differences in domestic institution, development paradigm and foreign policies applied by each countries did hamper the expansion of trade and investment between the two in the past. Despite some reforms, these differences are still the hurdles in the process of bilateral economic cooperation.

Second, with the process of regionalization and globalization, both the countries are facing severe competition in trade with other countries in the region and the world as well. This competition would lower the level of goods to be traded between the two countries and the lower level of capital to be invested in either country.

Third, the similarity in the traded items would also hamper the expansion of the bilateral trade between the two countries. Both the countries have almost the similar items to export so there is lack of competition in the export of these products to either country.

Fourth, apart from the gains, the operation of the FTA between ASEAN and India in general, and between Vietnam and India in particular, could pose some threat to some industries in each countries, because under the FTA, without full liberalization and building of the competitive strengths for industries it is unlikely to benefit the economies, and it would harm the weak industries.

Fifth, the connectivity between the two countries could also pose problem for expansion of bilateral trade and mutual investment. The two countries are quite far in distance and there is no direct flight between the countries, which would be a hindrance to mutual cooperation.

Sixth, the low level of general development existing in both the countries is also problematic for enhancing the bilateral cooperation. Both Vietnam and India are in the lower strata of the middle income group countries in the world with outmoded and backward infrastructure.

Seventh, shortage of the knowledge-based and high-tech industries in both the countries could not help much to develop economic cooperation, to expand bilateral trade and to promote mutual investment.

Conclusion

Vietnam and India enjoy very good relations politically and diplomatically for a long time dating back to their independence. However, there is still limitation in economic cooperation in both the countries. With the economic reforms and policy adjustment made by them in the last decades of the 20th Century, the bilateral economic relation started to show sign of expansion and development. Even though, it took more than a decade to the early years of the 21st century, the trade and investment relation between the two countries showed their expansion and development. Now, bilateral trade has increased rapidly and mutual investment started to boom.

With the process of regionalization and globalization in the form of FTA signing between ASEAN and India together with the Look-East Policy by the Indian Government as well as the movement of the India-East Asian integration, the tendency of the economic cooperation between the two countries seems to move upwards. New areas of cooperation can be identified such as steel and services, oil and gas, pharmaceutical and drug, transportation, agriculture, information technology and knowledge-based industries, and the bilateral trade with the operation of FTA, Mekong-Ganga cooperation frame-work, pan-Asian transportation, and corridors and gateways development.

However, despite these possible areas of cooperation, there are some challenges before the two countries such as the differences in domestic institution, growth paradigm and foreign policies applied by either country, the severe competition in the era of regionalization and globalization, the similarity in the traded item by both the countries, the lack of connectivity, the low level of general development as well as lack of knowledge based industries in both the countries. These challenges would obstruct the development of the bilateral economic cooperation. Once all these challenges are addressed, the development of the bilateral cooperation would be achieved.

NOTES

1. Nguyen Canh Hue, "Several Views on the Vietnam India Relation since 1945", *Southeast Asian Studies Review*, vol. 51, no. 6, 2001, pp. 61-63.
2. Nguyen Huy Hoang, "Looking back to thirty years of Vietnam India Economic Relation", *Southeast Asian Studies Review*, vol. 51, no. 6, 2001, pp. 13-18.
3. GSO of Vietnam (various years), "Export and Import Goods", http://www.gso.gov.vn/default_en.aspx, accessed on 24 September 2010.
4. Dang Ngoc Hung, "Vietnam and India: Economic, Trade, and Science and Technology Cooperation", *Southeast Asian Studies Review*, vol. 51, no. 6, 2001, pp. 19-26.
5. Institute of World Economics and Politics Working Paper (2005), "Trade and Investment between Vietnam and India", http://www.cuts-citee.org/PDF/Backgdr-Vietnam.pdf, accessed on 21 September 2010.
6. Consulate General of Vietnam, "Vietnam – India Relations", http://www.vietnamconsulate-mumbai.org/en/nr070521165956/news_object_view?newsPa.., accessed on 20 September 2010.
7. Newsletter Archives, "Monthly Economic and Commercial Report for the Month of January 2009", http://www.tradeindia.com/newsletters/country_focus/country_focus_17_march_2009_vietnam.html, accessed on September 29, 2010.
8. Khanh Lan, "To increase the Two-way Trade between Vietnam and India to USD 3 billion", *New Newspaper of the Vietnam Communist Party*, 8 March 2010.

3

India-Vietnam Bilateral Trade & Investment and Opportunities for Expanding Economic Relations

Shantanu Srivastava

Looking at the post independence period, India and Vietnam have always stood by each other in all bilateral and multilateral issues like true friends even if they were looked upon with disdain by certain countries of the world. Prime Minister Nehru visited Hanoi in 1954 and India opened its Consulate General in Hanoi the same year. Vietnam opened its Consulate General in Delhi in 1956 which was followed by the visits of President Rajendra Prasad to Hanoi in 1957 and President Ho Chi Minh to New Delhi in 1958. Full diplomatic relations were established between the two countries in 1972.

India strongly supported and assisted Vietnam in its efforts for economic reconstruction since the liberation of Saigon in 1975. The two countries set up the India-Vietnam Joint Commission in 1982 for Economic, Scientific & Technical Cooperation. The Joint Commission meets once in two years, alternately in New Delhi and Hanoi, the last meeting having been held in New Delhi in February 2007 during the visit of H.E. Mr. Pham Gia Khiem, Deputy Prime Minister and Foreign Minister of Vietnam. The Joint Commission Meeting which was due in 2009 in Hanoi could not take place and the same was scheduled in November 2010. India provides scholarships for nearly 100 Vietnamese students every year under the Indian Technical and Economic Cooperation (ITEC) program and the two countries exchange cultural troupes regularly under the Cultural Exchange Program. The year 2007 witnessed the signing of the agreement to establish Strategic Partnership between the two countries during the state visit of H.E. Mr. Nguyen Tan Dung, Prime Minister of Vietnam to India in the month of July.

The years from 1975 until the late 1980s were difficult years for Vietnam as it had just emerged from over 30 years of freedom struggle and was trying to reconstruct its economy which was ravaged by long years of war. During the 6th Communist Party Congress in December 1986, the Government of Vietnam introduced a new economic policy, commonly known as 'Doi Moi', and this open door economic policy proved to be a real success story for Vietnam and for the whole developing world to emulate. The 7th Party Congress adopted the program on national reconstruction and the 8th Party Congress in 1996 saw the ending of the socio-economic crisis and encouraged the country to boost the national industrialization and modernization program. The 9th Party Congress in 2001 prepared a ten-year strategy for socio-economic development. These were landmark decisions that hastened the process of international economic integration, made Vietnam one of the fastest growing economies in the region and an attractive destination for Foreign Direct Investment (FDI).

Vietnam and the US established diplomatic ties in 2000. During the visit to Vietnam in November 2000, President Clinton announced the lifting of the trade embargo and a couple of years after that USA lifted the ban on investments in Vietnam.

In 1982, bilateral trade between India and Vietnam was entirely dependent on the 'line of credit' from the Government of India to the Government of Vietnam, which has been coming at regular intervals since 1977. There was no other meaningful trade between the two countries outside of those credits. Starting from the first credit of 400 million Rupees in 1977, until the year 2000, substantial amounts were allocated to Railways and Textile sectors. Later on tea machinery was also added in the list of projects. These being tied credits, all supplies were made from India. Vietnam Railways received diesel locomotives, wagons and coaches under those credits, Hong Gai and Cam Pha coal mines received hopper wagons and some textile mills like Nam Dinh, Vinh Phu, Thang Loi etc. received spinning and finishing equipment. Tea machinery was supplied to a few provinces like Son La, Nghe An etc.

None of the above three sectors managed to create any visibility in Vietnam. Nor did they lead to any new opportunity for the business communities of the two countries to cooperate further. The large amount of money that was given as soft loan (interest rate: 1.75% per annum; period: 20 years including a grace period of 5 years) failed to generate any further export to India in the three sectors.

During 1996-98 period, a complete sugar mill of 1,250 tcd capacity was set up in Can Tho province under the Indian 'line of credit'. This was a very successful project that not only created visibility but also provided opportunities for Indian companies to supply sugar machinery to Vietnam outside the credit.

It is interesting to note that from 1988 to 1992, repayments of these credits were made by Vietnam in terms of rice which was purchased by some private sector Indian and Thai companies. These companies exported rice to third countries and made payments to the Indian Government based on certain discount formulas which were finalized before every deal.

The remainder of the 1990s did not witness much growth in bilateral trade. By 1996, bilateral trade between India and Vietnam was only US$ 100 million and by 1999, it crawled to US$ 150 million. Out of this, India's exports to Vietnam were above 90% and Vietnam's exports to India were below 10%. By the year 2000, bilateral trade rose to a little over US$ 200 million. However, the new decade brought new life into the bilateral trade and became the turning point for the two countries. This was partly due to the globalization of the world economy, massive growth of Vietnam's economy and also due to better awareness amongst the Indian business community about Vietnam.

The awareness was made possible to an extent by the Indian Business Chamber in Vietnam which was set up in Ho Chi Minh City in August 1998 (formally licensed in February 1999), followed by a chapter in Hanoi in December 1999. It is noteworthy that during the visit to Hanoi in January 2001, Prime Minister Atal Bihari Vajpayee expressed the desire to increase the bilateral trade from US$ 200 million to US$ 500 million in the next 5 years. This appeared to be an optimistic and difficult target at that point of time. However, the trade actually grew more rapidly between 2001 and 2006 and the figure rose to 1,000 million USD in the year 2006, though the share of Vietnam's exports to India still remained at a low 14% of the total. In

2009, the bilateral trade exceeded US\$ 2,000 million, with India's exports at over 80% and Vietnam's exports to India at slightly below 20%.

The first FDI project from India to Vietnam came in the late 1980s when ONGC-VL (earlier Hydro Carbons India Ltd) started their first overseas venture off the coast of Vung Tau in the southern part of Vietnam. The whole of 1990s and 2000-05 period witnessed slow years as far as FDIs from India is concerned, though companies like KCP, Nagarjuna, Ranbaxy, United Phosphorus and Godrej accounted successful ventures. They were joined by NIIT and Aptech a few years later with their training centers in Hanoi, Ho Chi Minh City and some other cities. A new momentum was created in 2007 when Tata Steel signed an MOU with the Vietnam Steel Corporation for a major investment project worth over US\$ 5 billion. As of 2010, nearly 30 Indian entities have invested in Vietnam, though most of the investments are very small in size. India currently ranks 29th amongst the 86 investing countries in Vietnam. Essar, which had also shown interest in investing in a steel plant in Vietnam, seems to have lost momentum due to the recent global economic crisis.

Growing Competition from China: An Important Issue for Indian Companies

China is gradually increasing its economic presence and visibility in Vietnam through projects in infrastructure, energy and telecommunications. An 8.5 sq. km. trans-border Economic Co-operation Zone linking Pingxiang city (in South China's Guangxi Zhuang autonomous region) to Vietnam's Langson's province is being set up. Besides being an industrial zone, this Economic Co-operation Zone will also allow trading of goods made in China and Vietnam, which can freely enter this Economic Co-operation Zone. Goods manufactured in this Economic Co-operation Zone will enjoy tax benefits, when they enter either country.

A multi-mode (road, rail and river way) Economic Corridor called "Two corridors & one beltway" is also being built. The first corridor, Kunming (Yunnan province) – Lao Cai – Hanoi – Hai Phong – Quang Ninh, it is believed that the railway track built with French assistance more than 100 years ago will be repaired. The river way will be on Red River and Thai Binh rivers. This corridor connects 4 cities of Yunnan province of China (Kunming, Yuxi, Houghe and Weushan) and 9 provinces/major cities of Vietnam (Lao Cai, Yen Bai, Phu Tho, Vinh Phuc, Hanoi, Hung Yen, Hai Duong, Hai Phong and Quang Ninh) by road, rail and river way. The roadway will be from Kunming to Hekou in Yunnan and Lao Cai – Hanoi highway + the highway no. 5 from Noi Bai airport to Ha Long Bay. The second corridor, Nanning – Lang Son – Hanoi – Hai Phong – Quang Ninh, connects three cities of Guanxi China (Nanning, Chongzou, Ping Xing) and eight province/major cities of Vietnam (Lang Son, Bac Giang, Bac Ninh, Hanoi, Hung Yen, Hai Duong, Hai Phong and Quang Ninh). This economic corridor will use road and rail links. The railway line will be from Nanning to Lang Son, Lang Son – Hanoi and Hanoi – Hai Phong – Quang Ninh, and road is from Nanning to Lang Son, highway # 1A, highway # 5, Noi Bai – Ha Long highway. The destination is Quang Ninh.

This Economic Corridor Project will help in promoting co-operation in industry, energy, transport, mining (Iron Ore & Bauxite and Coal), trade, science & technology, education & culture and tourism. Also, a 295 m highway bridge over the Red River is being built. Likewise, the 110 KV and 220 KV (linking China's Yunnan province with Lao Cai province of Vietnam) transmission lines and transformer stations are being built linking Tuyen Quang province of Vietnam with the Yunnan province of China, to enable Vietnam to import electricity from China when required. The Chinese companies are also actively involved in the power sector – especially hydro power, sugar industry, pharmaceuticals, mining, transport and tourism.

Possible Impact on Indian Business

India's major competition in Vietnam comes from China. There are three main categories of countries as viewed by the business community in Vietnam: (a) USA / Europe / Japan; (b) ASEAN / Korea / Taiwan; and (c) India/China. The scale of China's commitment to build economic ties with Vietnam and create visibility is indeed very high. As India is clubbed with China, in terms of level of technology and correspondingly the price, it is faced with a direct competition from China. India has to take the competition from China seriously and take measures to make itself more competitive. This entails issues like quality, price, after sales service, long term relationships and lines of credit, both G-to-G and through commercial banks. In addition to China, competition also comes from ASEAN countries like Singapore, Malaysia, Indonesia and Thailand, East Asian countries like Japan, South Korea, Taiwan and Turkey from the emerging CIVITS group, both in terms of level of technology and price.

To further boost and sustain the rising India-Vietnam bilateral trade, India needs to lay due emphasis on the export of Vietnamese goods to India. This will give a major impetus to the bilateral trade. In 2009, Vietnam's exports to India were less than 20% of the total and Indian effort should be to expand this to the level of at least 30% in the next 5 years. Further, a very large number of Indian companies (close to 70 Indian companies) have established representative offices in Vietnam. However, not a single Vietnamese company has opened a representative office in India till date. This successful Indian model in Vietnam should be replicated by Vietnamese companies in India. There is a general sentiment of love and friendship in Vietnam towards India. India would like this sentiment to be translated into enhanced business cooperation in the same proportion. India should invite Vietnamese business organizations to come forward and open representative offices in India for promotion of their exports. It is a positive sign that in 2009, 25 Vietnamese companies participated in the India International Trade Fair at Pragati Maidan, New Delhi.

Signing of the FTA between India and ASEAN is a great leap forward and it will create innumerable opportunities for boosting trade between India and ASEAN in general, and between India and Vietnam in particular. The Government of India and the governments of ASEAN countries must hasten the process of extending this to the service sector. All barriers in the service sector must be removed as quickly as possible so that business communities in our countries can work on a level playing field in this sector as well.

Another important aspect in India-Vietnam economic relations is increase in Indian investments. Indian companies should explore investment opportunities in the fields of ethanol, renewable sources of energy, transport, pharmaceuticals, breweries, distilleries, agriculture, forestry, tourism, education and healthcare etc.

While it is expected that investments from India would keep growing, there should be a movement in the other direction as well, i.e., Vietnam's investments in India. The time is ripe and Vietnamese companies must head towards India and explore investment opportunities. Some of the companies that participated in the Trade Fair should consider setting up manufacturing facilities in India. Other sectors could be hotel, tourism, pharmaceuticals, leather shoes, textiles, garments and handicraft etc. This will give them a competitive edge in this large and lucrative market, and also in export, as all the raw materials are available in India and there is no need to depend on imported raw materials.

In addition to growth in bilateral trade and investment, tourism needs to be developed as well. This can contribute substantially to the promotion of people to people contact and in turn influence business relations positively. Both countries offer a variety of attractions in terms of history, socio-cultural centers, adventure and scenic beauty. To promote tourism, it is imperative that both sides explore the possibility of setting up direct flights between the two countries. Another important area of possible cooperation is higher education, research and human resource development. India can become a preferred destination for Vietnamese students who want to avail high-quality professional education.

Banking arrangements are an important facet of international business especially with regard to payment guaranties, bid bonds, performance bonds etc. Bilateral trade between India and Vietnam having reached the critical mass, it is now time that an Indian bank opens a full branch in Vietnam. State Bank of India ran a highly inefficient Representative Office in Ho Chi Minh City for almost seven years in the 1990s and finally wound up the operations. Both their presence as well as their departure went largely unnoticed. Comparatively the Bank of India is more active through their Representative Office in Ho Chi Minh City which was opened in 2002. It has planned to convert the Representative Office to a branch but there are procedural impediments which perhaps need to be taken up at the government level.

India's main competition is from China and some other big Asian players. While it may or may not be possible for India to match the extent and scale of their involvement in Vietnam, India should try and ensure that the line of credit is utilized in big projects where there is visibility and which can potentially lead to the promotion of India's exports to Vietnam. One very good example is BHEL's ongoing Nam Chien Project for setting up a 200 MW Hydro Power plant in Vietnam which is financed under the line of credit from India for electro–mechanical equipment. The line of credit immediately before this, which covered the years 2003-06, was also partly utilized for a few power plants and this paved the way for many more similar projects from India, outside the credit. As noted earlier, most of India's previous credits have neither created visibility nor have they led to promotion of exports from India in those fields. Therefore, it is recommended that we should utilize our future lines of credit for infrastructural projects of medium to large size.

Tata Steel's proposed FDI project in iron ore and steel mill is of strategic importance to Indian business interests in Vietnam. Reportedly, there are road blocks in the issuance of the investment license. Efforts should be made to have the matter resolved soon. Indian telecom companies like Airtel, Reliance and Idea should invest in the field of telecommunication in Vietnam.

Concluding Remarks

In 2010, Vietnam which held the Presidency of ASEAN, celebrated the 1,000th anniversary of Thang Long – Hanoi and enjoyed a high rate of economic growth. However, all is not well as the country is facing an expanding credit bubble and mounting inflation This has been caused mainly by the extra soft loans offered by the banks to fuel growth, most of which have been given to large but not necessarily efficient government companies. This matter is of concern and is expected to be high on the agenda during the 11th Congress of the Communist Party in January 2011.

Vietnam has attracted international investors and foreign investment has flowed to manufacturing, infrastructure, utilities and real estate sectors, the focus being on the growing middle class and its ability to spend money. While FDI in 2010 has exceeded 12 billion USD, in terms of authorized capital, sustaining this momentum will be a challenge due to high inflation, which is currently at about 10% (down from over 25% during the second half of 2008 and early 2009) and the growing credit bubble.

Large amount of foreign exchange also flow into Vietnam from exports, tourism and remittances from overseas Vietnamese. However, a good part of those foreign currency inflows does not end up in the banking system. Several companies hold on to dollars and gold rather than selling them for the local currency, the Vietnamese Dong. It is unlikely that the sentiment on Dong will pick up soon to shift the trend away from holding on to dollars to selling them to banks. The State Bank of Vietnam has tried to rein in inflation by tightening the monetary policy.

The last decade brought immense growth and diversification to India – Vietnam cooperation. Bilateral trade grew many folds and FDI also witnessed a sharp increase. However, a huge reservoir of opportunities still remains untapped and it is necessary for the governments and business communities of the two countries to explore new areas for widening the bandwidth of cooperation. The main impediments are inadequate information about the true potential, lack of understanding of cultural differences, and lack of ability to understand and adapt to the vastly different ways of doing business. Language is also a barrier.

While the 20th century belonged to the West, the 21st century belongs to Asia. Amongst the Asian countries, India and Vietnam are amongst the fastest growing economies in the world. Vietnam is expected to become one of the top 20 economies by the year 2025 and by the same time India is expected to become the third largest economy in the world. Therefore, there is a lot at stake for both the countries and a lot on the platter for both the countries to work on as partners in progress.

BILATERAL POLITICAL ENGAGEMENTS

Important Vietnamese Delegations to India
- President Ho Chi Minh in 1958.
  (He also transited at Calcutta for a day on his way to Moscow in 1948, but this was not a state visit).
- Prime Minister Pham Van Dong in 1978 and 1980.
- Party General Secretary Le Duan in 1984.
- Party General Secretary Nguyen Van Linh in 1989.
- Party General Secretary Do Muoi in 1992.
- Prime Minister Vo Van Kiet in 1997.
- President Tran Duc Luong in 1999.
- Party General Secretary Nong Duc Manh in 2003.
- Prime Minister Nguyen Tan Dung in 2007.
- Vice President Nguyen Thi Doan in 2009.
- President of the National Assembly Nguyen Phu Trong in 2010.

Important Indian Delegations to Vietnam
- Prime Minister Nehru in 1954.
- President Rajendra Prasad in 1956.
- President R. Venkataraman in 1991.
- Vice President K.R. Narayanan in 1993.
- Prime Minister Rajiv Gandhi in 1985 (Hanoi) and 1988 (Ho Chi Minh City for half a day), both the times accompanied by Mrs. Sonia Gandhi.
- Prime Minister Narasimha Rao in 1994.
- Prime Minister Atal Bihari Vajpayee in 2001.
- Speaker of Lok Sabha Som Nath Chatterjee in 2007.
- President Pratibha Devi Singh Patil in 2008.
- Prime Minister Manmohan Singh in 2010 (ASEAN+3).

Vietnam's Trade with India as against Total Trade (million US$)

	Total Export	Export to India	Total Import	Import from India
2005	32447.2	97.8	36761.1	596.0
2006	39826.2	137.8	44891.1	880.3
2007	48561.4	179.7	62764.7	1357.0
2008	62685.1	389.0	80713.8	2094.3
2009	57096.3	419.6	69948.9	1634.8
Upto July 2010	44521.0	474.0	54676.0	1000.0

Source: Ministry of Industry & Trade, Vietnam.

BILATERAL TRADE

India's Main Exports to Vietnam

Animal Feed, Pharmaceutical Formulations & Raw Materials, Machinery & Equipment, Steel, Plastic Resins, Agro-Chemicals, Textiles, Garment & Shoe Accessories, Cotton Fiber & Yarn, Tobacco and Truck Tires etc.

Vietnam's Main Exports to India

Coal, Black Pepper, Coffee, Tea, Cinnamon, Rubber, Electronic Components, Footwear, Wooden Furniture, Textiles and CDs etc.

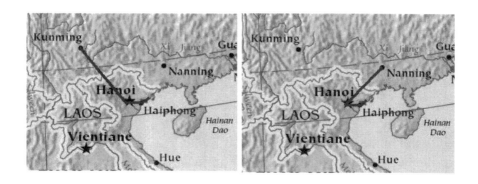

4

Emerging Trade Dynamics between India and Vietnam: What are Vietnam's Bilateral Trade Interests?

Saroj K. Mohanty

India and Vietnam are emerging as fast growing economies in the world during the last three decades. The resurgence of the Vietnamese economy in terms of its growth performance is only comparable with China, India (Qoia, 2008) and Russia in recent years. One of the important drivers of growth has been its export sector and the country stands out as one of the top ranking economies of the world in its trade openness.

Vietnam's sustained growth over the last two and half decades has captured the attention of the world as a vibrant economy, demonstrating its solid growth and also its future potential. The economy continues its high growth trajectory since introduction of its ambitious economic reforms *doi moi* ('renovation') in 1986, a major programme to initiate transition towards the market economy. The sweeping reforms brought in radical changes in diversifying portfolios of exports, attracting Foreign Direct Investment (FDI), promoting agricultural growth and strengthening role of state-owned enterprises, facilitating conditions for private sector participation, among others. Country's reforms became more focused on trade reforms in the 1990s when it joined the Association of Southeast Asian Nations (ASEAN) under the ASIAN Free Trade Area (AFTA) and the US under the Bilateral Free Trade

Agreement (BTA). The reform process was consolidated further with its accession to World Trade Organization (WTO) in January 2007.

With rapid economic growth and domestic policy reforms, Vietnam is emerging as an attractive destination for trade and investment. It is becoming a target for high technology investment from the US and also emerging as a major technology export market in Asia for the US (Athukorala, 2009). The economy has picked up strongly in institutionalising its legal and regulatory framework which is supportive of its domestic trade environment. It has not only provided level playing field to its domestic players, but also created conditions for attracting trade, investment, skill and technology to boost its domestic growth.

During the last two decades, the Vietnamese economy emerged as a resilient economy, growing at the rate of 7-8 per cent per annum despite intermittent recurrence of global shocks. During the period of the 'Asian Financial Crisis' in the late 1990s and global slump during 2001-03, the Vietnamese economy was least affected. But the recent episode of global slowdown affected the economy in 2009, and is expected to recover[1] in 2010 (ESCAP, 2010). During the post-crisis period, the external sector of the country performed better in taking the first mover's advantage in global trade.

From India's perspective, Vietnam continued to be important on two counts. Firstly, there are strong synergies between two countries since both them are growing very fast over a long period of time. Their strong integration with the global economy is combined with their expanding domestic economy. Their robust demand for final products and industrial intermediates could propel growth dynamics in each others economy. Therefore, evolving strong economic relationship with the emerging economies could be important for India to maintain high real GDP growth. Secondly, world economy has started booming during the post-recovery period (World Bank, 2010a) and collaborative approach of emerging countries could be helpful in operating jointly in third market to take the first mover's advantage. Association with Vietnam can help India in reaping the benefit from the global recovery.

But future bilateral economic cooperation is largely depending upon the current pattern of bilateral trade. Though the present level of bilateral trade is much below their trade potential, sustainability of current pace of bilateral trade is largely contingent on reduction of trade asymmetry. The future of the bilateral trade will be mostly governed by addressing the trade asymmetry issue effectively and harnessing trade opportunities existing in each others' economy.

The paper begins with analysing comparative macroeconomic performances of India and Vietnam; emphasizing their strategic responses to present global recovery in Section 2. Evolving bilateral trade relationship between these two countries is discussed in Section 3, focusing on emerging problems with further strengthening of their trade relationship. Section 4 presents changing dynamics of their trade regimes, highlighting undergoing reforms in the areas of tariffs and Non-Tariff Barriers. Section 5 examines the specific economic interest of Vietnam in India, particularly by estimating trade potential of Vietnam in the Indian market for further economic engagement. The key findings are summarised in the final section.

A New Macroeconomic Dynamism Emerging

India and Vietnam have passed through a phase of economic transition during the last two decades and their development strategies were immensely influenced by high growth profile of the East Asian countries who have used export-led growth strategy as their major policy plank since the 1970s (ADB, 2005). As reform processes made significant headway, both the economies have gradually integrated themselves with the global economy. Despite having different political regimes, the outward-oriented trade strategies pursued by both countries are now almost non-reversible in nature.

Despite commonality in policy regimes, both countries differ significantly in their accomplishment in economic and social sector development in recent years. They have diverse resource endowments, and there exist a great deal of complementarities which can be harnessed to strengthen economic cooperation between them. As both of these countries are emerging countries, their requirements for import and export capabilities have been highly diversified. There is large domestic demand for qualitative products as purchasing power of the middle income group is expanding persistently. With strong domestic demand, these countries have pursued export-led growth strategy during the period of reforms. They have effectively insulated their economies from the periodic global external shocks which appeared intermittently in 2001-03 and 2007-09.

Despite excellent track record of macroeconomic fundamentals in both countries to maintain high economic growth, particularly during the period of global crisis, there are many areas of concerns which need to be addressed. Soaring inflationary situation, deteriorating current account deficit, volatility in inflow of remittances, fragile financial sectors, etc., are some of the weaknesses which may be examined for understanding the level of vulnerability in these two economies. In the post-recovery phase of the present episode of recession, greater cooperation is required between fast growing economies to reap the advantages of first movers in a more coordinated manner. However, the experience suggests that robustness of bilateral cooperation is largely contingent upon performance of individual countries. In this context, macroeconomic performances of both countries are examined.

Dynamic Macroeconomic Setting

The macroeconomic performances of both the countries were robust during the present decade, despite variations in their level of economic accomplishment due to several reasons including external shocks. They are emerging as the two fastest growing economies in the world.[2] Vietnam grew at the rate of 8-9 per cent per annum during the last two decades and the momentum remained steady despite intermittent recurrence of global shocks. Both the countries have been improving their shares in the global trade and FDI inflows over last decades. Though the size of the Vietnamese GDP is less than one-tenth of India, its share in the global output (in terms of Purchasing Power Parity) is improving significantly during the last three decades as shown in Figure 1. In the current economic literature, incredible growth performances of India and China are often cited[3]. India has significantly improved its share in the Gross World Product (GWP) during the last two decades, but Vietnam has outshone India in this regard. Interestingly, Vietnam's share in GWP has been rising faster than India since 1995, though its share is yet to exceed more than ½ per cent of GWP by 2010.

The GDP of Vietnam made a three-fold rise within a span of less than a decade to reach US$ 90.6 billion in 2008. In real terms, the gross output registered an average growth rate of 7.4 per cent during the period 2000-08. The domestic economy was not affected by the trivial slowdown of the global economy during 2001-03. The average nominal capita income surpassed the benchmark level of US$ 1000 in 2008, and expanded at an average rate of more than 6 per cent per annum during the period 2003-08. Similarly, slowdown of the Indian economy during the period 2001-03 had depressed growth performance of India's per capita income, but it could recover from economic downturn in the latter period until the commencement of the present episode of recession.

Figure 1: Share in the World GDP

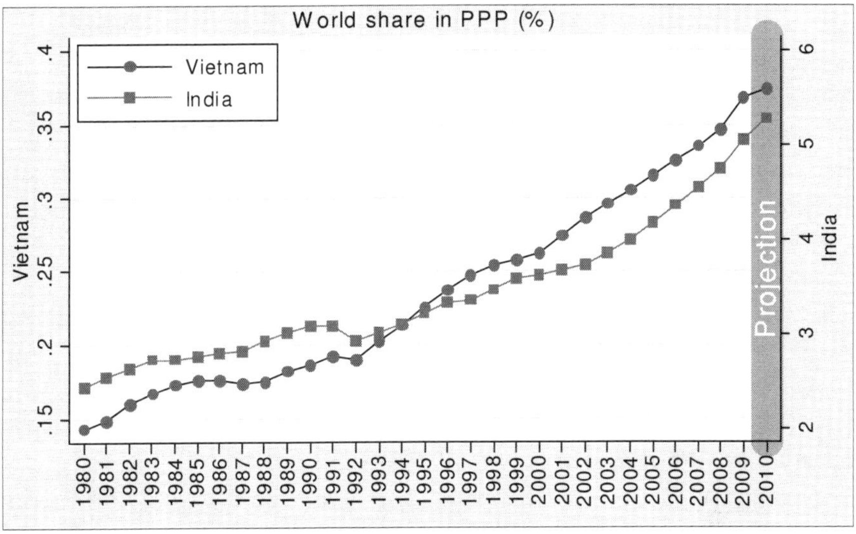

Source: Author's calculation based on World Economic Outlook, October, 2010.

The track record of resource management has been effective in both the countries. High growth in these countries has been the outcome of high savings and investment ratios which are increasing steadily during the last few years. The average saving rate of India is close to 40 per cent whereas the corresponding figure for Vietnam is around 35 per cent in recent years. However, investment ratio is either approaching or exceeding 40 per cent per annum in both countries. The policy of maintaining higher investment rate as compared to its savings rate is to gear up its level of economic growth in a sustainable manner. High investment rate has contributed to brisk growth in both the countries, especially in the latter half of the present decade. While the resource gap is very narrow in India, it is relatively pronounced in Vietnam, thereby leaving space for inflationary tendency to grow in Vietnam.[4] FDI has been flowing steadily to both the countries and becoming a credible source of resource inflows during their reform period.[5] This trend has been robust in recent years despite global downturn. Contribution of net inflows of FDI to GDP was around 2 per cent for India and 4 per cent for Vietnam before the onset of the present episode of recession. However, this figure has reached 3.6 per cent for India and 10.6 per cent for Vietnam in 2008, while the world economy was reeling under high level of uncertainties.

There is high degree of divergences between both countries in their economic structures. They have witnessed considerable shrinkage of their agricultural sector during the last quarter century. In India, share of agricultural sector in total GDP was 20.4 per cent in 2007, reduced just by half since 1985. The sectoral contribution of the industrial sector was 29.5 per cent in 2007, but it declined to 28.8 per cent in 2008 with the weakening of the global demand for industrial product. The manufacturing sector holds a small share in the overall GDP of India. It was almost stagnated at around 15 per cent in the first half of the present decade but a sign of improvement in sectoral share is observed in 2008. The bulk of domestic output is shared by the services sector. At present, the sector is contributing nearly 54 per cent of GDP. Lopsided sectoral development in India has a potential treat to employment generation in the country. On the contrary, production sectors are more uniformly spread in Vietnam as compared many countries in the developing world. Contribution of the agricultural sector to GDP declined from 40.2 per cent in 1985 to 20.4 per cent in 2007. There is improvement in the contribution of the agricultural sector to GDP at the cost of contraction of the industrial sector due to recession in 2008. Share of the services sector was hovering around 38 per cent in the present decade.

Shift in the development strategies towards export-oriented policies in both the countries has enabled them to place their economies on high growth trajectory. Rise in total factor productivity also played an important role for maintaining high growth during the last two decades (Doah et al, 2002; Thanh and Duong, 2007). Moreover, twin factors such as domestic demand and exports have been the driving force behind the 'growth miracle' in these countries. Exports of Vietnam have been increasing phenomenally from US$ 5.4 billion in 1995 to US$ 48.6 billion in 2007, showing a nine-fold increase in just more than a decade. In 2001, country's imports and exports were almost at the same level but trade gap expanded rapidly during the decade, indicating fast industrialising nature of the economy. Despite growing merchandise trade deficit, there has been constant increase in foreign exchange reserves during the decade. Its foreign reserve can sustain its imports for more than three months despite global recession in 2008.

In the present decade, Vietnam grew faster than India and progressed very consistently during the period. Like India, the resilient Vietnamese economy could effectively manage global recession by averting the anticipated adverse impact of it. The economy witnessed slowdown in its economic growth performance rather than plunging into deep depression like many countries in the industrial world. The World Bank has forecast robust growth for both the countries in 2010 (World Bank, 2010a). The estimation[6] of the World Bank indicates that real GDP growth rate of Vietnam is likely to improve from 5.3 per cent in 2009 to 6.5 per cent in 2010 and the corresponding expected growth estimate is reported as 9.7 per cent for India in 2010.

The vast literature on Vietnam presents growth dynamics of the economy during the last two and half decades since inception of its major reforms, 'Doi Moi' in 1986. The reform programme paved the way for both private sector development and opening the economy to FDI (Schaumburg-Müller, 2002). The economy started rolling very fast with the appropriate blending of phased industrialisation along with focused attention on social sector development. Country's development strategy with a 'human face' has been the hallmark of its economic success. This has enabled the economy to maintain high growth with greater degree of social justice.[7]

Most of the emerging countries including India and Vietnam have shown remarkable progress during the last two decades. Their relative performance vis-à-vis other major emerging countries in the world is an issue for discussion. This may indicate the extent of dynamism in these countries and also provide justification for their cooperation for mutual advantage. We have examined the issue by taking 24 most dynamic economies of the world in the analysis. As countries differ in terms of their GDP sizes, they are brought into a comparable form by indexing them at a given level. GDP (in constant US$) of each country is indexed to 100 in 1992. The indexed GDP (in constant US$) figures of selected countries[8] are presented in Figure 2. This presents relative growth performance of individual countries during the last three decades.

The results show that Vietnam is one of the fastest growing economies next to Russia and China during the period 1992-2008. India has ranked fifth in the world after Vietnam and the UAE in its growth profile during the same period. Other countries like Argentina, Egypt and Singapore are lagging behind India and Vietnam in their growth trajectories despite being high performing economies in the world during the last three decades. The Vietnamese economy is so resilient that it has resisted global slowdown during 1997-98 and 2001-03 by maintaining sustained growth where major emerging economies had to undergo economic downturn.

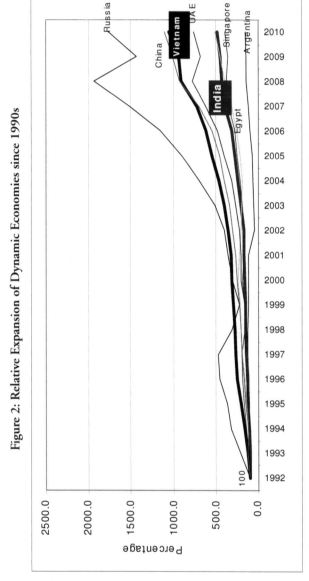

Figure 2: Relative Expansion of Dynamic Economies since 1990s

Note: GDP figures are in constant US$ with the base year 2000. Each GDP series is indexed to 100 for the year 1992.

Source: *World Economic Outlook*, October 2010, World Bank.

Though Vietnamese economy has sound economic fundamentals like India, it is still grappling with certain structural constraints. It is a common problem of developing countries that high growth rate is closely linked with possibility of overheating of economy. Despite high growth, Vietnam had low level of inflation in the early part of the decade. Moderate inflationary pressure built up since the middle of the decade and it became alarming to touch the level of 23.1 per cent in 2008. In fact, mild inflation is conducive to growth, but high inflationary pressure may cut existing level of competitiveness of a country and seriously affect real effective exchange rate. Vietnam was comfortable with its current account situation until 2006. The situation has deteriorated during the 'global financial crisis'.

Both the countries have shown strong macroeconomic fundamentals where both countries are likely to be on high growth trajectory in the medium term. With expanding domestic demand, strong resource base and high stake in the global market, both the countries can immensely benefit from tapping synergies existing between them. India and Vietnam are already engaged in Free Trade Agreement (FTA) under the broader cover of India-ASEAN FTA. More bilateral initiatives are to be initiated to tap the existing trade opportunities between both countries.

India-Vietnam Bilateral Economic Relationship
Trends in Bilateral Trade

Like many emerging countries, the export sector has played an important role in India's recent surge in the global economy. India has embraced both multilateralism and regionalism to access global market and also opening its domestic market for global players. In the process, India has been a net trade deficit economy since beginning of its trade reforms. Its bilateral trade linkage with Vietnam is examined in this section.

India-Vietnam bilateral trade resumed growth rapidly during the past few years and picked up significantly after its accession to WTO in 2007. Bilateral trade grew by nearly 8 times from US$ 273 million in 2001 to US$ 2.2 billion in 2009 as presented in Table 1. The bilateral outlook indicates that the two-way trade is expected to reach US$ 14.6 billion by 2015.[9]

Vietnamese trade with the rest of the world can be broadly categorized into three phases. The first phase (1990-99) is associated with low level of trade with greater degree of volatility. The second phase is marked with surge of trade with rising trade deficit. In the recent phase (2005-09), import grew rapidly than exports, leading to diverging trade deficit. Exports need to be promoted to arrest rising level of imports. Exports contributed 65 per cent of imports in 2009, and declining share of exports in imports had been observed since 2005 when the world economy was booming without any major external shock. The trade deficit issue has been an area of concern for the country in recent years.

Bilateral trade with India has also followed similar pattern as its trade linkages with the rest of the world. Bilateral trade was low during 1990-99 and imports increased during 2000-05. Both exports and imports started growing simultaneously during 2005-09. Bilateral imports of Vietnam increased faster than imports during the period 2000-05 over 1990-99, whereas the trend was reversed during the period 2005-09 over 2000-05. Though the level of bilateral trade was low, but Compound Annual Growth Rate (CAGR) of bilateral trade flow has been much higher than its overall trade average during the last two decades. As bilateral exports are picking up in recent years, the share of bilateral trade deficit with India with the overall trade deficit of Vietnam with rest of the world has been declining from 14.7 per cent in 2006 to 5 per cent in 2009. The volume of bilateral trade with India is growing with reduced trade deficit, which is a healthy sign between bilateral trade relationships.

Table 1: Trends in Vietnam's Bilateral Trade with India: 1990-2009 (Mn US$)

Year	World			India		
	Exports	**Imports**	**Balance**	**Exports**	**Imports**	**Balance**
2001	15025.1	16218.0	-1192.9	45.4	228.0	-182.6
2002	16707.3	19745.2	-3037.9	52.0	324.7	-272.6
2003	20144.9	25261.1	-5116.2	32.3	457.1	-424.9
2004	26485.0	31968.8	-5483.8	78.6	593.5	-514.9
2005	32447.1	36761.1	-4314.0	97.8	596.0	-498.2
2006	39826.2	44891.1	-5064.9	137.8	880.3	-742.5
2007	48561.4	62764.7	-14203.3	179.7	1357.0	-1177.3
2008	62685.1	80713.8	-18028.7	389.0	2094.4	-1705.4
2009	55046.4	84913.4	-29867.0	340.3	1832.3	-1492.0

Source: Direction of Trade Statistics, Online, IMF, Washington D.C.

At present, bilateral export basket of Vietnam has been very narrow as compared to its overall trading with the rest of the world. For example total number of products exported by Vietnam to India was 322 items whereas it was exporting 3,124 of products to the rest of the world during 2004-08 at 6-digit HS. Vietnam can export several other globally competitive products to India to have wider market access in India. Its export items to India have been highly concentrated as shown in Table 2. Export of anthracite coal alone constituted 22 per cent of total exports of Vietnam to India in 2008. Similarly, top 4 items comprised of 50 per cent of total bilateral exports, 14 items 70 per cent, and 34 items 80 per cent in 2008. Most of the high export earning items are primary and resource intensive products. Among the exportable items of Vietnam, many of them are not exported consistently. The time series bilateral exports of Vietnam indicate that most of high export earning items are added to the export basket recently and contributing to the growth of bilateral exports. Export of certain top ranking products picked up recently include phosphorus, urea, primary batteries, polyvinyl chloride, natural rubber, polyvinyl chloride, heterocyclic compounds, among others.

Table 2: India's Top 50 Import Items from Vietnam in 2008

(Thousand US$)

HS6	Description	2004	2005	2006	2007	2008
270111	Anthracite Coal	17958	18815	38965	32731	80554
251010	Natural calcium phosphates, etc.	0	0	0	4313	74418
090111	Coffee, not roasted, not decaffeinated	5101	18254	7317	4558	14763
280470	Phosphorus	0	0	1786	2720	13640
720421	Waste and scrap, stainless steel	1374	2518	8306	6287	11723
852290	Parts and accessories of apparatus	0	3	292	2677	10377
310210	Urea, wthr/nt in aqueous solution	0	0	0	0	9678
850680	Primary cells & primary batteries nes	432	195	128	0	8879
090411	Pepper of the genus Piper, ex cubeb pepper	11178	11310	10051	10300	7836
090610	Cinnamon and cinnamon-tree flowers	2654	2230	5547	6073	7670
400122	Technically specified natural rubber (TSNR)	2088	4530	974	2149	5287
330741	Agarbatti & other odoriferous preparations	228	954	2525	3444	5055
850710	Lead-acid electric accumulators	0	32	122	1797	4818
390421	Polyvinyl chloride nes, not plasticised	0	640	353	0	2773
850720	Lead-acid electric accumulators nes	4015	623	1216	3220	2569
293359	Hetercycl compds cntg pyrimidin rng/piperazine	0	0	0	918	2287
440349	Logs, tropical hardwoods nes	15	29	0	71	2178
090910	Anise or badian seeds	1190	10708	2019	1753	2176

(Contd.)

HS6	Description	2004	2005	2006	2007	2008
890110	Cruise ships, excursion boats etc	0	0	0	0	2169
630492	Furnishing articles of cotton, not knitted or crocheted	115	315	320	55	2126
252100	Limestone flux; calcareous stone for lime or cement	52	1014	749	1640	2018
401162	Herring bone tyres, ind equip, rim<61 cm	0	0	0	409	2016
252210	Quicklime	0	0	2	86	1965
390410	Polyvinyl chloride, not mixed with any other substances	0	593	13	0	1801
640319	Sports footwear of leather	353	1406	2599	2183	1686
380510	Gum, wood or sulphate turpentine oils	116	224	377	911	1678
292242	Glutamic acid and its salts	0	0	0	1054	1623
640699	Parts of footwear nes	3	113	441	219	1460
340290	Surface-active preparations, washing and cleaning	25	3	0	53	1396
640411	Sports footwear w outer soles of rubber or plastics	439	1093	1838	1661	1374
251512	Marble & travertine, merely cut, by sawing	89	3773	2966	1271	1360
500400	Silk yarn (other than yarn spun from silk waste)	211	259	601	688	1322
640610	Uppers and parts thereof, other than stiffeners	24	18	162	222	1317
090220	Green tea (not fermented) in packages	0	0	0	40	1289
380610	Rosin	670	781	1234	1675	1240
850110	Electric motors of an output not exceeding 37.5 W	0	0	128	519	1203
300410	Penicillins or streptomycins and their derivatives	0	0	0	10	1195
600532	Dyed wide warp knit synthetics	0	0	0	23	1132
293299	Heterocyclic compounds with oxygen hetero-atoms	852	6979	3291	807	1117
540269	Yarn of synthetic filaments, multiple, nes, not put up	0	6	0	0	1109
843790	Pts of clean/sort mach etc	3	164	140	367	1101
293999	Vegetable alkaloids and salts, nes	0	106	0	986	1100
848390	Parts of power transmission equipment	0	3	3	0	1071
853931	Fluorescent lamps, hot cathode	1046	5021	4865	1786	1068
261510	Zirconium ores and concentrates	0	16	107	606	1040
700510	Float glass etc in sheets	159	505	1017	723	979
091030	Turmeric (curcuma)	822	1996	2958	1938	939
481840	Sanitary articles of paper	1467	1698	508	655	939
350699	Glues or adhesives, prepared nes	0	42	59	379	890

Source: PCTAS CD, 2010, ITC, Geneva.

India's Bilateral Imports from Vietnam

As an emerging economy, India's demand for energy-related imports has increased manifold during the last two decades. Nearly 70 per cent of its domestic crude demand[10] is imported from rest of the world. Demand for certain critical minerals has been growing steadily during the period. Besides, it has strong demand for manufacturing products. The sectors which are most important for India during 2004-08, are minerals, chemicals, gems & jewellery, base metals, machinery and automobiles sector with the rest of the world. Growth of imports has been significant in most of these sectors. Largest growth in one of the major import sectors was noticed in the mining sector where imports increased by CAGR 112.4 per cent during the period 2004-08. Growth of imports has been robust in major sectors like automobiles and machinery during the same period.

Vietnam's exports to India have been diversified, and certain sectors continue to dominate in the bilateral trade. Growth of India's bilateral imports from Vietnam has been very robust during the period 2004-08. Country's export basket has been dominated by primary, resource-based and manufacturing sectors. It is important to note that structure of India's bilateral imports from Vietnam is consistent with its imports from rest of the world. India's imports from Vietnam comprise of agricultural, mining and manufacturing products. In sectors where India is heavily dependent on rest of the world are also those on which India is also dependent on Vietnam for import. For example, sectors like minerals, chemicals, machinery, automobile, etc., are important for India from both world and Vietnam during 2004-08. Vietnam exports small quantities of agricultural products and such products constitute nearly 10-11 per cent of its total bilateral exports. These products are mostly concentrated in the fruit and vegetable sector. Besides, others sectors are also emerging significant such as plastic products, textiles & clothing, etc for India's bilateral imports from Vietnam.

Dynamics of Bilateral Trade Imbalances

However, trade gap is gradually narrowing down since 2005; the absolute level of trade deficit of Vietnam is close to US$ 30 billion. Trade imbalance in any form has been an important issue for the country. Vietnam has strong trade ties with industrialised countries, and it has favourable trade with many countries in the EU and the US. Though it has low trade linkages with the developing countries, it has trade deficit with many countries in Asia.

Vietnam's bilateral trade deficit with India has been low in the overall trade deficit in 2009. In 2001, bilateral trade deficit with India exceed 15 per cent of the total trade deficit of Vietnam, and declined steadily until 2004. Again it went up to 14.7 per cent of the overall deficit of the country in 2006, and started receding consistently to touch 5 per cent in 2009 with increased volume of bilateral trade despite global recession.

With some countries, Vietnam has large trade surplus and with some large trade deficit in 2009. It maintained large trade surplus (more than 1 per cent of its overall trade deficit) with 9 countries and trade deficit with 10 countries in 2009. It maintained largest trade surplus with the US (i.e. 28.2 per cent of its total trade deficit) and largest trade deficit with China (i.e. 45.6 per cent of its total trade deficit) in 2009. With respect to China, bilateral trade deficit of Vietnam with India has been very low in 2009 as shown in Figure 3. Vietnam's bilateral trade deficit with India was 5 per cent of its overall trade deficit in 2009. At least 5 countries had larger bilateral trade surpluses with Vietnam than India. However, attempt has to be made to ensure that bilateral trade has to grow rapidly along with trade balance to sustain bilateral trade relationship.

Figure 3: Vietnam's Trade Deficit with Selected Countries

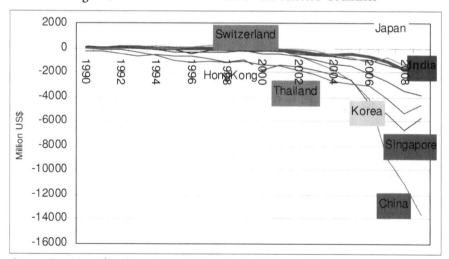

Source: Direction of Trade Statistics, Online, IMF, Washington D.C.

Trade Regimes: On a Path of Persistent Liberalisation

Experiences of both the countries have indicated that persistent and irreversible trade reforms have a lasting effect on their endeavour to keep these economies on high growth path. With its highly inward-oriented and protected trade regime during the first four decades of its independence, India maintained an annual 'Hindu Rate' of growth of 3.5 per cent despite massive development efforts (Rodrick and Subramanian, 2004). However, economic reforms in India in the early 1990s brought sea change in her economic policies (Ahluwalia, 2002). Deepening of liberalisation process has gone so far in India that it is one of the fast liberalising countries in the developing world. It appears strange, but it is true that India's tariff regime is, rather, more liberalised than China in the manufacturing sector since 2008 (Mohanty, 2010a) and most other sectors are converging very fast in recent years. Similar is the case for the NTBs.

Like India, Vietnam has achieved major strides in liberalising its trade policy to a large extent. It is believed in Vietnam that India still maintains a protected trade regime despite of its resurgence as strong outward-oriented economy and such a protected trade regime is coming on the way of accessing India's vast market. Therefore, this is one of the most important reasons for having persistent bilateral trade imbalances during the last two decades.

In fact, India has a liberalised trade regime and its global imports are growing very fast in diversified sectors, ranging from primary and resource-base sectors to various levels of technology intensive sectors during the last two decades (Mohanty and Chaturvedi, 2006). It is a net trade deficit country in merchandise trade with respect to rest of the world. As an emerging economy, its trade structure is highly diversified across the geographical space. For example, India has large trade surplus with countries like the US, United Arab Emirates, etc., and also trade deficit with smaller countries like Angola, Myanmar, Guinea, Papua New Guinea, Congo (both), Gabon, Togo, Cote d'Ivoire, Bhutan, Bermuda, etc., in 2009. As a dynamic country, Vietnam's bilateral trade deficit may be reversed with higher level of trade flows with India.

Both countries have potential to raise two-way trade and reverse the existing trade asymmetry. Both the countries have yet to introduce most of their globally competitive products in each others' market due to scores of reasons. Perhaps, more liberal trade regimes may have positive effects on bilateral trade flows. A brief profile of trade regimes existing in both the countries are discussed below.

Liberalised Tariff Regimes

Experiences of developing countries indicate that tariff policies are often the expressions of country's production structure. Though both the countries have strong synergies in trade, their production structures differ significantly across sectors. Therefore, these two countries have strong points of divergence with regard to sectoral protection in recent years. These countries have strong and divergent policies in liberalisation of their agricultural sector. India considers agricultural sector as an important sector for the economy from the point of 'livelihood security', though sector's contribution to GDP has been low. The sector shares 17.5 per cent of India's total GDP, but it absorbs less than ¾ of its total labour force in 2008. For protecting the interest of rural poor, agricultural sector is protected which has emerged a broad national policy in the WTO negotiation (RIS, 2007).

Agriculture in Vietnam is more liberalised than many developing countries including India. Since growth momentum has been sustained over a period of time and merchandise trade is an important source of growth, agriculture plays an important role in its export performances. It is one of the most open economies in the world. In terms of trade openness, it had a low ranking in 2003, but improved its position[11] to the 8th place in world ranking in 2008. Merchandise export alone was 173 per cent of its GDP and trade in services was 16.6 per cent of GDP in 2008 (World Bank, 2010b). India's trade in merchandise trade and services constitute 67.3 per cent of GDP in 2008 despite being considered as a fast emergence trading nation in the world.

The mineral policy has been very important for both countries. Vietnam has been exporting mineral resources to meet the pressing demand of resource constraints for industrialisation. On the other hand, India is a 'mineral scarce' economy, taking into account its future demand for industrialisation. It has liberalised its mining sector to allow import of minerals, and also not imposing restrictions on its exports of mining products. As India decides to bring down its average tariff close to ASEAN and Chinese level, unilateral tariff liberalisation in the manufacturing sector is an important feature of trade liberalisation in both the countries.

Overall Liberalisation in the Tariff Regime

Both the countries initiated trade liberalization in the mid-80s, where reform process was much faster in Vietnam than in India until 2004. The pace of liberalisation was reversed in India's favour since 2004, when external sector started booming along with the world economy. Since 2005, India's overall level of tariff declined significantly and remained lower than that of Vietnam.

In 1999, Vietnam's overall average tariff[12] was 18.9 per cent as against 28.4 per cent in India as shown in Table 3. As liberalization continued, simple average tariff[13] declined to 12.7 per cent for Vietnam, whereas it came down to 10.4 per cent for India in 2007 Vietnam made significant progress in liberalizing the agricultural sector whereas this sector remained protected in India. In the present decade, both countries have taken conscious decisions to liberalise their trade regimes unilaterally to facilitate their integration with the world economy. It is important to mention that overall import weighted average tariff rate in India is lower than Vietnam in the mining and manufacturing sector in recent years. While overall manufacturing tariff was 12.0 per cent for Vietnam, the corresponding statistics for India was 9.9 per cent in 2007. Mining sector is relatively more liberalized in India than Vietnam. The overall import weighted tariff indicates that both countries have made major strides in bringing down the level of tariffs since 2001. Tariff liberalization was almost stagnant after 2005 for Vietnam, whereas import weighted tariff was brought down significantly in India, particularly in the mining and the manufacturing sectors in 2007.

Table 3: Structure of Import Weighted Tariffs at the Aggregate Level

(in per cent)

Country	Sector	1999	2001	2004	2005	2007
Vietnam	Agriculture	46.1	39.1	28.1	29.8	17.2
	Mining	36.9	12.3	15.1	15.0	14.3
	Manufacturing	14.0	15.6	13.3	13.3	12.0
	Overall	18.9	17.4	14.4	14.7	12.7
India	Agriculture	29.1	58.7	66.3	55.7	65.4
	Mining	21.5	17.2	12.1	10.7	5.9
	Manufacturing	31.8	28.5	25.6	12.8	9.9
	Overall	28.4	26.5	22.8	13.4	10.4

Source: Author's calculation based on Trains Wits, Online, World Bank, Washington DC.

As India and Vietnam are almost at similar levels of tariff regimes, further tariff liberalization may not be a critical negotiating point for India in order to secure better market access in Vietnam and vice-versa. If preferential reduction of tariff takes place between both countries, it may be more advantageous to Vietnam in agricultural sector than India. Considering the small export basket of India in Vietnam, peak tariff and preferential tariffs could be detrimental to the export interest of India. Vietnam is gradually following regionalism, and extension of tariff preferences to more regional partners could prevent India in accessing Vietnamese market and materializing its export potential. If Vietnam continues to maintain peak tariff on certain products which are of export interest to India, and continues to provide tariff preferences to many competing suppliers from emerging countries, India may find difficulty in accessing Vietnamese market.

Trends in NTBs in India

Liberalisation registered in NTBs is no less than customs tariff in India. Substantial progress has been made in liberalising its NTBs over a period of time. The pace of unilateral liberalisation picked up fast in the latter half of the present decade. In India, quantitative restrictions (QRs) are construed hard core NTBs. In 2003, the level of quantitative restriction has come down nearly to 4 per cent of its total number of tradable products at 10-digit HS as shown in Figure 6. Under the provision of Article XX, and XXI of GATT, such restrictions are permitted under various grounds such as health, safety, essential security, etc. (Mohanty, 2006). The number of national lines subject to different forms of quantitative restriction comprise of 568 out of 11,671 lines in 2003 at 10-digit HS. As the reform process is in progress, the level of quantitative restrictions has declined further.

Historically, the level of NTBs remained very high during the pre-reform period, and smilar trend continued in the 1990s. Among the total number of tradable items, the share of hard core NTBs was more than 30 per cent in 1996, which declined significantly in the latter part of the 1990s as shown in Figure 4. The hard core NTBs consist of prohibited and restricted items in India. The proportion of the prohibited items to the total number of national lines was very small in 2000. The share of restricted and Special Import License (SIL) remained substantial in the mid-nineties, but declined sharply towards the late nineties.

Because of reduction of NTBs, the share of national lines under the free category rose significantly in the early 2000. Though regulatory control was strong on account of domestic compulsions, comprehensive economic reforms have brought down NTBs to a significant level. This has contributed to the surge in import bill of India along with its exports. India's total import bill

Figure 4: Declining Trend in NTBs in India

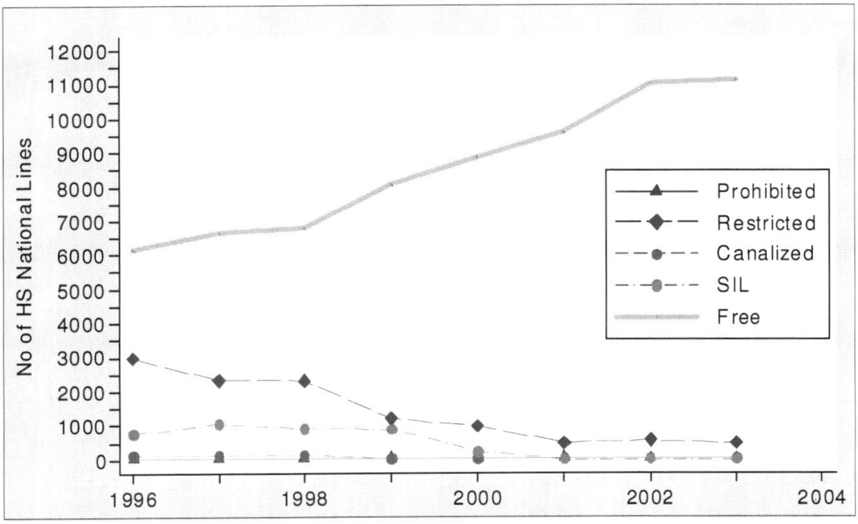

Source: Mohanty (2006).

was US$ 217 billion in 2007, and India provided enormous market access to Asian countries. Vietnam may take advantage of the large and growing Indian domestic market which is characterised by more transparent trading environment. The specific constraints that Vietnamese exports are facing to push its exports in the Indian market may be worth examining.

Opportunities to Access Indian Market
Vietnam's Export Potential in India

Vietnam has vast opportunities to access Indian market since it has large trade potential in diversified sectors. Similar is the case for India in Vietnam (Mohanty, 2010b). As discussed in the previous section, the current level of bilateral trade is below their trade potential. These two countries have shown their global competitiveness in different lines of products, but they are yet to venture into each others' economy for gaining market access despite being competitive in several lines of products globally.

Estimates of trade potential based on partial general equilibrium analysis[14] indicates that Vietnam has large trade potential in the Indian market and such trade potential can be achieved in the medium term. As noted earlier, the growth rate of bilateral trade flows between both has been very large, much above their overall trade with the rest of the world. This has been the reflection of large trade potential of both the countries in each others' market. The rate of bilateral trade flow had been very fast between 2003 and 2008, and trade flow declined to some extent in 2009 due to global recession. In the phase of recovery, bilateral trade flows should pick up, but fresh initiatives are to be taken to achieve certain reasonable trade targets.

However, the core issue remains trade bilateral trade balance between both the countries. There are other issues which need specific attentions. How trade imbalance can be addressed? Can Vietnam improve its export performance in India to reverse its current level of bilateral trade deficit? Which are the products/sectors to be emphasized to improve Vietnamese exports in India? What are the other regional initiatives in trade sector to overcome the impasse existing between both the countries?

Estimation of trade potential of Vietnam in India is to address some of the broad issues discussed above. Vietnam has not tapped its market potential fully. Vietnam's bilateral export with India was 0.62 per cent of its total exports and corresponding figure for import was 2.6 per cent in 2008. The corresponding figures are more attractive for certain European countries, the US and China. For reversing the problem of trade imbalances without interrupting the present flow of bilateral trade, focus on growth of Vietnam's exports along with balanced growth of bilateral flow of trade may be emphasised in the medium term. For addressing trade imbalance, Vietnam should substantially improve its presence in the Indian market by enlarging its current export basket and replacing less efficient suppliers in the Indian market through competition.

Sectoral Distribution of Vietnam's Export Potential

India considers Vietnam as the future powerhouse of global trade. In order to move towards achieving the objective of greater engagement with the country, India may be intended not only to reduce current level of bilateral trade imbalances by providing wider market access, but also to increase the volume of bilateral trade to achieve scale economies in the medium term.

In this study, the estimation based on conservative estimate indicates that trade potential of Vietnam is much higher than the actual trade. If trade potentials are translated into actual, Vietnam can reverse its current bilateral trade deficit with India in the medium term. Empirical estimation indicates that Vietnam's export potential[15] is around 127 per cent of its current imports from India in 2009. In case present trade potential is realised, Vietnam may emerge as a trade surplus country vis-à-vis India.

Distribution of export potential is not uniformly spread over all the major trade sectors since Vietnam has acquired competitiveness in certain lines of production as shown in Figure 5. The agricultural sector has very little trade potential in India as compared to mining and the industrial sectors. Vietnam can access Indian agricultural market to the extent of US$ 85 million based on India's import profile in 2008. It constitutes nearly 3.6 per cent of the total potential of the country in India. In the agricultural sector, largest trade potential is in the fats and oil sector followed by fruits and vegetables. Trade prospects are large in the fruits and vegetables sector where the trade potential has increased sharply during the period 2004-08. The bulk potential is in the industrial sector followed by the mining sector. While mining and industrial sectors share 13.2 and 83.1 per cent of the total trade potentials respectively in the total trade potential of US$ 2.34 billion in 2008.

**Figure 5: Sectoral Trade Potential of Vietnam in India, 2008
(in million US$)**

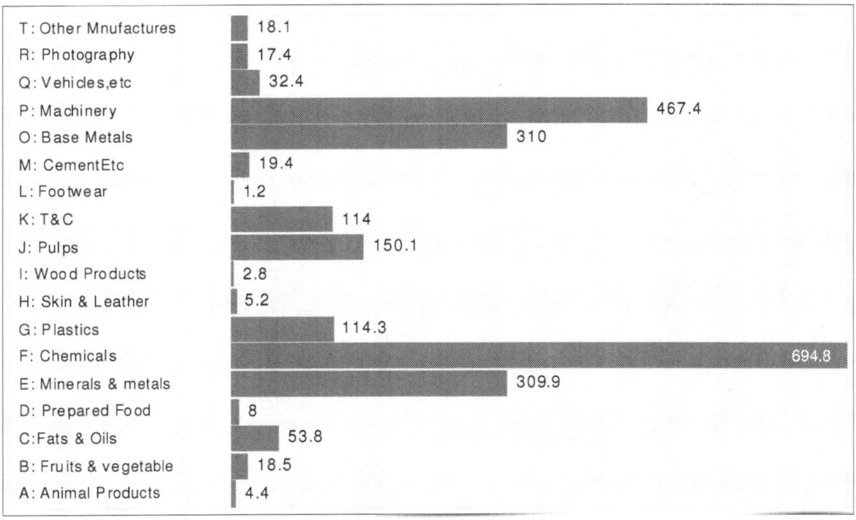

T: Other Mnufactures	18.1
R: Photography	17.4
Q: Vehicles,etc	32.4
P: Machinery	467.4
O: Base Metals	310
M: CementEtc	19.4
L: Footwear	1.2
K: T&C	114
J: Pulps	150.1
I: Wood Products	2.8
H: Skin & Leather	5.2
G: Plastics	114.3
F: Chemicals	694.8
E: Minerals & metals	309.9
D: Prepared Food	8
C: Fats & Oils	53.8
B: Fruits & vegetable	18.5
A: Animal Products	4.4

Source: Estimated by the author based on PCTAS 2010 CD, ITC, Geneva.

Distribution of Vietnam's trade potential across the non-agricultural sector of Indian market indicates that some sectors can have strong stack in the Indian market. It is evident from the sectoral distribution that mineral export is likely to dominate the future trade with India. Surging demand for industrial raw material/intermediates in the Indian domestic market will be the most determining factor for the expected growth of exports from Vietnam.

As an emerging country, India's import interest for industrial intermediates includes wide spectrum of products ranging from primary, resource-based, labour intensive to technology intensive products. The major sectors where Vietnam may have export interests in India could be chemicals, machinery and base metals. Other sectors have moderate level of trade potential such as textiles & clothing, pulps, plastic products and automotive. In the total trade potential of Vietnam in India, four sectors, such as machinery, base metals, chemicals and minerals share ¾ of the total trade potential existing in 2008. Incidentally, these sectors registered high bilateral export growth to India during the period 2004-08. Among these four lead sectors, chemical is the single largest sector in terms of Vietnam's total trade potential in India and potential in this sector was growing at the CAGR of 70.1 per cent during the same period. In case these potentials are realised by Vietnam, bilateral trade gap between the countries can improve very fast.

Conclusion

India and Vietnam are emerging as two resilient economies in the world, restraining effectively the adverse effects of recent global recession on their economies. Despite mounting pressure of global slowdown, GDP growth rates of India and Vietnam were 5.7 per cent and 5.3 per cent respectively against global average of –0.6 per cent in 2009 (World Bank, 2010). Their real GDP, inflow of FDI, trade, foreign remittances, among others, had grown phenomenally during the last two decades. Growth records of China and India are known in the contemporary economic literature, but Vietnam is emerging as the third fastest growing economy in the world after Russia and China since 1992. Export has been the driver of their 'growth miracle' during the reform period and has enabled them to integrate with the global economy. India and Vietnam are expected to grow fast at the rate of 9.7 per cent and 6.5 per cent respectively with the partial recovery of the global economy in 2010 (World Bank, 2010). Deep engagement between these economies at the backdrop of global recovery could be beneficial to harness the existing synergies between them.

The past experience indicates that bilateral trade has been growing rapidly, but with a low base. It made an 8-fold increase during the period 2001-09 and expected to touch US$ 14.6 billion by 2015 with a business-as-usual scenario. Though structure of bilateral trade passed through various phases, trade picked up significantly during the period 2005-09 over 2000-05. Bilateral trade increased from US$ 273 million in 2001 to US$ 2.5 billion in 2008. In fact, growth rate of their bilateral trade is much higher than their overall growth rate of trade with rest of the world.

With upsurge of bilateral trade, there is large trade asymmetry taking place in favour of India, causing trade friction between both the countries. Vietnam's bilateral trade deficit with India was 5 per cent of its overall trade deficit with the rest of the world in 2009. There are positive indications shown in their recent trade relationship where the ratio of bilateral trade deficit to total bilateral low of trade is declining with expansion of the volume of bilateral trade. This shows that trade asymmetry will continue to decline with rising volume of bilateral trade flows. This is a positive development towards bilateral trade cooperation in the medium term.

In the context of trade prospects of both the countries, two vital issues need immediate attention. What is the size of trade potential of Vietnam in India and in which sectors? Can it be possible to minimise the present level of trade asymmetry along with rise in the level of trade? To what extent potential trade of Vietnam can be realised keeping in view the protected trade regime existing in India?

These issues are empirically examined in the study. There is a strong undercurrent going on in several countries that India is continuing to have a protected trade regime as it was in the 70s and 80s. In fact, trade regime in India is overwhelmingly liberalised during the last two decades of reforms. It is almost reaching the level of ASEAN in several broad sectors and aiming to reach the EU tariff level soon. In the manufacturing sector, India is rather more liberalised than China (Mohanty, 2010a). By 2005, overall import-weighted tariff of India was lower than Vietnam. Agricultural sector in India is more protected than Vietnam on account of 'livelihood security' issue. But India is more liberal in tariff protection than Vietnam in broad sectors such as mining and manufacturing sectors until 2007. India's NTBs are at the minimum, which is consistent with the provisions of the WTO. However, low protection would allow Vietnam to compete with other competitors in the Indian market and also force domestic Indian producers to compete with foreign suppliers to create more congenial environment for improving production efficiency.

The empirical analysis has provided the evidence that Vietnam has large trade potentials in India. Using the Vinor's framework (1950), trade potential is estimated to be based on 'trade creation', applying the principle of price competitiveness. The study suggests that Vietnam has effective capabilities to venture into several sectors in the Indian market where it has to export yet. The recent surge in Vietnam's exports to India is due to introduction of new products in the Indian market (such as, natural calcium phosphate, urea, heterocyclic compound, etc.) and consolidating its strength on the existing export products (such as anthracite coal, coffee not roasted, batteries, cinnamon and technically specified rubber). Similarly, there is large trade potential in these products which can be supplied to the Indian market. Expansion of the bilateral export basket of Vietnam may support the endeavour to break product concentration of certain products in the Indian market. With a conservative estimate, total trade potential of Vietnam in India is US$ 2.23 billion in 2008 alone. In case this trade potential is realised into actual export, the bilateral trade surplus will tilt towards Vietnam. It may be noted that India has trade deficit with several small countries across the globe including Myanmar, Guinea, Papua New Guinea, Congo(s), Gabon, Togo, Bhutan, Bermuda, etc. It is possible that a vibrant country like Vietnam can effectively resolve its bilateral trade asymmetry with its competitive strength.

Notes

1. According to the recent forecast (ESCAP, 2010a), Vietnam's real growth rate could be 5.8 per cent in 2010.
2. In a recent study, Qiao (2008) has got the empirical evidence that Vietnam is the fastest growing economy among N11 countries. Similarly, India has been identified as the the fastest growing economy in the world only next to China (World Bank, 2010a).
3. For example see, Li and Zhang (2008) and Felipe, Lavina and Fan (2008).
4. Vietnam has mobilised resources through deficit finance to raise public investment in order to boost economic growth during the 2000s (World Bank, 2007). The annual budget deficit increased from an average of 3.5 per cent of GDP in the 1990s to an average of 4.8 per cent of GDP after 2000.
5. For understanding dynamics of FDI on overall development of Vietnam during the last two decades, see Le Viet (2002), Phan and Ramstetter (2006), Vu Bang, Byron and Noy (2006) and Nguyen (2006).
6. The recent forecast of World Bank for the global economy is reported in *World Economic Outlook, October 2010.*
7. There are a few studies documented economic success of poverty alleviation through trade liberalization. For example see, Glewwe et al (2000), Niimi et al. (2003) and Benjamin & Brandt (2004).

8. We have selected top performing countries from the list of 24 fast growing countries of the world during the last three decades. These 24 countries are selected from all the continents of the world.

9. The projection is estimated by the author based on average growth rate of bilateral trade during the period 2005-09.

10. India's oil consumption is growing at the rate of 13 per cent per annum. While domestic production was 0.807 million barrels per day, the domestic consumption was 2.57 million barrel day in 2006. Country's proven reserve is expected to last for 15 years from now. See http://escapefromindia.wordpress.com/2008/01/01/india-imports-about-70-percent-of-its-oil/

11. Other countries having higher ranking in trade openness are: Singapore, Hong Kong, Luxemburg, Seychelles, Liberia, Maldives and Belgium.

12. During the nineties, Vietnam's trade policy was complex with import protection of final goods remained at a high level. Trade openness enforced after 2003, mostly through exports (Niimi et al., 2003; Justino and al., 2008 and Coello, 2008).

13. *Trains Wits* database is used for tariff analysis where latest data available for Vietnam is for 2007. Though latest data available for India is for 2009, we are presenting tariff statistics for 2007 for comparative analysis.

14. Vinor (1950) developed a framework to estimate trade potential in a liberalized tariff regime. The twin concept of trade creation and trade diversion are familiar in the contemporary literature of international trade.

15. Trade potential is estimated using UNDTAD (2010) database.

REFERENCES

Ahluwalia, Montek S. (2002), "Economic Reforms in India since 1991: Has Gradualism Worked?," *Journal of Economic Perspectives*, American Economic Association, vol. 16(3), pages 67-88, Summer.

Athukorala, Prema-chandra (2009), Transition to a Market Economy and Export performance in Vietnam, The Arndt-Corden Division of Economics, Research School of Pacific and Asian Studies, May, Working Paper No. 2009/05, Australian National University.

Asian Development Bank (2005), Asian Development Outlook 2005, Asian Development Bank, Manila.

Balassa, B. (1965), "Trade Liberalisation and 'Revealed' Comparative Advantage", *The Manchester School*, Vol. 33, pp. 99-123.

Benjamin, D., and L. Brandt. 2004. "Agriculture and Income Distribution in Rural Vietnam under Economic Reforms: A Tale of Two Regions". In Glewwe, P., N. Agrawal, and D. Dollar (Eds) "*Economic Growth, Poverty and Household Welfare in Vietnam*", World Bank, pp. 133-186.

Coello B. (2008) Agriculture and trade liberalization in Vietnam. Working Paper 75, Paris School of Economics.

Dat, Tran Tho (2004), '*Part II – National Reports: Vietnam*', in Asian Productivity Organization (ed.) Total Factor Productivity Growth: Survey Report, Tokyo, Japan, 2004.

Doah, Le Dang, Vo Tri Thanh, Pham Thi Lan Huong, Dinh Hien Minh, and Nguyen Quang Thang, *Explaining Growth in Vietnam*, Global Research Project, Global Research Network, 2002.

ESCAP (2010), Economic and Social Survey of Asian and the Pacific 2010: Sustaining Recovery and Dynamism for Inclusive development, UN ESCAP, Bangkok.

Felipe, J., E. Lavina and E.X. Fan (2008). "The Diverging Patterns of Profitability, Investment and Growth of China and India During 1980-2003", *World Development*, 36(5), 741-774.

Glewwe, P., M. Gragnolati, and H. Zaman. 2000. Who gained from Vietnam's boom in the 1990's? An Analysis of Poverty and Inequality Trends. *World Bank Policy Research Working Paper Series* No. 2275.

Greenway, David, T Hyclak, and R. Thornton (1989), Economic Aspects of Regional Trading Arrangement, Harvester Wheatsheaf, New York.

Justino, P., Litchfield J. and Pham H.T. (2008), "Poverty Dynamics During Trade Reform: Evidence From Rural Vietnam," *Review of Income and Wealth*, Blackwell Publishing, vol. 54(2), 166-192.

Le Viet Anh (2002), FDI-Growth Nexus in Vietnam, mimeo, Graduate School of International Development, Nagoya University.

Li, Yuefen and Bin Zhang (2008). "Development Path of China and India and the Challenges for their Sustainable Growth", *The World Economy*, 31(10), 1277-1291.

Mehta, R. (2005), India-Vietnam Trade: Current Relations and Prospects, RIS Discussion Paper # 105, December, Research and Information System for Developing Countries (RIS), New Delhi.

Mehta, R. and S.K. Mohanty (2001), "WTO and Industrial Tariff: An Empirical Analysis for India", Monograph Series, Research and Information System for the Non-Aligned and Other Developing Countries (RIS), New Delhi.

Mohanty, S.K. (2010a), India China Bilateral Trade Relationship, Study conducted for the Reserve Bank of India, Mumbai.

Mohanty, S.K. (2010b), "Trade Implication of Close Economic Cooperation between India and Vietnam: Can Bilateral Trade Asymmetry be Corrected?" (Forthcoming).

Mohanty, S.K. (2006), 'South Asia as a Global Force in Trade', in Trade, in *Tariff and Customs in South Asia*, (ed.) Imtiaz Alam, South Asia Policy Analysis Network, Pakistan, 2006.

Mohanty, S.K. and Robert Arockiasamy (2010), Prospects for Making India's Manufacturing Sector Export Oriented, RIS Study for the Ministry of Commerce and Industries.

Mohanty, S.K. and Sachin Chaturvedi (2006), "Rising Tiger and Leaping Dragon: Emerging Global Dynamics and Space for Developing Countries and Least Developed Countries", *IDS Bulletin*, 37(1), Jan., pp. 62-70.

Nguyen Phi Lan (2006), Foreign Direct Investment in Vietnam: Impact on Economic Growth and Domestic Investment, Mimeo, Centre for Regulation and Market Analysis, University of South Australia.

Niimi, Y., Puja Vasudeva Dutta and Alan Winters (2003), "Trade Liberalisation and Poverty Dynamics in Vietnam," PRUS Working Papers 17, Poverty Research Unit at Sussex, University of Sussex.

Phan Minh Ngoc and Eric Ramstetter (2006), Economic Growth, Trade and Multinational Presence in Vietnam's Province, Mimeo, The International Center for the Study of East Asian Development, Kitakyushu University.

Qiao, Helen (Hong) (2008), "Vietnam: The Next Asian Tiger in the Making," *Global Economic Papers* No 165, April 17, Goldman Sachs.

RIS (2007), World Trade and Development Report: 2007, Oxford University Press.

Rodrick, Dani and Arvind Subramanian (2004), "From 'Hindu Growth' to Productivity Surge: The Mystery of the Indian Growth Transition", *NBER Working Paper No. 10376*, National Bureau of Economic Research, Cambridge, MA.

Schaumburg-Müller, Henrik (September 2002), Foreign Direct Investment in Vietnam: Impact on the Development of the Manufacturing Sector, Paper for the EADI 10th General Conference in Ljubljana, Slovenia.

Thanh, Vo Tri and Nguyen Anh Duong, *Studies of Total Factor Productivity in Vietnam: A Review*, CIEM, Hanoi, ADB Contract No. A11280, Sep 2007.

UNCTAD (2010), PCTAS 2010 CD, Geneva.

Vinor, Jacob (1950), The Customs Union Issue, Cornegie Endowment for International Peace, New York.

Vu Bang Tam, Gangnes Byron and Ilan Noy (2006), Is Foreign Direct Investment Good for Growth? Evidence from Sectoral Analysis of China and Vietnam, Mimeo, Department of Economics, University of Hawaii-Manoa.

World Bank (2007), World Bank, *Taking Stock – An Update on Vietnam's Economic Development*, prepared by the World Bank for the Midyear Consultative Group Meeting for Vietnam, June 2007.

World Bank (2010a), World Economic Outlook, October, World Bank, Washington DC.

World Bank (2010b), Direction of Trade Statistics, Washington DC.

5

Recent Developments in the South China Sea: Implications for Regional Security and Cooperation

Tran Truong Thuy

The significance of South China Sea has been widely recognized by several stakeholders engaged in maritime navigation, natural resource exploitation, environmental protection, and international law. The South China Sea disputes relating to the Paracel Islands, Spratly Islands and maritime zones associated with these groups of islands remain as one of the many potential flashpoints that could cause regional instability. Since 1990s, efforts have been made by regional countries to stabilize the situation and seek the opportunities for cooperation in the South China Sea area. These efforts have resulted in, among others, the ASEAN Declaration on the South China Sea in 1992, the adoption in 2002 of the Declaration on the Conduct of Parties in the South China Sea (DOC), according to which all signing parties pledged to seek peaceful solutions to disputes and conduct maritime cooperation in order to maintain regional stability in the South China Sea under the principles of the Charter of the United Nations, the 1982 UN Convention on the Law of the Sea (UNCLoS), the Treaty of Amity and Cooperation in Southeast Asia (TAC), the Five Principles of Peaceful Coexistence, and other universally recognized principles of international law.

However, the parties have not ceased activities that complicate the situation. Tensions have occasionally arisen and claimants continue to protest each other's moves in the South China Sea and regional cooperation is far from desirable. It is in this context that this chapter attempts to focus on the efforts made by regional countries to stabilize the situation and promote cooperation in the South China Sea. Also it is important to analyse implications of recent developments in the South China Sea for regional security and cooperation and ascertain why the implementation of the signed documents, especially the DOC, has been incomplete. It is also important to explore some solution-oriented suggestions for promoting regional cooperation.

Existing Documents Governing Behaviors of Parties

Prior to the DOC, the TAC and the Treaty on the Southeast Asia Nuclear Weapon-Free Zone concluded in 1976 and 1995 respectively were the main legal instruments governing behaviours of the parties concerned in the South China Sea. The fundamental principles guiding the contracting parties in the TAC include the settlement of differences by peaceful means, non-resort to the threat or use of force and the promotion of effective cooperation among the concerned parties.[1]

Association of Southeast Asian Nations (ASEAN) members first adopted their common stance on the South China Sea dispute in the ASEAN Declaration on the South China Sea signed in Manila in 1992. The declaration demonstrated ASEAN's concerns over the tension between Vietnam and China after the latter licensed the Creston Energy Corporation (from the United States) to exploit oil in Vanguard Bank on Vietnam's continental shelf and passed its Law on the Territorial Sea on 25 February 1992 stipulating China's absolute sovereignty over both the Paracel and the Spratly islands. The Declaration called on the parties concerned to settle the dispute by peaceful means, exercise restraint and cooperate in applying the principles enshrined in the TAC as a basis for establishing a code of international conduct over the South China Sea. In addition, all parties concerned were invited to subscribe to this Manila Declaration.[2] Vietnam, a non-ASEAN country at the time, supported Manila Declaration. China, however, reiterated its position on its refusal to accept multilateral discussion of the issue and its view that the Paracel and Spratly Island disputes did not concern ASEAN.

Bilaterally, China and the Philippines reached an agreement on an eight-point Code of Conduct in their Joint Statement on Consultations on the South China Sea and other Areas of Cooperation in August 1995. The fourth annual bilateral consultative dialogue between Vietnam and the Philippines also produced a nine-point Code of Conduct in October 1995.[3]

The 1995 Chinese occupation of Mischief Reef in the Spratlys, a reef well within the Philippines' Exclusive Economic Zone, marked a change in China's policy toward the South China Sea. Previously, China only resorted to force twice, namely in 1974 and 1988 against Vietnam, a non-ASEAN country. After the Mischief Reef incident, ASEAN sought initiatives that could prevent existing disputes from escalating into conflicts.

The Declaration on the Conduct of Parties in the South China Sea

The idea of a regional Code of Conduct (COC) was officially endorsed at the 29th ASEAN Ministerial Meeting (Jakarta, 21-27 July 1996) in the hope that it would provide the foundation for long-term stability in the area and foster understanding among the countries concerned.[4] The ASEAN Foreign Ministers expressed their concerns over the situation in the South China Sea in the joint communiqué and underlined that the parties concerned should apply the principles of the TAC as the basis for a regional code of conduct in the South China Sea to build a secure and stable regional environment. 'Recent developments affirmed the need of a COC in the South China Sea and this will lay a foundation for long term stability and foster understanding among claimant countries', stated the Communiqué.[5] At the 6th ASEAN Summit (Hanoi, 15-16 December 1998), ASEAN leaders agreed to formulate the Code of Conduct in the South China Sea.[6]

Although a binding code of conduct had been considered to be the primary goal, after almost 5 years of negotiations, ASEAN and China eventually only reached a political document. On 4 November 2002 in Phnom-Penh, ASEAN and the People's Republic of China signed the DOC. The signing of DOC in 2002 was a result of a long process of engagement of ASEAN toward China into a framework of governing state-to-state relations and dispute settlement, confidence-building measures, and cooperation activities.[7]

The DOC, therefore, is not a document to resolve disputes but to create favourable condition and opportunities for the parties concerned to seek resolutions. The DOC can help build a cooperative and friendly environment by confidence-building measures, paving the way for a long-term solution.

This document can serve as a basis for cooperation in the South China Sea.[8] The DOC is composed of three main components, namely the basic norms governing state-to-state relations and dispute settlement, confidence-building measures, and cooperation activities.

Point 4 underlines the duties of the parties concerned to resolve their territorial disputes by peaceful means, without resorting to the threat or use of force, through friendly consultations and negotiations by sovereign states directly concerned, in accordance with universally recognized principles of international law, including the 1982 UN Convention on the Law of the Sea. Concrete measures are listed in point 5 in which the parties concerned undertake to exercise self-restraint in the conduct of activities that would complicate or escalate disputes and affect peace and stability including, among others, refraining from inhabiting the currently uninhabited islands, reefs, shoals, cays, and other features.

Regarding second component of DOC – confidence-building measures, in point 2, the parties are committed to exploring ways for building trust and confidence on the basis of equality and mutual respect. Point 7 in the DOC underlines the need for the parties concerned to continue their consultations and dialogues concerning relevant issues, including respecting the Declaration, to promote good neighbourliness and transparency and establish harmony, mutual understanding and cooperation.

Concerning cooperative activities, pending a comprehensive and durable settlement of the disputes, the DOC states five areas for the parties concerned may explore and undertake, including: (a) marine environmental protection; (b) marine scientific research; (c) safety of marine navigation and communication; (d) marine search and rescue; and (e) combating transnational crime, including but not limited to trafficking in illicit drugs, piracy and armed robbery at sea, and illegal traffic in arms. These areas, which are considered of less sensitivity, can help the parties concerned build mutual trust and confidence.

The DOC was signed as a step towards the adoption of a more binding COC which defines the rights and responsibility of the parties concerned to further promote peace, stability and development in the region.

Developments in the South China Sea after signing the DOC

The DOC was signed in the hope that it would provide the foundation for long-term stability in the area and foster understanding among the countries concerned. However, as commented by Nguyen Hong Thao, "it is naïve to believe that because of the DOC, the parties have ceased activities to complicate the situation."[9] Although there has been some improvement in relations between China and Southeast Asia, tensions have occasionally arisen and claimants continue to protest each other's moves in the South China Sea.

ASEAN-China Relation

At the seventh ASEAN-China Summit on 8 October 2003 in Bali, Indonesia, both sides signed Joint Declaration of the Heads of State/Government of the Association of South East Asian Nations and the People's Republic of China on Strategic Partnership for Peace and Prosperity with the declared purpose of fostering friendly relations, mutually beneficial cooperation and good neighbourliness between ASEAN and China by deepening and expanding ASEAN-China cooperative relations in a comprehensive manner in the 21st century.[10] On the same day, China officially became the first non-ASEAN country to join the TAC, thus encouraging China to commit to settle disputes by peaceful means and avoid threatening behavior or use force. ASEAN countries highly appreciated these developments, which was a major contribution to regional peace, security and development. In 2005, Chinese leader Hu Jintao visited Indonesia, Brunei, and Philippines to promote friendship and cooperation and to assuage concerns about Chinese intentions. All of these developments, combined with other activities within Chinese "charm offensive" toward Southeast Asia, including the 2001 proposal to establish a China-ASEAN Free Trade Area (CAFTA), have helped reduce the Chinese threat perception in the region.

Implementation of DOC

To translate the provisions of DOC into concrete cooperation activities, in the Plan of Action to implement the joint declaration on ASEAN-China strategic partnership for peace and prosperity in 2003, which was formulated to serve as the "master plan" to deepen and broaden ASEAN-China relations and cooperation, among other things, ASEAN and China declared to pursue joint actions and measures to implement the DOC in an "effective way".[11] The actions and measures include: (i) to convene regular ASEAN-China

Senior Officials Meeting (SOM) on the realisation of the DOC to provide guidance for and review the implementation of the DOC, and (ii) to establish a working group to draw up the guidelines for the implementation of the DOC and to provide recommendations to the ASEAN-China SOM on policy and implementation issues.[12] The first ASEAN-China SOM on the implementation of the DOC in Kuala Lumpur on 7 December 2004 decided to set up a Joint Working Group (JWG) to study and recommend confidence-building activities.[13] The ASEAN-China JWG is tasked to formulate recommendations on: (a) guidelines and action plan for the implementation of the DOC; (b) specific cooperative activities in the South China Sea; and (c) a register of experts and eminent persons who may provide technical inputs, non-binding and professional views or policy recommendations to the ASEAN-China JWG; and (d) the convening of workshops, as the need arises.[14] At the first meeting of ASEAN-China JWG on DOC in Manila on 4-5 August 2005, ASEAN presented a draft of guidelines for discussion. This proposal consists of seven points:

(a) The implementation of the DOC should be carried out in a step by step approach in line with the provisions of the DOC.

(b) ASEAN will continue its current practice of consulting among themselves before meeting China.

(c) The implementation of the DOC should be based on activities or projects clearly identified.

(d) The participation in the activities or projects should be carried out on a voluntary basis.

(e) Initial activities to be undertaken under the ambit of the DOC should be confidence building measures.

(f) The decision to implement concrete measures or activities of the COC should be based on consensus among parties concerned and lead to the eventual realization of a DOC.

(g) In the implementation of the agreed projects under the DOC, the service of the experts and eminent persons if deemed necessary will be sought to provide specific inputs on the project concerned.

The main issue is that the ASEAN wants to deal with China as a group and to "consult among themselves" before meeting with China, while China prefers consultations with "relevant parties", not with ASEAN as a bloc. After several meetings of ASEAN-China JWG, ASEAN-China SOM, ASEAN country coordinator with China, Informal Consultations, a consensus on paragraph 2 of the guideline has not been reached.

In January 2010, Vietnam took over the rotating chairmanship of ASEAN. At a press conference after summit meeting in Hanoi in April 2010, Prime Minister Nguyen Tan Dzung announced that ASEAN and Chinese officials had agreed to hold meetings to "discuss solutions to push the implementation of the DOC".[15] At the recent meeting of the ASEAN-China joint working group in Ha Noi, both sides reaffirmed their commitment to full respect and realization of the DOC in the South China Sea.[16] But no real progress was made – parties merely came back to the starting point.

At the 43rd ASEAN Foreign Ministers Meeting in Hanoi on 19–20 July 2010, ASEAN Ministers "stressed the importance of maintaining peace and stability in the South China Sea," "reaffirmed the importance of the DOC," "underscored the need to intensify efforts to ensure the effective implementation of the Declaration," and "looked forward to the Regional Code of Conduct in the South China Sea (COC)." ASEAN Ministers also tasked ASEAN Senior Officials to work closely with their Chinese counterparts to reconvene the ASEAN-China SOM on the DOC at "the earliest opportunity."[17] In response, at the ASEAN-China Foreign Ministers Meeting, China's Foreign Minister Yang Jiechi agreed to implement the DOC, but declared that an ASEAN-China SOM meeting on DOC will be held in an "appropriate time".[18] At the 17th Asian Regional Forum (ARF) on 23 July, thirteen foreign ministers (including five from ASEAN countries) brought up the South China Sea issue and supported the ASEAN-China DOC. U.S. Secretary of State, Hillary Clinton, said that "the United States has a national interest in freedom of navigation, open access to Asia's maritime commons, and respect for international law in the South China Sea". She said the United States supports a collaborative diplomatic process, supports the 2002 ASEAN-China DOC, encourages the parties to reach agreement on a COC, and is "prepared to facilitate" initiatives and confidence-building measures consistent with the DOC.[19] In response, Yang Jiechi highlighted the ability of the DOC to enhance mutual trust and to create favorable conditions and good atmosphere for final solution to the disputes. But he insisted that the South China Sea issues should not be internationalized, that the DOC should not be viewed as between China on one side and ASEAN on the other, and that disputes should be handled on a bilateral, not multilateral, basis. He also pointed out that there have been JWG consultations on DOC, and "when the conditions are ripe", a SOM can also be held.[20]

Actions Taken by Claimants on the disputed areas

The DOC was signed in the hope that it would provide the foundation for long-term stability in the area and foster understanding among the countries concerned. However, as stated by Nguyen Hong Thao, it is naïve to believe that because of the DOC, the parties have ceased undertaking activities that complicate the situation.[21] Tensions have occasionally arisen and claimants have continued to protest each other's moves in the South China Sea.

Claimants have continued to construct structures in the disputed features in the South China Sea. Malaysia used soil to raise the level of Swallow Reef in order to construct an airstrip and other resort facilities. In November 2003, the Fillipino naval forces discovered markers erected by China on some uninhabited features of Spratly.[22] In addition, Taiwan erected 'a simple bird-watching stand' in 2004 and constructed a runway on the disputed island of Itu Aba in 2006.[23] In December 2006, China plated new markers on the Paracel Island, which Vietnam protested, calling their construction "invalid."[24] In December 2007, China established the city of Sansha for administrating the Paracel and Spratly Islands (and the submerged reef of Macclesfield Bank), which triggered strong official protest from Vietnam as well as anti-China demonstrations in Hanoi and Ho Chi Minh City. In January 2010, Hanoi condemned China's decision to establish local governing bodies in the Paracel Islands and develop the islands's tourism industry as a violation of Vietnamese sovereignty.[25] Later, China passed the "2010-20 Grand Plan for Construction and Development for the International Tourism Island of Hainan," under which the Spratly and Paracel Islands will be incorporated in a multi-purpose ocean complex, air and sea tourist routes bound for Paracel will be promoted, and registration for the right to use uninhabited islands will be encouraged. In June 2010, Vietnam Ministry of Foreign Affairs (MOFA) spokesperson condemned the Chinese plan as a violation of its sovereignty and contradictory to the spirit of DOC. She quoted provision five of the DOC: "The parties undertake to exercise self-restraint in the conduct of activities that would complicate or escalate disputes and affect peace and stability including, among others, refraining from any action of inhabiting the presently uninhabited islands, reefs, shoals, cays, and other features, and to handle their differences in a constructive manner."[26]

Every year, China continues to send research vessels to conduct maritime research programs in areas adjacent to the coast of other countries in the South China Sea.[27] In July 2007, the Chinese Navy dispatched one warship in the southern part of the South China Sea in order to compel Vietnam to stop its hydrographic campaign for gathering the data needed to determine the extension of its continental shelf.

Occasionally, China conducted firing exercises in a disputed area of the South China Sea, the most recent living drill conducted immediately after ARF meeting in Hanoi in July 2010.

China's Unilateral Fishing Ban

China has annually unilaterally declared its fishing ban in the South China Sea for two months, June and July, which had been applied since 1999. In 2006 and 2007, there were several reports of incidents of Vietnamese fishermen being killed or wounded by Chinese patrol vessels and gunboats. Over 2009, Chinese forces have repeatedly detained Vietnamese fishing boats near the Paracel Islands, which both countries claim, and have demanded a fine of $10,000 for the release of the fishermen.[28] To enforce its jurisdictional claims in the South China Sea, Beijing announced in early April 2010 the dispatch of two large fishery patrol vessels to the Spratly Islands to protect Chinese fishing vessels, the first time it has done so outside the period of its unilateral fishing ban in the sea that usually takes place between May and August.[29]

Tensions over Energy Developments

After signing the DOC, tensions over energy developments have continued to occur. China and ASEAN states have actively involved international companies to exploit the energy reserves of their claims in order to fulfill the need of their rapid economic growth. Occasionally, when international energy companies undertake exploration in zones awarded by one country but claimed by another country, especially within the U-shaped claim line of China, activity has been halted by diplomatic protest and even naval intervention.

In November 2004, China sent the research vessel Nanhai 215 with oil drilling platform Kantan 3 to an area about 2 nautical miles east of the median line between the coasts of Vietnam and China's Hainan Island. Vietnam's MOFA spokesman made a protest and requested China to "refrain from complicating the situation" and not to move the Kantan 3 oil drilling platform to the area, claiming that it "lies entirely within the exclusive economic zone and continental shelf of Vietnam."[30]

In October 2004, China's Foreign Ministry spokeswoman protested Vietnam just a day after the announcement of the discovery of oil by a partnership of companies comprising Petronas Carigali Overseas of Malaysia, American Technology Inc. Petroleum (ATI), Singapore Petroleum Co., and PetroVietnam's Petroleum Investment and Development Co (PID) in the 14,000-square-kilometer area of Blocks 102 and 106 in the Yen Tu field, about 70 kilometers east of Vietnam's Hai Phong seaport.[31] Starting in the summer of 2007, China told a number of foreign oil and gas firms to stop exploration work with Vietnamese partners in the South China Sea or face unspecified consequences in their business dealings with China.[32] In April 2007, China's Foreign Ministry spokesman protested Vietnam's concession and cooperation with British Petroleum to build a gas pipeline near the southern coast of Vietnam that China considered "adjacent maritime zones" of the Spratly Islands.[33] China readily slipped back into its legally dubious historic claim to most of the South China Sea and the nationalist rhetoric that accompanies it.[34] Foreign Ministry spokesperson Qin Gang said, "any unilateral action taken by any other country in these waters constitutes infringement into China's sovereignty, territorial rights and jurisdiction."[35] Vietnam reaffirmed that the area covered by its project with BP is located in Vietnam's Exclusive Economic Zone (EEZ) and continental shelf. All conducted activities are in conformity with international law and practices, particularly UNCLOS and the spirit of DOC.[36] In the spring of 2007, under Chinese pressure, BP stopped its exploitation activities on the gas fields of Moc Tinh and Hai Thach on continental shelf of Vietnam. In 2008, there were many press reports that U.S. energycompany ExxonMobil had been threatened by China. From 2007 to 2010, China has also frequently protested other exploration activities conducted by international energy companies, including BP in bloc 117; PGS (Norway) in bloc 122; Chevron (US) in bloc 122; Pogo (US) in bloc 124; ONGC (India) in bloc 127; Indemisu (Japan) in bloc 04-3; CoconoPhilips (US) in bloc 133; Pearl Energy (UK) in bloc 06-1; Knoc (South Korea) in bloc 11-4; and Gazprom (Russia) in blocs 111 and 113.[37] A spokesperson from Vietnam's MOFA confirmed that in the case of ExxonMobile, "these (awarded blocs) are totally under the sovereignty right of Vietnam and in line with the 1982 UN Convention on the Law of the Sea," and "Vietnam will ensure all the legitimate interests of foreign investors when they operate in Vietnam." Vietnam "welcome[s] and shall facilitate all cooperation with foreign partners, including Chinese investors operating in Vietnam, on the basis of full respect for our sovereignty."[38]

In 2009, China also objected to the Philippines's drilling in the Reed Bank area, about 60 miles (100 kilometers) west of Palawan, which may contain 3.4 trillion cubic feet of gas and 450 million barrels of oil.[39] Malaysia and Brunei also dispute over the development of a gas field in an area where their claims overlap. Identical blocs were awarded to different companies: Malaysia awarded exploration rights to Murphy Oil, while Brunei awarded similar rights to Royal Dutch Shell and Total.[40] On the Chinese side, in 2007 Beijing opened the concession and invited bids for 22 petroleum blocks in the South China Sea in areas up to 1000 miles from Hainan.[41]

China's "Core National Interest"

The most recent significant development in the South China Sea is that in March 2010, senior Chinese officials told U.S. high-ranking visitors that China had put the South China Sea into its "core national interest" category of non-negotiable territorial claims – in the same level as Taiwan and Tibet.[42] It possibly means that Chinese authority has to defend its newly categorized national interest in the South China Sea by all costs, including the use of force. An editorial headlined "American shadow over South China Sea" in the *Global Times*, a newspaper viewed as a mouthpiece of China's Communist Party, stated that "China will never waive its right to protect its core interest with military means."[43] If this position is adopted officially by Beijing, it clearly goes against spirit and text of the DOC.

These developments reaffirmed the limits of the DOC in preventing the occurrence of tensions, incidents, and skirmishes in the South China Sea.

The Agreement for Joint Marine Seismic Undertaking in the South China Sea between China, Philippines and Vietnam – Cooperation and Controversy

Although existing documents, especially the DOC, can not prevent the occurrence of tensions that open opportunities for cooperative activities in the South China Sea. This section will analyze one of the achievements within spirit of regional cooperation – the Agreement for Joint Marine Seismic Undertaking in the South China Sea.

During the visit of Wu Bangquo, Chairman of China's National People's Congress, to Philippines in 2003, the two national petroleum companies, the Chinese National Offshore Oil Company (CNOOC) and the Philippines National Oil Company (PNOC), discussed joint actions in the South China Sea.[44] As a result, an "Agreement for Seismic Undertaking for Certain Areas in the South China Sea" between two national oil firms was signed on 1 September 2004 during the visit of Philippines President Gloria Arroyo to Beijing. However, Beijing and Manila did not make public the content of the agreement.

After Vietnam's protest, the bilateral agreement was expanded and included the national oil and gas corporation, PetroVietnam. The "Tripartite Agreement for Joint Marine Seismic Undertaking in the Agreement Area in the South China Sea" was signed by Vietnam Oil and Gas Corporation (PETRO Vietnam), PNOC and CNOOC in Manila, on 14 March 2005.[45]

This Agreement established a precedent for a multilateral cooperative arrangement in the disputed area in the South China Sea. Parties characterized that the agreement on JMSU "manifests responsible diplomacy to ease tension and promote confidence building" in the disputed islands chain.[46] Philippines President Gloria Arroyo described this agreement as a "historic breakthrough" in developing the area of conflict among ASEAN and China into a possible energy source: "This is a historic event because it is the first, it is the breakthrough in implementing the provisions of the code of conduct in the South China Sea among ASEAN and China to turn the South China Sea into an area of cooperation rather than an area of conflict".[47]

According to this Agreement, three companies affirmed that the signing of the tripartite agreement would not undermine the basic positions held by their respective governments on the South China Sea issues.[48] The three national oil companies started with less sensitive issue in dealing with energy resources. The parties would hold "pre-exploration activity" with "a view of engaging in a joint research of petroleum resource potential of certain areas of the South China Sea".[49] The three companies would equally share the costs of 15 million US dollar joint marine seismic undertaking in the South China Sea.[50] Avoiding public criticism, all parties kept secret details of the seismic study in accordance with the Agreement. According to Article 10 of the Agreement, "all relevant documents, information, data and reports with respect to the joint marine seismic undertaking shall be kept confidential during the Agreement Term and within five (5) years after its expiry and shall not be disclosed by a Party to any third party without the written consent of the other Party."[51]

Once the details of Agreement was published,[52] a controversy broke out within and outside the Philippines. Critics in the Philippines raised the issue of treason against the Arroyo government, which was alleged of "sellout" of Philippines territory. The main objection to the Agreement related to the area of joint research. According to an annex attached to the Agreement, the three oil companies would undertake a joint research of petroleum resource potential in an area over 142,886 square-kilometers in the South China Sea, which included large part of disputed Spratlys. The Agreement also covers 24,000 square kilometers of undisputed Philippine territory, closest to its coastline.[53] Critics claimed that by allowing others to operate within the Philippine continental shelf the Philippines claim to the area was weakened. At the end of the 3-year term of the JMSU, due to domestic politics in the Philippines, no new definitive agreements were agreed on. The JMSU agreement expired in July 2008.

Outer Limit of Continental Shelf Submissions and Its Implications

Controversy over the JMSU agreement coincides with developments in the South China Sea in the last 2-3 years, related to the deadline 13 May 2009. The deadline was set by a subsequent agreement of the States Parties to the UNCLOS for states to lodge claims extending their continental shelves beyond the 200 nautical mile limit to The United Nations Commission on the Limits of the Continental Shelf (CLCS).

On 6 May 2009, Malaysia and Vietnam submitted a joint proposal to the CLCS in respect to an area seabed in the southern South China Sea located seaward of their 200 nautical miles EEZ limits.[54] On the following day, Vietnam made a separate submission in relation to northern parts of the South China Sea.[55] China immediately protested both submissions as a violation of its sovereignty and called on the UN commission to reject it. After almost three months, on 4 August 2009, the Philippines also protested submissions to CLCS made by Vietnam and Malaysia. Vietnam and Malaysia immediately protested the notes by the Philippines China.

China also made a submission of preliminary information to the CLCS relating to the East China Sea. Chinese preliminary information included the statement that China reserved the right to make submissions on the outer limits of the continental shelf that extends beyond 200 nautical miles in "other sea areas."[56] This statement possibly referred to areas in the South China Sea.

The Philippines also made a partial submission to the CLCS for areas of outer continental shelf seaward of its 200 nautical miles EEZ limit in the Benham Rise region in the Philippine Sea. The Philippines, however, reserved the right to make additional submissions for unspecified "other areas at a future time."[57]

The developments around the submissions of relevant countries to CLCS created several implications for the situation in the South China Sea in general, and for cooperative development of energy resources in particular.

The submissions to the CLCS by Malaysia and Vietnam arguably clarified the borders of their claims of continental shelf from the mainland. Furthermore, it seems that Vietnam and Malaysia do not consider any features in the Spratly Islands (and the Paracel Islands in the case of Vietnamese submission) as islands, as defined in Article 121 of UNCLOS. If any of the South China Sea islands is capable of generating EEZ and continental shelf rights, there is no area of outer continental shelf beyond 200 nautical miles for submission to CLCS.[58] The fact that Vietnam did not make any comments on the contract between the Filipino government and Forum Energy in the area within the Reed Bank basin reconfirmed Vietnam's aforementioned consideration.

If this clarification of Malaysia and Vietnam's claims regarding the disputed islands would be adopted by all the South China Sea parties, it would significantly simplify the dispute overall by substantially narrowing the maritime claims associated with the disputed islands.[59] There would be an entire area in the central part of the South China Sea, which could be described as 'the continental shelf doughnut' combined by the outer limits of continental shelf from the nearest island or mainland of surrounding South China Sea countries, which is open for cooperative developing maritime resources.

This simplified and dispute-solution-oriented interpretation of Vietnam and Malaysia about 'regime of features' of Spratly was shared by other surrounding South China Sea countries but not by China. In the note protesting the submissions of Vietnam and Malaysia to CLCS, China asserted its "indisputable sovereignty over the islands in the South China Sea and the adjacent waters, and enjoys sovereign rights and jurisdiction over the relevant waters as well as the seabed and subsoil thereof."[60] Attached to the note was a map showing China's U-shaped claims to virtually the entire South China Sea. This possibly means that China uses an alternative claim, besides its historical claim, based on an EEZ and continental shelf from islets of Spratly that it also claims.

Regarding the position of the Philippines, during the process of preparing the submissions on the outer limit of continental shelf, the Philippines passed the Archipelagic Baselines bill on 10 March 2009, which revised the existing straight baselines and brought them into conformity with the rules for archipelagic baselines set out in the UNCLOS. Under the new law, the disputed Kalayan islands group and Scarborough Shoal remain part of Filipino territory, but under a "regime of islands."[61] In August 2009, in notes protesting both the submission by Vietnam and the joint submission by Vietnam and Malaysia to CLCS, the Philippines did not refer to any possible continental shelf generated from the disputed Kalayan islands, but that "the submission for extended continental shelf by Vietnam lays claim on areas that are disputed because they overlap with those of the Philippines,"[62] (extended continental shelf beyond the 200 nautical mile limit from archipelagic baseline[63]) and "joint submission for extended continental shelf by Vietnam and Malaysia lays claim on areas that are disputed not only because they overlap with that of the Philippines, but also because of the controversy arising from the territorial claims of some of the islands in the area including North Borneo."[64] Arguably, it means that the Philippines do not consider any features in the Spratly Islands as an island, as provided in Article 121 of UNCLOS. Therefore, these features are incapable for generating EEZ and continental shelf rights.

Concerning the Indonesian position, in a note circulated in the UN on 8 July 2010, to protest nine-dotted-lines-map attached to China's afore-mentioned note, Indonesia stated that "those remote or very small features in the South China Sea do not deserve exclusive economic zone or continental shelf of their own," and "the so called nine-dotted-lines-map...clearly lacks international legal basis and is tantamount to upset the UNCLOS 1982."[65]

Brunei also seems to share the view of other concerned countries in ASEAN. In preliminary information concerning the outer limits of its continental shelf, submitted to CLCS on 12 May 2009, Brunei stated that the country has made significant progress towards preparation of a full submission, but it can only provide the full submission after the date of

13 May 2009. "Brunei's full submission to the Commission will show that the edge of the continental margin, lying at the transition between the Dangerous Grounds and the deep ocean floor of the South China Sea, is situated beyond 200 nautical miles from the baselines from which Brunei's territorial sea is measured."[66] It possibly means that Brunei will fix the outer limit of extended continental shelf beyond 200 nautical miles from the baseline of land territory without taking consideration of claimed islands in the Spratly Islands.

Concluding Remarks

A long process of engagement of ASEAN towards China into a framework of governing state-to-state relations and dispute settlement, confidence-building measures, and cooperation activities has resulted in a series of signed documents between parties, including the DOC in the South China Sea. However, these documents can not prevent the occurrence of tensions in the region and have not contributed too much for regional cooperation in the South China Sea.

As the most powerful country, China sets the tone for the dispute in the South China Sea.[67] As Beijing adopted a more accommodating stance in the South China Sea disputes, the DOC was reached in 2002 and a relatively calm situation in the region was lasting for almost half of decade after that. However, since 2007, as Beijing corrected its policy toward the South China Sea issue with more assertive approach, the situation was tense again.

For regional security and development, China and ASEAN should successfully implement the DOC and Beijing should accept a binding regional COC, which would ensure smaller parties that force will not be used, making them more confident to proceed with the cooperative activities in the South China Sea.

NOTES

1. Treaty of Amity and Cooperation in Southeast Asia, Indonesia, 24 February 1976, www.aseansec.org/1217.htm
2. ASEAN Declaration on the South China Sea, Manila, Philippines, 22 July 1992, www.aseansec.org/1196.htm
3. Nguyen Hong Thao, 'Vietnam and the Code of Conduct for the South China Sea', *Ocean Development and International Law*, vol. 32, issues 1-2 (2001), pp. 105-130.
4. The idea of a COC was previously put forward in the 1992 ASEAN Declaration and the workshop series on managing potential conflicts in the South China Sea in 1991-2000.

5. Joint Communiqué of the 29th ASEAN Ministerial Meeting, Jakarta, 20-21 July 1996, www.aseansec.org/1824.htm

6. Section 7.16, Hanoi Action Plan, www.vpa.org.vn/ENGLISH/activities/ac_asean.htm

7. For more details on process of negotiation on COC/DOC, see Tran Truong Thuy, "Compromise and Cooperation on the Sea: The case of Signing the Declaration on the Conduct of Parties in the South China Sea", in Tran Truong Thuy (Ed.), *The South China Sea: Cooperation for Regional Security and Development*, TheGioi Publisher, 2010.

8. Robert C. Beckman, "Legal Regimes for Cooperation in the South China Sea," In *Security and International Politics in the South China Sea: Towards a Co-operative Management Regime*, ed. Sam Bateman and Ralf Emmers, (London: Routledge, 2009), p. 227.

9. Nguyen Hong Thao, "The Declaration on the Conduct of Parties in the South China Sea: A Vietnamese perspective, 2002-2007," In *Security and International Politics in the South China Sea: Towards a Co-operative Management Regime*, ed. Sam Bateman and Ralf Emmers, (London: Routledge, 2009), p. 211.

10. Joint Declaration of the Heads of State/Government of the Association of Southeast Asian Nations and the People's Republic of China on Strategic Partnership for Peace and Prosperity, Bali, Indonesia, 8 October 2003. http://www.aseansec.org/15265.htm

11. Plan of Action to Implement the Joint Declaration on ASEAN-China Strategic Partnership for Peace and Prosperity. http://www.aseansec.org/16805.htm

12. Ibid.

13. ASEAN-China Senior Officials Meeting on the Implementation of the Declaration on the Conduct of Parties in the South China Sea, Kuala Lumpur, 7 December 2004. http://www.aseansec.org/16888.htm

14. Terms of Reference of the ASEAN-China Joint Working Group on the Implementation of the Declaration on the Conduct of Parties in the South China Sea. http://www.aseansec.org/16885.htm

15. http://phapluattp.vn/20100409113013464p0c1013/asean-va-trung-quoc-se-som-hop-ve-van-de-bien-dong.htm

16. ASEAN, China confirm to observe DOC, http://news.gov.vn/Home/ASEAN-China-confirm-to-observe-DOC/20104/7005.vgp

17. Joint Communiqué of the 43rd ASEAN Foreign Ministers Meeting. http://asean2010.vn/asean_en/news/47/2DA8FF/Joint-Communique-of-the-43rd-ASEAN-Foreign-Ministers-Meeting

18. Personal interview.

19. Remarks at Press Availability, Hillary Rodham Clinton, Secretary of State, Hanoi, Vietnam, July 23, 2010. http://www.state.gov/secretary/rm/2010/07/145095.htm

20. Foreign Minister Yang Jiechi Refutes Fallacies On the South China Sea Issue, http://www.fmprc.gov.cn/eng/zxxx/t719460.htm

21. Nguyen Hong Thao, "The Declaration on the Conduct of Parties in the South China Sea: A Vietnamese perspective, 2002-2007," In *Security and International Politics*, ed. Sam Bateman and Ralf Emmers, 2009, p. 211.

22. Ibid.
23. Ralf Emmers, *Geopolitics and Maritime Territorial Disputes in East Asia*, (London: Routledge, 2010), p. 74.
24. Ibid.
25. Statement by the Spokesperson of Ministry of Foreign Affairs of Vietnam on 4th January 2010. http://www.mofa.gov.vn/vi/tt_baochi/pbnfn/ns100104182947# KvsTE0ShBsOB
26. Regular Press Briefing by Vietnam MOFA's Spokesperson on 24th June, 2010. http://www.mofa.gov.vn/en/tt_baochi/pbnfn/ns100624185700#JVew0HAfgRkg
27. Nguyen Hong Thao, "Declaration on the Conduct", p. 211.
28. "Vietnam protests Chinese ship seizure". *Earth Time*, 30 March 2010, http://www.earthtimes.org/articles/show/316377,vietnam-protests-chinese-ship-seizure.html
29. Ian Storey, China's "Charm Offensive" Loses Momentum in Southeast Asia, *China Brief*, Volume: 10 Issue: 9, April 29, 2010. ttp://www.jamestown.org/single/?no_cache=1&tx_ttnews[tt_news]=36324&tx_ttnews[backPid]=7&cHash=897d20a7fa
30. Nguyen Hong Thao, "Declaration on the Conduct", p. 211.
31. Tran Dinh Thanh Lam, "Vietnam oil find fuels China's worries", In *Energy Bulletin*, 26 October 2004, www.energybulletin.net/node/2838
32. Scot Marciel, "Maritime Issues and Sovereignty Disputes in East Asia" Testimony before the Subcommittee on East Asian and Pacific Affairs, Committee on Foreign Relations, United States Senate, July 15, 2009. http://foreign.senate.gov/hearings/hearing/20090715_2/
33. Ibid.
34. Mark Valencia, 'Wither the South China Sea dispute?" (Paper presented at the Workshop "the South China Sea", Hanoi, 2009.
35. "China reiterates sovereignty over islands in South China Sea," www.xinhuanet.com, 3 February 2007.
36. www.mofa.gov.vn
37. Personal communications with Vietnam MOFA's and PetroVietnam's officials.
38. Vietnam signals it wants ExxonMobil deal despite China warning. (AFP) – 24 July 2008. http://afp.google.com/article/ALeqM5heDDtUDkdvnfpdxGI91DdmaxA7aw
39. Mark Valencia, 'Wither the South China Sea dispute?"
40. Leszek Buszynski, "The South China Sea: Avenues toward a Resolution of the Issue," (Paper presented at the Workshop "the South China Sea", Hanoi, 2009.
41. Nguyen Hong Thao, "Declaration on the Conduct", p. 212.
42. Chinese Military Seeks to Extend Its Naval Power, www.nytimes.com/2010/04/24/world/asia/24navy.html?_r=1&scp=1&sq=Chinese%20Military%20Seeks%20to%20 Extend%20Its%20Naval%20Power&st-cse
43. http://opinion.globaltimes.cn/editorial/2010-07/555723.html
44. Nguyen Hong Thao, "Declaration on the Conduct", p. 216.
45. Answer to correspondent by Mr. Le Dzung, the Spokesman of Vietnam MOFA on 14 March 2005, http://www.mofa.gov.vn/en/tt_baochi/pbnfn/ns050314164241
46. Palace says agreement with China not a sellout of RP sovereignty, http://www.pia.gov.ph/default.asp?m=12&fi=p080308.htm&no=26

47. Philippines, China, Vietnam to conduct joint marine seismic research in South China Sea. http://english.people.com.cn/200503/15/eng20050315_176845.html

48. "Tripartite Agreement for Joint Marine Seismic Undertaking in the Agreement Area in the South China Sea" (JMSU).

49. "Tripartite Agreement for Joint Marine Seismic Undertaking.

50. Ibid.

51. Ibid.

52. Barry Wain, "Manila's Bungle in The South China Sea", *Far Eastern Economic Review,* January/February 2008.

53. "Spratly Deals Cover 6 Philippine Islands", http://www.pinoypress.net/2008/03/10/six-spratly-islands-occupied-by-philippines-covered-in-controversial-deals/

54. http://www.un.org/Depts/los/clcs_new/submissions_files/submission_mysvnm_33_2009.htm.

55. http://www.un.org/Depts/los/clcs_new/submissions_files/submission_vnm_37_2009.htm.

56. http://www.un.org/Depts/los/clcs_new/submissions_files/preliminary/chn2009preliminaryinformation_english.pdf

57. http://www.un.org/Depts/los/clcs_new/submissions_files/submission_phl_22_2009.htm

58. UNCLOS provides for two categories of feature under Article 121 governing the "regime of islands": islands that are capable of generating the full suite of maritime zones, including the exclusive economic zone and the continental shelf, and "rocks which cannot sustain human habitation or economic life of their own shall have no exclusive economic zone or continental shelf."

59. Clive Schofield and Ian Storey, *The South China Sea Dispute: Increasing Stakes and Rising Tensions,* Jamestown Foundation Occasional Paper, November 2009, 23

60. http://www.un.org/Depts/los/clcs_new/submissions_files/submission_mysvnm_33_2009.htm and http://www.un.org/Depts/los/clcs_new/submissions_files/submission_vnm_37_2009.htm.

61. www.lawphil.net/statutes/repacts/ra2009/ra_9522_2009.html

62. http://www.un.org/Depts/los/clcs_new/submissions_files/vnm37_09/vnm_re_phl_2009re_vnm.pdf

63. A Philippine official confirmed this consideration with author during private conversation in Manila in July 2010.

64. http://www.un.org/Depts/los/clcs_new/submissions_files/mysvnm33_09/clcs_33_2009_los_phl.pdf

65. www.un.org/Depts/los/clcs_new/submissions_files/mysvnm33_09/idn_2010re_mys_vnm_e.pdf

66. www.un.org/Depts/los/clcs_new/submissions_files/preliminary/brn2009preliminary information.pdf

67. Clive Schofield and Ian Storey, "*The South China Sea Dispute: Increasing Stakes and Rising Tensions,*" p. 46.

6

Developments in South China Sea and its Impact on India

Vijay Sakhuja

A series of high decibel politico-diplomatic exchanges have showcased the growing tension between United States, the global power and China, a rising power. The current spat involves the South China Sea wherein the two sides have referred to their stakes as 'national interest' and 'core interests' respectively. It is also a continuation of series of incidents at sea between the maritime forces of the two countries. Further, US arms sales to Taiwan have cast a shadow on their bilateral relations.

The other South China Sea claimants i.e., Brunei, Malaysia, Philippines, Taiwan and Vietnam have watched with mounting anxiety the unfolding of recent politico-diplomatic exchanges between China and US. They are apprehensive of China's assertiveness; Beijing has been conducting regular patrols in the region to reinforce its fishing rights in South China Sea, engaged in large scale military exercises, and forward deployed a variety of sophisticated naval platforms including submarines and fighter jets from islands particularly at the Sanya naval base on Hainan. Besides, the fast pace of China's naval and missile modernisation reflecting Beijing's agenda to dominate regional affairs has sent discomforting signals to the smaller nations in Southeast Asia. The claimants are also concerned about China's *volte-face* of its earlier stated position on the joint development of resources in South China Sea.

The reverberations of developments in South China Sea have been felt in India too. Although not a claimant to any territory in South China Sea, the region gains salience for India in the political, economic and strategic context due to the safety and security of its maritime trade that transit through the region. India has high stakes in the sea-lanes of the region that are critical for its economic vitality. New Delhi's concerns also arise from the Chinese articulation of its 'core interests' which Beijing may expand to include the disputed areas in India's northeast.

This paper attempts to highlight the contemporary developments in South China Sea and its impact on India. It begins by briefly tracing the past skirmishes/clashes at sea between China and the other South China Sea claimants and the formulation of the '2002 Declaration on the Conduct of Parties in the South China Sea' (DOC). Thereafter, the paper examines the recent developments in the South China Sea and the reaction of regional and extra regional powers to the events in the region. Finally, the paper examines India's interest and response to the events in South China Sea.

South China Sea: Past Incidents

In the past, South China Sea has witnessed show of force, saber rattling and clashes at sea between China and the other claimants. In 1974, the Chinese were in occupation of the Amphitrite Group in the Eastern Paracel and South Vietnam occupied the Crescent Group in the Western Paracel. The South Vietnamese government announced oil exploration contracts in eight blocks in the western edge of the Spratly Islands to Shell, Exxon, Mobil and a consortium of Canadian oil companies and also declared the Spratly Islands as the administrative unit of South Vietnam and deployed troops on five of the islands. China had laid claims to all the islands in the area and acted in response by taking over the Crescent Group on 17-20 January 1974.[1] Between 1979 and 1982, the Vietnamese made several attempts to regain control of the islands, but failed.

The second clash between claimants took place in 1988 in which China and Vietnam clashed over the Western Spratlys. The Chinese occupied four reefs namely Fiery Cross, Johnson, Gaven and Cuarteron and the Vietnamese six reefs Pigeon, Ladd, Great Discovery, East London, Alison and Cornwallis South. In the ensuing clash between the two navies, Vietnam lost 3 ships, 30 men killed, 11 wounded, 70 missing.[2] The Chinese authorities observed "The armed conflict on March 14 was provoked entirely by the Vietnamese side when the Vietnamese navy made provocations against Chinese personnel conducting survey and study on the Chigua Reef and Vietnamese vessels opened fire on these people and on the Chinese vessels anchoring nearby… It was under such circumstances that the Chinese side was forced to make a limited counterattack in self-defense."[3]

In 1992, China enacted the Territorial Waters Law that lay claim to the entire South China Sea resulting in an angry reaction from the other claimants.

The third encounter between the claimants was over Mischief Reef involving China and the Philippines. In February 1995, the Chinese Foreign Ministry stated that "Structures had been built on the Reef by China to ensure the safety and lives as well as the production operations of the fishermen who work in the waters of the Nansha (Spratly) Islands. The Chinese side never detained nor arrested any Filipino ship nor established any military base on the Meiji (Mischief) Reef." After talks between China and the Philippines over the Mischief Reef failed, the Philippines Navy removed the markers put up by the Chinese on reefs, atolls and other features in the Philippines' claimed Exclusive Economic Zone.[4]

2002 Declaration on the Conduct of Parties in the South China Sea (DOC)

A non-binding multilateral agreement '2002 Declaration on the Conduct of Parties in the South China Sea' (DOC) with focus on the Spratly Islands has been in place since 2002. The DOC was signed at the end of the sixth China-ASEAN Summit in November 2002, wherein China and ASEAN countries agreed to work together to build trust and confidence, exercise restraint for creating a positive atmosphere for the eventual resolution of disputes, and to maintain peace and stability in the region. The DOC is based on the 'purposes and principles of the Charter of the United Nations, the 1982 UN Convention on the Law of the Sea (UNCLOS), the Treaty of Amity and Cooperation (TAC) in Southeast Asia and the Five Principles of Peaceful Coexistence' and lays the foundation for building an understanding among the partners on the necessity to ensure stability in the region.[5] Point 3 of the DOC[6] clearly state that the parties respect the 1982 UNCLOS provisions, freedom of navigation in and over-flight above the South China Sea . Further Point 4 notes that concerned parties agree to reduce tensions arising out of territorial and jurisdictional disputes among the claimants.

Although the DOC was a concrete step to institutionalize regional dialogue among the claimants and served for the de-escalation of military tensions in South China Sea, it appears that it was only a provisional political arrangement to dispel 'China Threat' among the claimant states.[7] There are fears that China would like to deal with the claimants on a one-to-one basis. The ASEAN countries are now arguing for "a more formal and legally binding code of conduct in the South China Sea" to bring about stability in the region.

Joint Marine Seismic Undertaking (JMSU)

In order to uphold the spirit of the 2002 DOC and abide by the 1982 UNCLOS, China, Vietnam and the Philippines agreed to jointly undertake oil exploration in the Spratly Islands. The respective petroleum companies i.e. China National Offshore Oil Corp (CNOOC), Vietnam Oil and Gas Corp and Philippine Oil Co agreed to conduct a seismic survey program in the region over an area of about 143,000 square kilometers.[8] It was also agreed to follow the "principle of equality and establish a committee to negotiate issues related to the exploration, with each nation sharing the expenditure for the survey."

It has been noted that "the JMSU has done little to mitigate Sino-Vietnamese tensions in the South China Sea as a whole."[9] This was so due to a series of incidents including Chinese objections to Vietnam allowing energy companies to develop two gas fields in the Con Son Basin, Chinese naval exercises in the Paracel Islands, firing at Vietnamese fishing boat, Chinese plans to allow tourist cruises to the Paracel Islands and under a domestic law, declaring South China Sea to be administered under Sansha. The latter led to protests in Vietnam over China's hegemonic behavior and declaring the Spratly and Paracel Islands as its sovereign territory.[10]

Recent Developments in South China Sea

In July 2010, the US Secretary of State Hillary Clinton noted that "The United States has a 'national interest' in freedom of navigation, open access to Asia's maritime commons and respect for international law in the South China Sea.[11] Further, "We [US] oppose the use or threat of force by any claimant." This was in response to China declaring the South China Sea as the "core interest" similar to Tibet and Taiwan.

China reacted sharply to the US-South Korea joint naval manoeuvres code named 'Invincible Spirit' off the Korean Peninsula in the Yellow Sea involving

200 aircraft, 20 ships and the nuclear aircraft carrier.[12] The US had argued that these exercises were in response to the sinking of the South Korean corvette Cheonan by a torpedo attack suspected to be the handiwork of the North Korean navy.

These articulations by the US and China sent out some very discomforting signals to the ASEAN countries. Interestingly, Beijing also sent out a veiled warning that "Few Southeast Asian countries would like to get in the middle of Sino-US tensions, but like many other regions, they are caught in a dilemma: economically close to China yet militarily guarded against China…Southeast Asian countries need to understand any attempt to maximise gains by playing a balancing game between China and the US is risky. China's long-term strategic plan should never be taken as a weak stand. It is clear that military clashes would bring bad results to all countries in the region involved, but China will never waive its right to protect its core interest with military means."[13]

Be that as it may, the United States' economic and military pre-eminence in the Asia Pacific is a given constant for the region and it is engaged in Asia through economic ventures, trade, and a variety of politico-military arrangements. Close US economic ties with the Asia Pacific region serve its economic interests and the region is a major trading partner in Washington's trans-Pacific trade. The US and Asia have become more interdependent, with foreign direct investment growing dramatically.

In fact, US prosperity depends upon the prosperity of its trading partners, a vibrant world economy and safe sea-lanes. US interests in the SLOCs of the South China Sea appear indirect, but they are indeed very important. The US would feel the pain of any disruption of Sea Laws of Communications (SLOCs) in the region. A 1996 study by the US Navy brought out that the US governments needed to commit itself to keeping the Asia Pacific strategic sea-lanes open to commercial shipping.[14] The study also noted that extended closure of these strategic highways could seriously harm Asian economies with which US has important trading links.[15] Washington has been careful not to get embroiled in territorial disputes arising out of UNCLOS III and strongly opposes the use of force. It is primarily concerned about the safety of maritime traffic. It appears that unless the security of its maritime traffic is threatened, it is not likely to be involved in regional conflicts.

China cautioned the US to stay out of the South China Sea dispute. The Chinese Foreign Ministry spokesperson stated, "We express great concern about any possible South China Sea announcement made by the United States and the ASEAN countries... We resolutely oppose any country which has no connection to the South China Sea getting involved in the dispute, and we oppose the internationalization, multilateralization or expansion of the issue. It cannot solve the problem, but make it more complicated,"[16] Meanwhile, Indonesia, though not a claimant to any South China Sea territory, is keen that US remain engaged in the region and the Indonesian Foreign Minister Marty Natalegawa has rejected China's stance that the US stay out of territorial disputes in the South China Sea and noted that "Indonesia, through ASEAN, is keen to ensure we have conditions conducive for negotiations to take place" so disagreements "can be resolved through peaceful means."[17] On their part, the Southeast Asian countries are worried how far the US would support them in South China Sea. It has been observed that amidst growing tensions between the US and China, "they would be forced to take sides."[18]

However, the recent tensions between the US and China appear to have reduced and officials from both sides had "finalized an agreement to work toward restoring military exchanges ahead of a planned visit by Chinese President Hu Jintao to Washington in January 2010."[19] It was agreed to resume defence consultative talks and "Both sides agreed that dialogue is essential to build mutual trust and reduce the chances of misunderstanding and miscalculation,"[20] Further, the US "suggested that as the military relationship matures, the two sides develop it in a manner that breaks the on-again, off-again cycle that has characterized the US-China military-to-military relationship to date."[21]

The tone and tenor of the statement at the end of the summit in New York between US and ASEAN heads of state, had also mellowed down. President Obama stated that "we've strengthened old alliances, we've deepened new partnerships, as we are doing with China, and we've re-engaged with regional organisations, including ASEAN,"[22] Both sides also stressed the need for "peaceful resolution of disputes" and "freedom of navigation" including in the South China Sea. China also expressed intention to revisit the '2002 DOC and the Chinese Ambassador to the Philippines was quoted as saying that "We are ready to work with other countries in ASEAN in formulating such a document."[23]

US is supportive of 'an enforceable DOC' that can ensure the safety of maritime traffic through the South China Sea and would not like to be entangled in the disputes among the claimants. Harry Thomas, the US ambassador to the Philippines has noted "I think we have to wait for ASEAN and China to agree to sit down and when ASEAN develops its goals and objectives, and if they ask for our assistance in specific items, we would be happy to assist."[24]

China Plants Flag on the Seabed in South China Sea

In August 2010, the Chinese State Oceanic Administration and Ministry of Science and Technology jointly announced that a mini submarine had successfully positioned the national flag at 3,700 meters under the sea in South China Sea.[25] Although the stated aim of the event was to conduct underwater resource survey and also to demonstrate China's undersea technological capability, the statement by one of the engineers of the China Ship Scientific Research Centre, who designed the hull of the submarine, is of concern. It was noted "It might provoke some countries, but we'll be all right. The South China Sea belongs to China. Let's see who dares to challenge that." The Chinese engineer further stated that "The closer to Philippines, the deeper the sea. We will put down national flags all the way until we reach their border... And then we will go beyond and aim for the Mariana Trench." It should be pointed out that the Mariana Trench is 11,034 meters and is located to the northeast of the Philippines.

The event can be discerned as an attempt by China to establish sovereignty over the South China Sea. It has been noted that "We [China] were inspired by the Russians, who put a flag on the floor of the North Pole with their MIR [deep sea submarine]." In 2007, Russia placed national flag on the seabed in the Arctic to demonstrate to the other Arctic claimants over its sovereignty in the Arctic. At that time, the Canadian Foreign Minister had remarked "This isn't the 15th century... You can't go around the world and just plant flags and say 'We're claiming this territory'."[26] With the Arctic ice melting, there are competing claims over to Arctic resources.

Although China has been able to display its technological prowess, it is believed that nearly 40 per cent of the equipment for the submersible were imported and the acquanauts received training overseas.[27] The seven feet wide submersible hull was acquitted from Russia, and advanced lights, cameras and manipulator arms were imported from the US. As early as 2005, six Chinese acquanauts (five pilots and one scientist) began deep sea dive training in the US.

India and South China Sea

There are several geo-economic and geo-strategic causal factors that shape India's interest in South China Sea. In spatial terms, South China Sea is a seamless sea space and offers connectivity to the broader Asia Pacific region. Since ancient times, South China Sea has offered connectivity for trade that had generated a complex trading system with a burgeoning trade among China, Southeast Asia and India. Besides, it facilitated cross-cultural linkages wherein Buddhist monks travelled from China through Palembang in Sumatra to Tamralipti in India. Significantly, geographical contiguity has been instrumental in harmonious relations among India, China and Southeast Asia.

As far as India's Look East Policy is concerned, India's relations with the ASEAN countries have acted as catalyst and served as an important driver of economic growth. The bilateral trade has grown from US$ 2.4 billion in 1990 to US$ 44.66 billion in 2008-09.[28] Both partners have expressed their commitment to strengthen economic cooperation to enhance bilateral trade to US$ 70 billion by 2012.[29]

In 2009, India and ASEAN signed the Free Trade Agreement (FTA) that came into force in July 2010.[30] This FTA is believed to be quite extensive covering a market of approximately 1.8 billion people and the plans envisage gradually cutting down tariffs over 4,000 product lines by 2016.[31] Further, nearly fifty percent of India's sea borne trade is east bound for countries in Southeast Asia, East Asia, east coast of US and Canada and transits through the South China Sea.

Given the above economic realities, India is an important stakeholder in the evolving security dynamics in South China Sea and any insecurity in the region could adversely impact India's trade and economy. New Delhi's economic vitality pivots on assured supply of energy and safe and secure trading routes in the region including the Straits of Malacca. It has high stakes in keeping the sea-lanes open in the region.

At another level, India has been engaged in offshore energy development projects in the South China Sea. The state owned ONGC Videsh Limited (OVL) in partnership with PetroVietnam and British Petroleum began exploration in South China Sea in 1992 and 1993 which resulted in the discovery of the Lan Do and Lan Tay gas fields that estimated to contain reserves of around 58 billion cubic metres that would result in three billion cubic metres of gas a year.[32] However, in the 1990s, due to financial crisis,

OVL had to sell its stake to BP. In 2010, due to Gulf of Mexico oil spill liability, BP announced plans to sell its energy assets in Vietnam and this prompted OVL along with Vietnam's PetroVietnam joined hands to bid for the BP's stake in Nam Con Son gas fields spread over 955-square kilometre including two offshore gas fields, a pipeline and power project.[33] The upstream part of the Nam Con Son project also referred to as Block 06.1 is about 370 km Southeast of Vung Tau on the southern Vietnamese coast. The Block 06.1 comprises of the Lan Tay (currently produces around 14 million standard cubic metres per day of gas) and Lan To gas fields which are currently under development. Reports indicate that the OVL has invested $217 million on the gas fields and could invest up to $377.46 million. OVL also has stakes in two other exploration blocks 127 and 128 in Vietnam.

An observation by a Filipino diplomat that "Many of the participants in the ARF are trading nations and, therefore, it is important for them to have unimpeded access to the waters in South China Sea" suggests that trading nations such as the United States, Russia, India, Australia and Japan are important stakeholders in the safety and security of the region.

Indian Navy and the South China Sea

India's Military Maritime Strategy defines area of interest and operations for the Indian Navy. It is quite natural that the Indian Ocean region gains primacy in its formulation and encompasses the sea space around the Strait of Bab-el-Mandeb – Strait of Hormuz – Straits of Malacca and the Cape of Good Hope.[34] The strategy also envisions South China Sea and the East Pacific Region as the secondary area of interest to the Indian Navy. According to the Military Maritime Strategy, these sea spaces would gain primacy in case of events and incidents that impinges on Indian interests.

As part of this strategy, the Indian Navy has been expanding its area of operations east into the South China Sea and the Pacific Rim, west towards the Strait of Hormuz, and, in the south, deep into the Indian Ocean towards the Cape of Good Hope. The political leadership has stated that India's "area of interest ... extends from the north of the Arabian Sea to the South China Sea." In 2000, the Indian navy announced plans to conduct naval exercises in the South China Sea clearly suggesting that Indian Navy had acquired the operational capability to conduct sustained presence in the area.

In the past, China has objected to Indian Navy's presence in the region. In 2000, China objected to Indian Navy exercising in the South China Sea.

A flotilla of Indian naval ships was on voyage to China, Japan and Republic of Korea and was also scheduled to engage in exercises with the PLA Navy. According to Indian Navy sources, "The Chinese have protested any navy carrying out exercises in the South China sea, whether it is the US Navy, Japan or Singapore. We told them that we are passing through and would even visit them and carry out Passex (exercise) and they received us warmly,"[35] This prompted a retired Indian official to observe that "Goodwill visits like these to China, Japan, Korea and Indonesia are to strengthen ties. India's moves are not aggressive or motivated with territorial designs" and a former Indian navy Chief remarked that the Chinese protests only amounted to "pressure tactics".

China's policy towards India has been one of eroding any possible India-US naval cooperation, as it perceives such cooperation would be inimical to its interests. In that context, China also reacted to the 2007 quadrilateral naval exercises in the Bay of Bengal and issued a demarche' seeking an explanation from New Delhi, Washington, Tokyo and Canberra on the purpose of holding a meeting on 24-25 May 2007 in Manila, Philippines. The Chinese Foreign Ministry spokesman Qin Gang noted "China believes that to enhance mutual trust, expand cooperation for mutual benefit and remain win-win, being open and inclusive is the global trend,"[36] referring to the evolving alliance among the democratic partners. In that context, Sun Shihai, Deputy Director of the Institute of Asia-Pacific Studies under the Chinese Academy of Social Sciences (CASS) has noted, "The so-called democratic alliance is not good for Asia... Any attempts to take China as a rival or contain China will not work".

'Core Interests' and the Himalayas

At another level, New Delhi's concerns also arise from the Chinese articulation of their 'core interest' to include Tibet and Taiwan. It is feared that China may continue to announce new 'core interests' that my involve territories in India that China lays claims. It has been observed that "By declaring the South China Sea a 'core national interest' and elevating it to the same status as Tibet and Taiwan, Beijing has marked another territorial claim. If this is not challenged, it will gradually gain de facto international acceptance, as its claims over Tibet and Taiwan have in the last six decades."[37] In fact, there have been periodic articulations in the Chinese media about Tawang. For instance, in 2009, during Prime Minister Dr. Manmohan Singh's visit to Arunachal Pradesh, *The Global Times* noted "Indian Prime Minister Manmohan Singh made another provocative and dangerous move. India will make a fatal error if it mistakes China's approach for weakness. The Chinese government and public regard territorial integrity as a core national interest, one that must be defended with every means,"[38] Further, a Chinese academic even suggested that "India would 'just' have to surrender the Aksai Chin plateau in Ladakh and Tawang and the border issue could be solved."[39] These views must be tampered with another Chinese academic arguing that China should release list of its core interests in a calibrated way, "As China becomes stronger, we can publicize by instalments those core interests that our country can effectively safeguard."[40]

The Indian Ministry of Defence Report 2008-09 has expressed concerns over Chinese military capabilities and observed that 'greater transparency and openness' is critical, but on a conciliatory note also stated that India will "engage China, while taking all necessary measures to protect its national security, territorial integrity and sovereignty."[41] There are natural fears in India about China's military modernisation and augmentation of military infrastructure along the borders and should China include the disputed territory, like the South China Sea, could be worrisome for India. China sees India as a potential rival and a competitor and has identified several pressure points to contain India.

India and Vietnam

Vietnam has a unique geographical and strategic location astride the hypothetical choke point between Sabah (on the island of Borneo) and the southern tip of Vietnam. Historically too, Vietnam has always been on the sea-route from China to India. As far as India is concerned, Vietnam offers a window to monitor shipping activity in the South China Sea and its ports serve as strategic support base for transhipment and logistics for the Indian shipping.

New Delhi's policy towards Vietnam attempts to expand both economic and military ties. In the broader strategic framework, maritime cooperation between New Delhi and Hanoi helps India to support its maritime activities. As far as the Indian Navy is concerned, Indian naval ships have on a regular basis visited Vietnamese ports on goodwill visits. These visits were useful in showcasing Indian naval shipbuilding capability, and Hanoi has shown interest in purchasing naval vessels from India. Further, both Indian and Vietnamese navies have carried out joint exercises.

Indian naval ships have on regular basis conducted exercises in the Pacific waters and these include exercises involving long-range maritime patrol aircraft staged from some Southeast Asian countries, submarines and forward deployed ships sustained by sea based logistics and friendly countries. However, it is unlikely that the Indian Navy would be able to sustain a combat capable force in South China Sea over a long period of time without support from friendly regional countries.

Vietnam has a history of operating Soviet/Russian aircraft. Significantly, bulk of the aircraft inventory of the Vietnam People's Air Force and Vietnam People's Navy is of Soviet/Russian origin and thus Vietnam has less difficulty in operating modern Russian aircraft like the Su 27 / Su 30 and Soviet / Russian naval platforms. In December 2009, during his visit to Moscow, the Vietnamese Prime Minister Nguyen Tan Dung signed a US$ 2 billion for purchase of 6 Kilo Class submarines and 12 SU-30MKK fighter jets.[42]

An option available to Vietnam is the Brahmos missile jointly developed by the Defence Research and Development Organisation, India and Federal State Unitary Enterprise "NPO Mashinostroyenia" (NPOM), Russia. According to the manufactures, the missile is suitable for fitment onboard the Su 30 aircraft and submarines (Kilo / Amur class). The Su 30 can be fitted with up to three missiles, one under the fuselage and the other two can be mounted on wing pylons after strengthening the support points. As far as submarines are concerned, up to eight missiles packaged in containers can be fitted on the Russian Amur class submarines.

In recent times, the Vietnam-US rapprochement has resulted in joint naval exercises and port calls. Perhaps what merits attention is that the US Navy embarked Vietnamese military and government officials onboard the USS George Washington for a series of "naval engagement activities" that included damage control and search and rescue exercises.[43] It is feared that 'any prolonged American presence could be viewed by the Chinese as a '*casus belli* and jeopardise the entire painstaking process of Sino-Vietnamese normalisation," It has also been observed the US requires "places rather than bases", keeping in mind that domestic pressures in Japan ad South Korea have been growing to push the US out of their respective countries and in the case of Vietnam Cam Ranh Bay fits the bill.

In the above context, India-Japan-United States-Vietnam naval cooperation gains salience primarily due to the issue of the safety and security of maritime trade that transit through the region. These countries have high stakes in keeping the sea-lanes open for their economic vitality that pivots on assured supply of energy and safe and secure trading routes in the region including the Straits of Malacca. Besides, their shipping has been facing a number of threats and challenges posed by non-state actors with transnational capabilities. In recent times, piracy has been on the rise in South China Sea and such an arrangement has the potential to cut down on piracy attacks.

Concluding Remarks

Washington has been careful not to get embroiled in territorial disputes arising out of UNCLOS III and strongly opposes the use of force and is primarily concerned about the safety of maritime traffic. It appears that unless the security of its maritime traffic is threatened, it is not likely to be involved in the regional conflicts.

The regional countries favour an amicable balance of power for peace and stability with assents on economic development and are apprehensive of regional tensions that could undermine regional stability which is critical for Asia's rise. However, there are fears that South China Sea may become, in the future, an arena for US-China rivalry.

NOTES

1. For an excellent understanding of the sequence of incidents leading to clashes, see Ang Cheng Guan, "The South China Sea Dispute Re-visited", Institute of Defence and Strategic Studies Working Paper No 4, August 1999.
2. "Naval Battle in Spratly 1988", available at http://en.academic.ru/dic.nsf/enwiki/9309751 accessed on September 6, 2010.
3. David Holley, "China, Hanoi Count Losses in Isles Clash" *Los Angles Times*, 17 March 1988.
4. "Chinese Territorial Assertions: The Case of the Mischief Reef", available at http://www.southchinasea.org/docs/Chinese%20Territorial%20Assertion%20The%20Case%20of%20the%20Mischief%20Reef.htm, accessed on 6 September 2010.
5. "China, ASEAN Sign Code of Conduct on South China Sea", *People's Daily*, 05 November 2002.
6. Point 3. The Parties reaffirm their respect for and commitment to the freedom of navigation in and over flight above the South China Sea as provided for by the universally recognized principles of international law, including the 1982 UN Convention on the Law of the Sea; Point 4. The parties concerned undertake to resolve their territorial and jurisdictional disputes by peaceful means, without resorting to the threat or use of force, through friendly consultations and negotiations by sovereign states directly concerned, in accordance with universally

recognized principles of international law, including the 1982 UN Convention on the Law of the Sea.

7. Zhai Kun and Wendy Wang, "The South China Sea Declaration: A Chinese Perspective", *RSIS Commentaries*, available at http://www.rsis.edu.sg/publications/Perspective/RSIS0842009.pdf accessed on 5 September 2010.

8. Chen Hurng-yu, "Taiwan Needs Spratly-deal Details", *Taipei Times*, 19 July 2005.

9. Ian Storey, "Conflict in the South China Sea: China's Relations with Vietnam and the Philippines", *Japan Focus*, 30 April 2008.

10. Andrew Symon, "China, Vietnam Churn Diplomatic Waters", *Asia Times*, 20 December 2007.

11. Mark Landler, "Offering to Aid Talks, U.S. Challenges China on Disputed Islands", *The New York Times*, 23 July 2010.

12. "Massive S. Korea, US Joint Naval Drills Enter 2nd Day", *Xinhua*, 26 July 2010.

13. John Chan, "S-China Tensions over South China Sea" available at http://www.wsws.org/articles/2010/aug2010/usch-a04.shtml accessed on 8 September 2010.

14. John H. Noer, *Choke Points: Maritime Economic Concerns in South East Asia* (Washington: NDU Press, 1996), p. 2.

15. Ibid., p. 4.

16. Ben Blanchard and Huang Yan, "China Tells U.S. to Keep Out of South China Sea Dispute", *Reuters*, 21 September 2010.

17. Daniel Ten Kate and Susan Li, "Indonesia Rejects China Stance That U.S. Stay Out of Local Waters Dispute", *Bloomberg*, 22 September 2010.

18. Barry Wain, "Asean Caught in a Tight Spot", *The Straits Times (Singapore)*, 16 September 2010.

19. "U.S., China to Resume Military Talks" available at http://www.spacewar.com/reports/US_China_to_resume_military_talks_999.html accessed on 26 September 2010.

20. Viola Gienger, "China, U.S. Turn to Maritime Agenda as Military Talks Resume", available at http://www.bloomberg.com/news/2010-09-29/china-u-s-resume-military-talks-after-break-over-sales-of-arms-to-taiwan.html accessed on 30 September 2010.

21. Ibid.

22. Stephen Collinson, "China Looms Over US-ASEAN Summit, *The Sydney Morning Herald*, 25 September 2010.

23. "China, ASEAN working on South China Sea code – ambassador", *Reuters*, 30 September 2010.

24. Jason Gutierrez, "US willing to help in South China Sea code of conduct: envoy", *AFP*, 4 October 2010.

25. Stephen Chen, "Submarine Plants Flag on the Ocean Floor", *South China Morning Post*, 27 August 2010.

26. "Russia Plants Flag Under N Pole", available at http://news.bbc.co.uk/2/hi/europe/6927395.stm accessed on 8 September 2010.

27. William J. Broad, "China Explores a Frontier 2 Miles Deep", *The New York Times*, 11 September 2010.

28. "Look East Policy", *Press Bureau of India*, 20 April 2010 available at http://www.pib.nic.in/release/release.asp?relid=60558 accessed on 30 August 2010.
29. "India-ASEAN Summit Commits to Fight Terrorism, Other Crimes", *Net Indian News Network*, New Delhi, 25 October 2009.
30. "FTA with ASEAN to Eliminate Duties on 80% of Traded Goods", *Times of India*, 14 August 2009.
31. "ASEAN-India Dialogue Relations", available at http://www.aseansec.org/5738.htm accessed on 12 May 2010.
32. T.S. Subramanian, "The Vietnam Connection", *Frontline*, Volume 20, Issue 01, 18-31 January 2003.
33. "BP's Vietnam project: Deora to support ONGC bid", available at http://business.rediff.com/report/2010/oct/01/bps-vietnam-project-deora-to-support-ongc-bid.htm accessed on 2 October 2010.
34. "Freedom to Use the Seas: India's Maritime Military Strategy", (New Delhi: Integrated Headquarters Ministry of Defence (Navy), 2007), pp. 59-60.
35. Gaurav C Sawant, "China Objects to Indian Presence in South China Sea", *Indian Express*, 14 October 2000.
36. Sidtharth Srivastava, "India Expands her 'hard power' Capabilities as Emerging World Power: U.S. Remains a Key Strategic Partner", available at http://www.worldsecuritynetwork.com/showArticle3.cfm?article_id=14599 accessed on 12 May 2010.
37. Claude Arpi, "China's Core Interests", *The New Indian Express,* 28 August 2010.
38. Claude Apri, "Why the Chinese are so Upset about Tawang", available at http://news.rediff.com/slide-show/2009/oct/20/slide-show-1-why-chinese-are-so-upset-about-tawang.htm accessed on 10 September 2010.
39. Ibid.
40. Willy Lam, "Hawks vs. Doves: Beijing Debates "Core Interests" and Sino-U.S. Relations", *China Brief,* Volume 10, Issue 17, 19 August 2010.
41. "India Wary of Sino-Pak Strategic Link-up in Occupied Kashmir", *Indian Express*, 12 July 2009.
42. "Vietnam Aims to Counter China with Sub Deal: Analysts", *Bangkok Post*, 17 December 2009.
43. "US and Vietnam Stage Joint Naval Activities", available at http://www.bbc.co.uk/news/world-asia-pacific-10925061 accessed on 10 September 2010.

7

Vietnam-China Relations: An Assessment

K. Raja Reddy

The good neighbourly relations between Vietnam and China, besides being mutually beneficial in terms of maintenance of peace and stability in the region, have been conducive to the promotion of economic growth of the two neighbours. But these relations had witnessed bouts of tension in the past as Vietnam and China fought bitter wars. Interestingly enough, time and again, the Vietnamese had been resisting the hegemonic attitude of the Chinese for the past two millennium years as the Chinese had imposed their economic, political, social and religious institutions on Vietnam during their oppressive rule on the Vietnamese from 111 B.C. to 939 A.D. For the next thousand years, the Chinese continued their subversive activities to make the Vietnamese subservient to them. However, the Vietnamese continuously fought against the Chinese to preserve their ethnic identity and to maintain political independence until the French conquered and colonized Vietnam. During the French occupation of Vietnam from the middle of nineteenth century to the middle of twentieth century, the Chinese had absolutely no scope to meddle in the affairs of the Vietnamese as the Chinese became weakened against the European powers. The present paper proposes to track the relations between Vietnam and China in the post-Second World War.

The chapter is divided into two parts; part one attempts to explain the impact of the communist victory in China and the People's Republic of China's (PRC) recognition imparted to Ho Chi Minh's Democratic Republic of Vietnam (DRV) as a reciprocal gesture to the latter's recognition of the PRC, accorded earlier. This part also discusses the issues of why the two decades of comradeship turned acerbic enough to lead to a bloody battle between the two nations in 1979 as well as how the reforms initiated in the two countries, enabled them to open up new avenues of cooperation that developed into partnership. Part two of the chapter discusses the issue of normalization of relations between Vietnam and China. This part considers the year 1991 as a landmark in the history of the bilateral relations between Vietnam and China because, having felt the need for enhancing their cooperation indispensable for resolving the territorial disputes to establish peace and stability in the region, both declared that they got their relations normalized. By 1995, Vietnam became a member of Association of South East Asian Nations (ASEAN). Membership of ASEAN not only enhanced Vietnam's clout in the region, but also enabled it to negotiate with China as if on a forting of equality, from a position of strength. Vietnam adopted a two-pronged strategy: one, to strengthen its bilateral relations with China and two, to settle unresolved issues with China through its multilateral relations.

Mutual Suspicion: Historical Evidence

The Vietnamese revolutionary leader Ho Chi Minh declared the dawn of independence in Vietnam and established DRV on 2 September 1945. The first encounter of the new government with China was the occupation of Vietnam, north of 16th parallel, by the nationalist Chinese forces under the arrangement of Allied Powers at Potsdam meeting to disarm the Japanese soldiers. Most of the Chinese soldiers, who had landed in Vietnam by the middle of September 1945, were so inordinately ambitious and so intractably undisciplined that as soon as they arrived, they unleashed looting, arson and violence in and around Hanoi. The top brass of the Chinese appeared that they had come to stay in the northern part of Vietnam to settle their national issues with the French, besides disarming the Japanese.[1] Commenting on this aspect Ellen J. Hammer, an eminent scholar on Indochina, observed:

> "Hanoi ... was in the grip of terror in January 1946 as pro-Chinese nationalist elements launched a campaign of violence against the Viet Minh and the French indiscriminately. The Chinese apparently expected to benefit from this situation, to discredit the Viet Minh in French eyes

so as to prevent any Franco-Vietnamese agreement which might lead to the loss of Viet Nam by China; and to put forward their own candidates for power through whom they hoped to gain control of the country. At the same time, the Chinese seemed to regard the insecurity of the French residents as strengthening the bargaining position of China in the negotiations with France which had just begun in Chungking."[2]

Following the Japanese surrender, France, which was anxious to reoccupy Vietnam, entered into negotiations with China that resulted in substantial gains to the Chinese. According to the agreement signed on 28 February 1946, France renounced her extraterritorial rights and concessions in China and also granted exemption from customs and transit duties to the Chinese goods shipped in Hai Phong harbor and Kunming Railway.[3] The Chinese agreed to leave Vietnam by 31 March 1946. The DRV observed a strategic silence as Ho Chi Minh was aware of the damage the Chinese could inflict if they over-stay. Soon thereafter, Ho Chi Minh made a wry comment to Paul Mus, the political advisor to the French High Commissioner, about the Chinese withdrawal from Vietnam and noted that "It is better to smell the feces of the French for a little while than to eat Chinese excrement all of one's life."[4] It was the historical experience of the Vietnamese about the Chinese. Gradually, Ho Chi Minh, with the help of Vo Nguyen Giap, the Commander of DRV forces, had succeeded in eliminating the baneful Chinese influence among the nationalist leaders in Vietnam as they became increasingly unpopular in the nationalist struggle.

The next phase, an important phase in Vietnam-China relations, was the period after the establishment of the communist rule in China. On 1 October 1949, the PRC came into being under the leadership of Mao Zedong. In a cable gram sent to Mao, Ho Chi Minh expressed the hope of developing closer Sino-Vietnamese relations "in order to promote the freedom and happiness of the two nations and defend world democracy and lasting peace in common."[5] In his reply, Mao stated: "China and Vietnam are on the frontline of an imperialist struggle. With the victorious development of the struggle for liberation of the peoples, the friendship between our two peoples will surely become closer day by day."[6] The communist victory in China gave hope to Ho Chi Minh that, with the help of the PRC and the Soviet Union, the communist victory in Vietnam would become a reality. In December 1949, one month after the PRC held the Conference of Asian Trade Unions, the DRV organized the first National Conference of Vietnam Trade Unions.

Symbolizing the solidarity of the three fraternal countries, large size portraits of Stalin, Mao and Ho adorned the rostrum. The Conference hailed the victory of the Chinese people and pledged to coordinate its activities with the Asian Trade Unions. It also stressed the need for an alliance of the working class with the peasantry and the army in the national liberation movement.

On 14 January 1950, the DRV sought recognition from the PRC, the Soviet Union and other socialist countries and on the following day Hanoi recognized the PRC. In turn, on 18 January, the PRC recognized the DRV and on the same day trade and military aid agreements were signed between the two countries. The Soviet Union accorded recognition on 31 January and the other socialist countries followed suit. Vietnam's struggle for independence and unity turned out largely to be a struggle between the Vietnamese communists and the non-communist nationalists. By the middle of 1950, there was an intense activity in the People's Army of the DRV as a wide array of military hardware including guns, mortars and other equipment started pouring into Vietnam from the PRC.[7] Equipped with modern Soviet weapons brought through China, the Vietnamese inflicted defeat on the French who got demoralized day by day. While extending this assistance, the PRC hoped that Vietnam would be aligned with China in advancing China's national interests. Geneva negotiations of 1954 were the best example to show as to how PRC sought to project its supremacy over Vietnam.

The Geneva negotiations of 1954, conducted to end the Indo-China conflict, caused much damage to Vietnam, at the behest of the PRC. Had the PRC not forced the DRV to accept the division of the country, perhaps the largest human loss after the World War II and an incalculable human suffering in the Vietnam War, could have been averted. Years later, it was revealed that the DRV had to compromise under intense pressure from the PRC and the Soviet Union on various issues at the Geneva Conference. Wilfred Burchett, a war journalist, who covered the Conference extensively, wrote to say that the two Socialist brothers, the PRC and the Soviet Union, were not solidly backing Vietnam at the Conference.[8] To quote Burchett:

> "During the Geneva Conference, on at least three points, China checked Vietminh [Vietnam Communists] ambitions, in a way which clearly recalls classical policy. Firstly, the June 16 proposal to disassociate the Laotians and Cambodian question from that of Vietnam which contributed, immediately after the Dien Bien Phu victory, to reinforce the prestige of the royal governments of Vientiane and Phnom Penh and, at the same

time, to ruin the hopes of the Vietminh to set up on the west and southwest flanks, revolutionary governments which would have been devoted to them. The same, on June 23 at Berne, in indicating to Mendes-France when he [Chou En-lai] said he would push the Democratic Republic of Vietnam to reconciliation with the Vietnam of Bao Dai and then on 19 July, at Geneva, in proposing a deal of two years of Vietnamese nation-wide elections..."[9]

Sharing the views of Burchett, C.P. Fitzgerald, a China expert, noted:

"It is known that this agreement owed much to the persuasion of the Chinese delegation, as was acknowledged by Mr. Eden, then Foreign Secretary, in the House of Commons. The Vietminh leaders were rather unwilling to evacuate large areas in the south where they had fought for years, and their military position justified the hope of Vietcong. But both Russia and China succeeded in convincing Ho Chi Minh that half a loaf was better than no bread..."[10]

By the middle of 1960s, irritants developed between China and Vietnam over the issue of Vietnamese relations with the Soviet Union in the wake of Sino-Soviet dispute. Ho Chi Minh maintained neutrality between the PRC and the Soviet Union, but the Chinese wished Vietnam to be with China only. Tatsumi Okabe, an expert on China, described: "In the 1960s when the Sino-Soviet conflict was intensifying Vietnam became an area of contest between China and the Soviet Union. China concentrated its efforts on attracting Vietnam to its side rather than in achieving an early settlement of the fight."[11] Vietnam declined to take sides between China and Soviet Union, even the aid to Vietnam supplied by the Soviet Union through China, reached the spot after much delay.[12] By 1968, the PRC paid less attention to the DRV.[13] The table below makes this fact amply clear:

DRV Delegates Exchanges with China and the Soviet Union, 1964-68

Governments	1964	1965	1966	1967	1968
DRV to PRC	34	17	26	13	5
DRV to USSR	17	11	13	17	18
PRC to DRV	17	17	8	2	0
USSR to DRV	8	8	6	10	6

The Chinese attitude towards the DRV vastly changed after Nixon's visit to China, which was followed by the conclusion of the Paris Agreements of 1973. However, China continued to deny any change of its policy towards the DRV. The upgradation of diplomatic relations between India and the DRV in 1972, was viewed as a DRVs move to redraw its strategic calculus in favour of DRV's closeness towards the USSR with which India had signed a "Friendship and Cooperation Treaty" in the previous year. The first aggressive demonstration of anger by China was the occupation of Paracel islands in January 1974, which were under the possession of Republic of Vietnam (South Vietnam). It was a veiled grim reminder to the DRV of Chinese future intentions.

The quick merger of two Vietnams, following the communist victory in South Vietnam in April 1975, was designed to avoid Chinese intervention in the matter of Vietnam's unification. According to Okabe: "In 1970s, China tried to keep Vietnam weaker by advising the Vietnamese not to unite with the South hastily and by keeping close ties with anti-Vietnamese Democratic Kampuchea [Cambodia]. When the Chinese felt that the Vietnamese were irreversibly tilted towards the Soviet Union, they punished the Vietnamese and withdrew aid and experts from Vietnam."[14] China exhibited its unhappiness over the developments in Vietnam by cancelling the supply of committed aid besides drastically cutting its further assistance for the reconstruction of the war ravaged Vietnam.[15] Though publicly refrained from exhibiting its displeasure, China supported the insidious acts of Pol Pot in Cambodia against Vietnam. Pol Pot regime claimed large portions of South Vietnam and indulged in border skirmishes and propaganda against the Vietnamese. Meanwhile, the issue of overseas Chinese in Vietnam, who desired to leave the country alleging persecution, further irritated the Chinese. By mid-1978, Beijing came to the conclusion that Vietnam had become a Soviet ally and, therefore, hardened its stand against Vietnam. China also decided to use the issue of ethnic Chinese in Vietnam as a catalyst to punish Vietnam. Robert S. Ross, a Western scholar, wrote: "The PRC's declaratory policy now demanded that Hanoi completely accommodate itself to Chinese demands – not only concerning the overseas Chinese but also concerning Kampuchea. By the second half of 1978 it openly sided with Phnom Penh, trying to deter Vietnam from overthrowing the Pol Pot regime."[16]

Vietnam knocked down Pol Pot regime and occupied Cambodia in December 1978 and the Chinese viewed it as a serious challenge to them as Pol Pot was a known China supporter. The new found friendship between China and the US was an encouragement for China's "punitive action" against Vietnam. On 17 February 1979, China launched its war against Vietnam and quickly advanced into border areas of Vietnam including Cao Bang, Lang Son and Lao Cai. As the casualties on the Chinese side were unexpectedly very huge, China pulled out its troops by 5 March. However, tension at the border continued, leading to border flare-up from time to time. China was highly critical of Vietnam's attitude towards Beijing in the post-war period. Chang Pao-min gave a graphic account of the Chinese version of the reasoning for China's attack on Vietnam:

> "The very fact that Vietnam had not treasured enough its cultural ties and traditional links with China and had not even hesitated to turn against China in Vietnam's better times caused great dismay and anger in China. Indeed, precisely because of its anticipation of Vietnamese loyalty, China could not tolerate, and would react strongly to a hostile Vietnam. This love-and-hate complex was in fact the underlying causes – though perhaps not easily comprehensible to Western observers – of China's military attacks in 1979. It also explained the accompanying and subsequent outpouring of all the emotion-charged accusations against Vietnam. China under the Communist regime, like any previous Chinese regime, had not been so concerned about a Vietnam seeking and defending its political independence from China, as turning itself into an anti-China outpost of actually or potentially hostile powers."[17]

History proved that the Vietnamese were irrepressible and that the Chinese attempts to contain Vietnam, once again failed.

Persisting Irritants vs Normalisation of Relations

The late eighties formed the reform period in all the communist countries. China's Deng Xiaoping inspired reforms were already a decade old and global changes have already reckoned this Asian giant to undertake confidence building measures for a meaningful engagement with the countries around, to establish peace in the region for its economic growth. Immediately after Tiananmen incident, Jiang Zemin the Chinese President, sought to introduce a series of foreign policy initiatives which were known as peripheral (Zoubian) diplomacy.[18] Accordingly, the global changes and the domestic imperatives prodded Vietnam and China to come to terms with each other, in the interests of both the nations and also to establish peace and stability in the region. By the beginning of 1989, contacts were established at high level. Paris Peace Process on Cambodia was one of the factors that facilitated the rapprochement. China's normalization of relations with the Soviet Union was another reason for Vietnam to come to terms with its northern neighbour.

The end of communism in Soviet Union and Eastern Europe alarmed both China and Vietnam to make an alliance immediately and sought to revive their socialist links and to normalise their relations.[19] The elder statesman of Vietnam Pham Van Dong, the General Secretary of the Vietnam Communist Party Nguyen Van Linh and the Premier Do Muoi had surfaced at Chengdu, the fifth largest city in China, on 3-4 September 1990, for a summit meeting with the Chinese leaders.[20] The secret meeting paved way for further discussions between the leaders of China and Vietnam. High level secret diplomatic parleys in 1990, culminated in a Summit meeting from 5 to 10 November 1991 and the two parties declared that the diplomatic relations were normalized.

Ever since that time to the present day, two contradictory trends appear in the relations between Vietnam and China. The progress of the bilateral relations has been substantial. The two ways high level visits have forged closer cooperation in economic, science and technology and cultural spheres. However, the relations, experienced periodic bouts of tensions with regard to unresolved territorial disputes.

On the positive side, the normalization of relations with China gave Vietnam a breather to look around and to promote its relations with ASEAN, the United States and others. As the Cambodian mill-stone was removed from the neck of Vietnam, the United States lifted its trade embargo in 1994 and the ASEAN accorded membership to Vietnam in the next year. As a member of ASEAN, Vietnam gained an enormous clout in the region. Meanwhile, Vietnam also normalized its relations with its former adversary, the US. These developments had their positive impact on the Vietnam-China relations.

Following the normalization, Vietnam and China inaugurated expert level discussions and in the following year visits of top officials took place. The land border disputes and the problem of Gulf of Tonkin were separated. A Joint Working Group (JWG) on land border disputes started negotiations in 1994 and after sixteen meetings, Vietnam and China concluded a treaty in 1999.[21]

During the visit of the General Secretary of Communist Party of Vietnam, Le Kha Phieu, to China in 1999, the two sides agreed on an important agenda for their future relations. Vietnam and China underlined the need for guidelines for "long term stability, future-oriented good neighbourly relations and comprehensive cooperation." This was hailed as "16 word principles" which was supposed to guide the relations between Vietnam and China in the 21st century. In the very next year, Vietnamese President Tran Duc Luong visited China and the two sides issued a Joint Statement describing the two countries as "good neighbours, good friends, good comrades and good partners."[22] The Joint Statement signed by Tran Duc Luong and Hu Jintao stated that the two sides "will refrain from taking any action that might complicate and escalate dispute, resorting to force or making threats with force." According to Carlyle A. Thayer: "The 2000 Joint Statement set out the long-term framework for cooperative bilateral state to relations with a permission for the regular exchange of high level delegations led by their respective State Presidents, Prime Ministers, other ministers, national legislatures and other political organizations."[23]

Another important milestone in the relations between Vietnam and China was the establishment of Steering Committee on Bilateral Cooperation set to discuss all aspects of the bilateral relations at the deputy Prime Ministerial level and this Steering Committee was to meet at the capitals alternately. During the visit of President Nguyen Minh Triet to China in May 2007, the two sides signed six cooperation documents and nine economic agreements. In 2008, both China and Vietnam declared that they raised their bilateral relations to that of strategic partnership. They agreed to take measures to increase trade to US$ 25 billion, by 2010. Vietnam and China also agreed to establish a Working Group to map out a five-year master plan for economic and trade cooperation.

With regard to the land border dispute, Vietnam and China made substantial progress. Chronological development is given below:

(a) 3 November 1991: A temporary agreement for the management of border disputes between Vietnam and China, signed.

(b) 19 October 1993: The basic principles for the management of border and territorial disputes accepted.

(c) 30 December 1999: Border Treaty, signed.

(d) 27 December 2001: The first border marker installed at Mong Cai facing Dong Xing, China.

(e) 31 December 2008: The Vietnam-China joint statement for the completion of the border demarcation and marker installation along the entire border, signed.

(f) 18 November 2009: Three accords for demarcation of the border installation of border marked and the arrangement of border gate management, signed. In all, 1971 marker posts have been installed.[24]

On 14 July 2010, three accords that defined the land border between Vietnam and China came into effect. These accords officially ended a 36-year land border settlement process between the two countries. On the occasion of a ceremony in honour of the accords at Thanh Thuy border gate in the northern part of Ha Giang province, Ho Xuan Son, the Deputy Foreign Minister observed: "The event today is a land mark in the history of Vietnam-China relations development."[25] It was also hoped that these accords would take Vietnam-China strategic partnership and comprehensive cooperation to a higher level. Around the same time, a similar ceremony was held across the border in China's Yunnan province.

The most contentious issue which soured the relations between Vietnam and China has been the question of sovereignty over the Paracel and Spratly islands in South China Sea. The two sides agreed to settle the issue through peaceful negotiations. Expert level talks were also held to improve the understanding of each other's stance. Since some of the ASEAN countries have claims over Spratly islands, ASEAN and China signed a Declaration of Conduct in the Eastern Sea (DOC) that led to Code of Conduct (COC) on 14 March 2005. But both Vietnam and China are not prepared to compromise over the sovereignty of these islands. The crooked way of taking the Vietnamese unawares in which the Chinese had occupied the Paracel islands in 1974, caused deep anguish to the Vietnamese especially as the latter were otherwise engaged, being in the midst of war in South Vietnam. There was pressure from the peoples of both the nations to remain firm on the issue of sovereignty. In Vietnam, the government and the people are very much apprehensive of the intentions of the Chinese steady buildup of its might in the region. When the Chinese planted new marks in December 2007, Hanoi openly rebuked China, and this was followed by the public protests in Hanoi and Ho Chi Minh City. The Chinese made an insolent retort by staking out a claim as follows: "China has indisputable sovereignty over the Xisha and Nansha [Chinese names for Paracels and Spratlys respectively] islands, and we have all the historical and legal evidence to prove it."[26]

Maritime stand offs from time to time, reflects the Vietnamese deep rooted animosity. The Chinese aggressive posture in preventing the companies of oil exploration working for Vietnam was seen as China's hegemonic tendency back in action though China pretended to be batting for a "harmonised world". Vietnam's security dialogue with the US in October 2008, was a clear signal for China of the future developments in the region. USS Mustin's port call at Danang's Tiensa port emphasizes the growing amity and cooperation between the United States and Vietnam. Given the economic potential of the region, China's maneuvers to utilize this potential as its strategic and security backyard to gain access to sea lanes to reach the Indian Ocean, are really matters of grave concern for the Vietnamese. The completion of a strategic Chinese submarine base on Hainan Island, just 200 km from the Vietnamese shore, would cause deep concern for Vietnam. In December 2009, Vietnam signed an agreement with Russia for a US$ 2 billion deal to acquire six kilo-class Russian submarine. Vietnam's multifaceted relations with India, particularly in the economic and defence, are growing at a rapid pace. Vietnam's defence contacts with India, the United States and Russia caught the keenly vigilant eyes of the Chinese much to the latter's annoyance.

Conclusion

The relations between Vietnam and China, though asymmetrical in terms of size, population and economic potential, have a great bearing on the region's peace and stability. The deep-rooted mutual suspicion and mutual animosity are based on the facts of China being an assertive power and Vietnam playing a counterforce to balance China as a foil. The Chinese attempt to cultivate Vietnam at the cost of the latter's legitimate national interests and national pride, failed miserably in the past. The 1979 war between the two is to be deemed a glaring example. When normalization of diplomatic relations became inevitable, in the wake of global changes, Vietnam responded positively to get engaged with China and to revive its socialist links. Vietnam clearly intended to follow China in its economic planning and get over from its economic and political isolation. The series of agreements concluded between Vietnam and China at the top level, provided adequate confidence to both the sides to negotiate unresolved issues. The economic cooperation has also been substantial and had achieved consistent progress.

What seemed to be a meaningful engagement between Vietnam and China fell short of the fruitfulness of being "good neighbours and good friends" as both of them were to stand guard against each other in the South China Sea whatever good intentions they cherished from time to time, being marred by mutual suspicion. As China tries to be assertive as usual, Vietnam seeks to get its strength enhanced by being a member of ASEAN and by courting the forging of strategic partnerships with countries as varied as the US, India, Australia and Japan. Undoubtedly, these partnerships carry a strong security bearing in the region though very much to the chagrin of the Chinese, whose tendency to monopolize the situations thus, affects the course of Vietnam-China relations by making it alternate between falling on evil days and getting restored to normalcy, obviously a mere semblance of normalcy.

NOTES

1. Ellen J. Hammer, *The Struggle for Indochina, 1940-55*, Stanford, 1966, pp. 134-137.
2. Ibid., pp. 137-138.
3. Ibid., p. 137.
4. Cited in King C. Chen, *Vietnam and China, 1938-1954*, Princeton, 1969, p. 99.
5. Ibid., p. 228.
6. Ibid.
7. Edgar O' Blanc, *The Indochina Wars, 1945-54: A Study in Guerrilla Warfare*, London, 1964, p. 121.
8. Wilfred Burchett, *The China-Cambodia-Vietnam Triangle*, Chicago, 1981, p. 50.
9. Cited in Ibid., p. 39.
10. C.P. Fitzgerald, *China and Southeast Asia since 1945*, London, 1993, p. 15.
11. Tatsumi Okabe, "China's Relations with Communist Countries and Parties," Robert A. Scalapino et.al (eds.), *Internal and External Security Issues in Asia*, California, 1986, p. 108.
12. C.P. Fitzgerald, p. 15.
13. C.P. Fitzgerald, p. 15
14. Tatsumi Okabe, p. 108.
15. Ramses Amer, "Sino-Vietnamese Relations: Past, Present and Future," in Carlyle A. Thayer and Ramses Amer (eds.), *Vietnamese Foreign Policy in Transition*, Singapore, 1999, p. 69.
16. Robert S. Ross, *The Indochina Tangle: China's Vietnam Policy 1975-1979*, New York, 1988, p. 173.
17. Pao-min Chang, "Sino-Vietnamese Relations: Prospects for the 21st Century," in Carlyle A. Thayer and Ramses Amer (eds.), *Vietnamese Foreign Policy in Transition*, Singapore, 1999, pp. 132-133.
18. Marc Lanteigne, *Chinese Foreign Policy*, Oxon, 2009, p. 109.
19. Alexander L. Vuving, "Changing Synthesis of Strategies: Vietnam's China Policy Since 1990," paper presented at the Conference on "Regenerations: New Leaders, New Visions in Southeast Asia,", Yale University, New Haven, November 11-12, 2005.
20. James W. Morley and Masashi Nishihara, "Vietnam Joins the World," in James W. Morley and Masashi Nishihara (eds.), *Vietnam Joins the World*, New York, 1997, p. 6.
21. Carlyle A. Thayer, "The Structure of Vietnam and China Relations," Paper presented at the 3rd International Conference on Vietnamese Studies, Hanoi, December 4-7, 2008, p. 3.

22. http://www.vnemba.org.cn/cn/nr050706234129, accessed on September 15, 2010.
23. Carlyle A. Thayer, "Vietnam and Rising China: The Structural Dynamics of Mature Asymmetry," *Southeast Asian Affairs 2010*, Singapore, 2010, p. 396.
24. http://english.Vietnamnet.vn/politics/201007/land-borders-finaly-defined-with-China-922503/, accessed on August 21, 2010.
25. Ibid.
26. Roger Mitton, "China-Vietnam ties remain more sour than sweet," http://www.asiasentinel.com/index.php?option=com_content&task=view&id=1546&Itemid=188, accessed on September 7, 2010.

8

Defence and Security Dimension of India-Vietnam Relations

Pankaj Jha

With South China Sea strategically brewing and the East China Sea witnessing renewed Sino-Japanese tensions, the question that needs to be asked at this juncture is whether peaceful rise of China is a myth. In view of the current circumstances, it is also important to envisage the possible dynamics of the relationship between China's peripheral countries like Vietnam and India which have been celebrating China's economic trickle down effects and peaceful rise notion. It is vital to understand the defence and security dimension of the ties between Vietnam and India in view of an assertive China. A number of articles in the public domain list the do and don't with regard to India's ties with the peripheral countries of China. While both Vietnam and India are strategically located, have fought wars against China, but the defence cooperation dimension has been subdued and underutilised to a large extent. At this juncture it becomes a key question that whether India and Vietnam can stand up to Chinese challenge or can act constructively in enmeshing China through economic interdependence and regional security architectures. With assertive China on the horizon and emerging challenges like energy security, security of sea lanes, non-traditional threats and the resurrection of US in Southeast Asia, the defence priorities need to be redefined. The questions and the possible answers have been discussed in this chapter which not only discuss the dynamics of the past relationship but also address the emerging challenges in the bilateral and regional security context.

India's ties with Vietnam date back in history and more often than not, are embedded in terms of ancient civilisation links, cultural ties as well as personal equations between the leaders of the two countries. But the major converging point has been the rise of China and the legacy of the war with China in 1962 and 1979 for both the countries. Even in the face of the perceived threat presented by China, India-Vietnam relationship remained essentially one of political and diplomatic support. Although India provided limited economic aid to Vietnam in the late 1970s and early 1980s, bilateral trade remained minimal until well after the Cold War. India also shied away from developing a security relationship, although there were influential calls within India to create an India-Vietnam axis to contain China, similar to the relationship between China and Pakistan (which India perceives is aimed at its containment). The Vietnamese did make at least one attempt to add a security element to the bilateral relationship. In 1978, Vietnamese General Giap, on his way to Moscow to negotiate Vietnam's Friendship Treaty with the Soviet Union, made an unpublicized halt in New Delhi to seek Indian assistance in the establishment of local arms manufacturing capability to reduce their increasing reliance on the Soviets but the Indian side politely shelved the request. It is not known if the Indian response reflected caution about the Soviet relationship or their traditional reticence about security ties with other countries outside of South Asia. Whether or not an India-Vietnam security relationship may have been possible during the 1970s and 1980s, India did not pursue the opportunity and security relations were limited to information sharing arrangements. India's support for Vietnam remained at political-diplomatic level even after the Chinese invasion of Vietnam in February 1979. Though there has been political understanding on a number of global issues but defence cooperation and the evolving strategic dimension has added an evolving new dimension to the relations.[1]

India's relationship with Vietnam also had a major impact on its relations with Southeast Asia. From the early 1970s, the burgeoning relationship between New Delhi and Hanoi was viewed with a degree of suspicion by Southeast Asian states in light of Hanoi's open hostility to Association of South East Asian Nations (ASEAN) and its apparent strategic designs on the remainder of Indochina. This came to a head with India's recognition of the

Vietnamese-installed Phnom Penh government in July 1980, an episode which set back India's relations with ASEAN for nearly a decade. India had at that time been seeking recognition as an official dialogue partner of ASEAN. In a major diplomatic slip, in June 1980, Indira Gandhi's government cancelled scheduled discussions with ASEAN and officially recognized the Vietnam-backed Heng Samrin government, becoming the first noncommunist state to recognize the regime. The ASEAN states interpreted India's action as proof of it toeing the Moscow-Hanoi line which not only placed India in opposition to the more hawkish ASEAN states such as Singapore and Thailand, but also as sabotaging attempts by Malaysia and Indonesia to work out a compromise settlement in Cambodia. The Indians viewed ASEAN's concerns as merely reflecting Sino-US demands. India's continuing support for Vietnam over Cambodia (together with its failure to condemn the Soviet occupation of Afghanistan) would bedevil Indian relations with Southeast Asia throughout the 1980s. India's unsuccessful attempts over the next decade to work with Hanoi to facilitate a Vietnamese withdrawal from Cambodia without strengthening China's regional position continued to place it at odds with the ASEAN states which, by and large, feared Vietnam as a Soviet regional proxy more than China. It was only with the collapse of the Soviet Union that India's relationship with Vietnam became a potential asset in its political and security relationships in Southeast Asia.[2] Further, the resolution of Cambodian conflict in early 1990s led to strengthening of the concept of regional security and enmeshment of Vietnam in the regional security structures.

Regional Security Structures – Much Ado about Nothing?

India's attempts at mending political fences in post-Cold War phase with Southeast Asia were accompanied by a more assertive regional strategic policy. In 1994 Prime Minister Narasimha Rao declared that: "India would like to be part of the evolving security framework in the region to assuage doubts arising from its potential military might as well as to contribute to the security edifice that was being crafted by the Asia-Pacific powers." India became a member of the ASEAN Regional Forum in 1996. India's Pokhran II nuclear tests in 1998 signaled a new strategic posture in which India was no longer confined to security threats in South Asia and wished to be judged as a competitor to China. Around the turn of this century, India began implementing what has since been called "Phase 2" of its Look East Policy, which included a more direct strategic engagement in East Asia. Over the following years, this included engagement by India on a political and security level with key states in East Asia including Vietnam, Japan, South Korea and Singapore. However, it should be of little surprise that India, given its longstanding political relationship with Vietnam, should make its first attempts at developing a security role there.[3]

The end of the Cold War brought about a major change in Vietnam's strategic thinking. For Vietnam, like India, the collapse of the Soviet Union meant the loss of a longstanding strategic guarantor against China which left it largely bereft of its traditional source of arms. However, the end of the Cold War also facilitated the resolution of the longstanding impasse over the Vietnamese occupation of Cambodia and the consequent improvement of relations with ASEAN states and China. Vietnam moved quickly in the new strategic environment to stabilize its regional security relationships, beginning with Southeast Asia. Vietnam signed the ASEAN Treaty of Amity and Cooperation in 1992 and was invited to join ASEAN in 1995. Beginning in the early 1990s, Vietnam also made significant efforts to improve relations with China. A "good neighborliness" treaty was signed in February 1999, leading to the resolution of the land border dispute in December 1999 and an agreement delimiting the maritime boundary in the Gulf of Tonkin in December 2000. While the boundary disputes in the South China Sea remain a major source of disagreement, in November 2002 China and ASEAN states (including Vietnam) signed the Declaration of the Code of Conduct on the South China Sea in which the parties committed to avoiding provocative actions and to the peaceful resolution of disputes.[4]

China figures prominently in diplomatic and military circles in India and Vietnam. In India, coalition compulsions have forced the strategic outlook to see China in a different way and at the same time accommodating the different opinions. In the case of Vietnam, the new found economic recognition as well as settlement of boundary dispute between them has shaped their policy towards China. Though India and Vietnam are apprehensive of China and this can be gauged from their policy documents, both have avoided making direct reference to China. The bilateral understanding on geopolitical front has evolved and the relations can be called good relations but falls short of being called strategic allies. The lack of bilateral defence alliance relationship and the not so comprehensive policy towards containment or even enmeshment of China have forced the India and

Vietnam to look at multilateral security structures which function at different levels and coefficients.

The two nations are members of the regional security organisation and have been working to make it a forum for dialogue and conflict prevention. Though the recurring interaction in a multilateral forum has been in ASEAN Regional Forum (ARF) but it expanded into many other areas which included the East Asia Summit (EAS) as well as the ASEAN+6 mechanism. Though organisations like ARF have been successful in promoting dialogue and providing a forum for discussion but it has been short in terms of conflict resolution.[5] The proposals by Australian Prime Minister Kevin Rudd of Asia Pacific Community and the former Prime Minister Hatoyama's East Asian Community were meant to create a different perspective about the regional security mechanism. Though the annual Shangri-La dialogue has been an International Institute for Strategic Studies (IISS) sponsored set up but it has brought the major stake holders in Asia under one roof. The evolution of the ASEAN Defence Ministers Meeting which has expanded to ADMM Plus (the first meeting took place in October 2010 in Hanoi) has created understanding as well as meaningful acceptance or rejection of the new forum. ADMM Plus in its initial meeting discussed non-traditional security issues so as to build consensus. There are fringe organisations like Trans Pacific Strategic Economic Partnership attempt to create economic engagement through tariff reduction but it has a strategic meaning embedded into it. It would be worthwhile to see the regional security structures evolving in the future. Even in the regional security structures India and Vietnam have been cooperating and this has manifested in the statements of the leaders of both countries. Vietnam has now been pressing for an institutionalised Code of Conduct for South China Sea while the Indian stance has been that China should resolve the South China Sea dispute amicably with the contesting partners showcasing the increasing involvement of India in the regional issues. India and Vietnam would like to address regional security issues through dialogue.

India's Multilateral Defence Initiatives and Vietnam

India has embarked on two multilateral initiatives in the form of 'Milan' a biennial naval meeting and the Indian Ocean Naval Symposium (IONS). The regional security concerns with regard to poaching, anti-piracy, armed robbery, maritime terrorism, coastal security have been discussed as well as PASSEX exercises with the participating nations had been conducted. Though these biennial naval liaison meetings were started in 1995 with only four nations participating but in 2010 about 13 nations participated including Vietnam. Three of the navies observing or participating in Milan-2010 (Vietnam, Malaysia and the Philippines) belong to nations engaged in territorial disputes with China over the resource-rich Spratly Islands of the South China Sea.[6] This demonstrates that there is increasing convergence between India and the littoral nations of Indian Ocean region and Southeast Asian region.

India also started the first meeting of IONS in February 2008. Under its rubric 'Conclave of Chiefs' was held in Delhi and Goa which ratified four principal objectives of promoting shared understanding on maritime issues, strengthening capability of all littoral nations states of the Indian Ocean, promote cooperative mechanisms and develop interoperability to counter disasters and provide relief throughout the region.[7] Though, Vietnam is not a participating nation of the IONS but five of the southeast Asian nations namely Indonesia, Thailand, Malaysia, Singapore and Myanmar have been participating in the annual meetings. On the pacific side, a similar structure like IONS exists which is known as Western Pacific Naval Symposium (WPNS) and Vietnam is a member of the grouping while India is an observer.

There is a growing recognition that within the maritime domain, initiatives such as IONS and the WPNS will inevitably be the major components of any pan Asian security construct. A handshake-in the immediate future-between the WPNS and the IONS is inevitable and will synergise maritime domain throughout the Asia-pacific.[8] In that case Vietnam and India are bound to play a greater role in those organisations. But the major issue have been the low naval strength of Vietnamese Navy and so it needs to be enhanced for playing a more responsible and capable role not only in its territorial waters but also in the maritime sphere of Southeast Asia. India has utilised defence diplomacy as an instrument of its larger geo strategic objectives in the southeast Asia and the liaison visits of the ships from both countries in the recent past and earlier also buttress the increasing defence interactions.

Defence Cooperation with Vietnam – Lacking Coherent Strategy

Defence relations between India and Vietnam have acquired importance against the backdrop of the Sanya submarine base and India's security concerns vis-a-vis China as the most likely area for the deployment of Chinese nuclear submarines would be Indian Ocean as well as East China Sea.[9] The only long-term threat to Indian security interests through Southeast Asia would be that of Chinese pressure on the Indochinese states. According to K. Subramanyam, "We have a large stake in ensuring that the pressure is contained. That has been our basic policy from the fifties. The only country that can do this is Vietnam, the most capable nation of the region. That is why where the strategic interests of India and Vietnam coincide."[10] There have been frequent military interactions between the two nations over the last four decades but defence interactions have not been pursued as a part of defence diplomacy.

In recent times, defence diplomacy has received considerable attention and seeks increased stability and security by changing attitudes and perceptions. It is this "disarmament of the mind" that characterizes defence diplomacy. Defence diplomacy covers a broad range of activities, including:

(a) MOD training courses and education programmes, including opportunities for overseas students to attend courses at military training establishments;

(b) Provision of Loan Service Personnel, Short Term Training Teams, and civilian and military advisers to overseas governments for extended periods;

(c) Visits by ships, aircraft and other military units;

(d) Exchange of visits by Ministers and by military and civilian personnel at all levels;

(e) Staff talks, conferences and seminars to improve mutual under-standing;

(f) Exchanges of civilian and military personnel;

(g) Military exercises.[11]

Taking cue from the above definition, India-Vietnam bilateral military relations are evolving process barring few elements of defence diplomacy.

The first significant step in expanding India-Vietnam relations beyond the traditional political alliance was taken in 2000 at the initiative of India. During a visit by Vietnamese Prime Minister Phan Van Khai to New Delhi in January 2000, the then Indian Defence Minister George Fernandes, part of the Bharatiya Janata Party (BJP)-led government, called for a renewed political relationship with a strong security focus, calling Vietnam India's "most trusted friend and ally." India called for a new relationship with Vietnam, with a significant security dimension, including joint defense training, supply of advanced weapons to Vietnam and a proposal for India's naval presence in the South China Sea through access to the Cam Ranh Bay naval and air base. Although the Indians were no doubt seeking new markets for their defense industry, they clearly hoped to develop a comprehensive security relationship with Vietnam. As will be discussed in detail later in the chapter, the Indian proposal for access to Cam Ranh Bay, which had followed earlier discussions between Indian and Vietnamese military officers in the early 1990s, did not receive support but both sides agreed to formalize a wide-ranging defense cooperation agreement. This provided among other things regular exchange of intelligence, joint coastguard training to combat piracy, jungle warfare and counterinsurgency training for the Indian Army (something particularly useful in dealing with the Naga insurgency in northeast India), repair of Vietnamese MiG aircraft, training of Vietnamese pilots and assistance for production of small and medium arms. When Indian Defense Minister George Fernandes visited Vietnam in March 2000, he offered to undertake policing sea lanes of communication in the South China Sea and noted that "A strong India, economically and militarily well endowed, will be a very solid agent to see that the sea lanes are not disturbed and that conflict situations are contained." Apparently, he was referring to the longstanding disputes between Vietnam and other littoral states with China in the South China Sea. As is well known, in 1988 the Vietnamese and Chinese navies clashed in the Spratly Islands, and several Vietnamese naval vessels were sunk. In 1992, Vietnam protested after China landed troops at Da Luc Reef and seized Vietnamese commercial vessels. There were more naval confrontations in the mid-1990s, and in 2007 the Chinese PLA navy sank an "armed" Vietnamese fishing boat as part of a dispute about the grant of oil exploration blocks. The Vietnamese were also involved in military incidents in the South China Sea with Taiwan in 1995 and the Philippines in 1998 and 1999. The disputed maritime boundaries in the South China Sea remain one of Asia's military flashpoints, and represent a clear and continuing strategic divide between China and Vietnam and the rest of Southeast Asia.[12]

In 2000, George Fernandes, the then Indian Defence Minister, signed a protocol on defence cooperation with Vietnam, which covered areas such as the institutional dialogue between officials of the two defence ministries, sharing of intelligence, naval exercises between the two countries and coordinated patrols by the Vietnamese Sea-Police and Indian Coast Guard, repair programmes for Vietnam Air Force planes, and training of Vietnamese

Air Force pilots by the Indian Air Force. Vietnam also sought Indian assistance in training its submariners and guerrilla warfare training of the Indian armed forces by their Vietnamese counterparts in 2003. In May 2003, India signed a Joint Declaration on a Framework of Comprehensive Cooperation between the two countries. The areas of cooperation included:

(a) Conduct of regular high-level meetings;

(b) Close cooperation in the United Nations and other international forums;

(c) Assistance with regard to safeguarding of mutual interests;

(d) Gradual steps to expand cooperation in the security and defence fields.[13]

Indian Defence Minister George Fernandes declared that India could supply Vietnam with warships and also anti-ship and air defense missiles. Pursuant to the agreement, Hindustan Aeronautics and Bharat Electronics were contracted to repair and overhaul up to 125 of the VPAF's Russian-built MiG-21s, including new avionics and radar to support Russian antiaircraft missiles. The Indian Navy also supplied spares for Vietnamese Osa II-class missile gunboats and other Russian built warships, and in October 2002 the Vietnamese requested India to provide submarine training for its navy.[14]

For its part, India has turned out to be a less than reliable weapons procurement partner, proving itself to be often uncompetitive, bureaucratic and politically hesitant in supplying weapons to Vietnam. While Vietnam was initially keen on sourcing the spares for many of its Soviet-vintage equipment from India, the Indians found themselves undercut by cheap suppliers from Belarus, Ukraine and Russia. Other deals have been lost through payment-related problems and Indian bureaucratic bottlenecks. Vietnamese defence personnel had complained of excessive bureaucratic caution in supplying military spares, coupled with highly complex and uncoordinated procedures required to export military goods. However, there was also an element of political caution by India particularly in relation to the supply of advanced missile technology. The Vietnamese have formally requested the supply of Indian Prithvi intermediate range ballistic missiles and Brahmos cruise missiles (both of which can be supplied under the Missile Technology Control Regime). The deployment by Vietnam of Brahmos missiles, in particular, would likely significantly enhance Vietnam's maritime capabilities. Although the Indians reportedly agreed "in principle" to the sale of Prithvi missiles as early as 2003, they have since stalled. The Vietnamese are believed to have indicated their displeasure at delays in the supply of Prithvi missiles. Interestingly, the Vietnamese Ministry of Public Security has purchased a small number of small arms from Pakistan in August 2007.[15] While it seems likely that India may supply Prithvi missiles to Vietnam, there is no indication that India will supply Vietnam with the Brahmos missiles.[16] There is problem of the joint manufacturers and end user agreement which dictates that the technology does not proliferate to the unintended countries.

The signing of the Strategic Partnership Agreement in 2007 showcased the new contours of India-Vietnam relations. Within the academic and strategic community a consensus is emerging that India must use its military might to safeguard its commercial interests. India's position with regard to Vietnam and the way in which it is going to nurture its relations with Vietnam remains a mystery. During the visit of Defence Minister A.K. Antony to Hanoi in December 2007 the two sides agreed to set up a joint working group to facilitate a Memorandum of Understanding (MoU) on defence cooperation. India agreed to transfer 5,000 items of naval spares belonging to the Petya class ships to Vietnam to make many of its ageing vessels operational. The Indian delegation also visited defence industries in Ho Chi Minh City. A Joint Working Group was also mooted for facilitating the realization of the MoU.[17]

The Vietnamese Defence Minister, General Phung Quang Thanh's visit to India during 4-8 November 2009 was seen as an effort to buttress and intensify bilateral ties between India and Vietnam, which have withstood post Cold War strategic permutations. This visit was seen as a milestone in furthering defence cooperation between the two countries, through annual defence dialogue. The visit was preceded by the first strategic dialogue between the two sides in October 2009. During the visit an MoU of Defence Cooperation between the two countries was signed.

While rising powers like China have utilized their strategic leverage vis-à-vis India's neighbours, India has been reluctant in pursuing its strategic objectives in a more pronounced manner. Dr Manmohan Singh's meeting with Vietnamese President Nguyen Minh Triet on the sidelines of the Sharm el-Sheikh Summit in Egypt in 2009 is proof that Vietnam is vital for India's 'Look East' strategy.

The visit of India's Army Chief to Vietnam in July 2010, first visit in the last 15 years, shows that Vietnam can offer good knowledge of the Chinese strategy and also fathoming the Chinese strategic impulse when dealing with adversaries. The visit was also seen as a way to buttress and enhance the defence ties between the two nations including sharing knowledge of network centric warfare and technology development for the Vietnamese small arms industry so that it is self reliant. Though the defence industrial complex in Vietnam is quite rudimentary and is of a low technology, but Vietnam has significant economic capabilities to develop a modern military industrial complex in the long run. Vietnam can also be an important market for India's indigenous aircraft and helicopter. The case of Tejas, light combat aircraft as well as light combat helicopter, a improvised version of HAL Druv can be explored.

What should the policy prescriptions for the India-Vietnam defence and security relationship be? With increasing importance of Vietnam in ASEAN, multilateral security organizations need to be strengthened in Southeast Asia. China should also be involved in a constructive manner. India should engage Vietnam because of low costs and its highly literate population. India should study Vietnamese ship building facilities and look for possible joint ventures. Vietnam's defence equipment is becoming outdated, so India should help in upgrading its military hardware. India should send technicians and fighter pilot trainers to Vietnam in the future. Vietnam and India use the same Russian and erstwhile Soviet platforms, so there is a possibility of selling aircraft spares and engine oils to Vietnam. There is a need for creating a database of aircraft spares and inventories to be shared with Vietnam on a real time basis. India must conduct more bilateral exercises with Vietnam for domain awareness as well as engaging the Vietnamese Navy in exercises in the South China Sea. India should look to export non-lethal military equipment and communication sets to Vietnam. Both countries can look for greater engagement between the Vietnam Marine Police and Indian Coastguards in anti-piracy operations as well as developing coordination. There is a growing need among Indian decision makers for engaging Vietnam in a more comprehensive way. Vietnam is a country with immense economic and strategic potential. The time is ripe for India to devise a specific Indochina policy because clubbing Vietnam into the Look East policy will not yield many dividends, if India wishes to have a strategic presence and a more participative status in the region.[18]

While China has made it very apparent that it has an Indian Ocean policy to protect its maritime interests and trade. India has also been participating in the regional maritime security initiatives with regard to anti-piracy operations but the deployment of Chinese ships for anti-piracy operations is a serious matter. The question is whether India should counter Chinese influence through South China Sea policy or it should keep a rather complacent posture on the issue. Though, Chinese have been building ports in Gwadar and Hambantota, India should also address its commercial concerns as well as security needs on a priority basis. India should also look for expeditionary role and shed the oft-repeated lack of resources rhetoric. Vietnam and India need to enhance their defence relationship to the next level and the starting point could be cooperation in developing defence industry in Vietnam and cooperating in ship building industry which is one of the developed areas in Vietnam.

Conclusion

The defence and security ties between the two nations has been predicated on the two major factors; first the comparative importance given to their respective relations with China and second the lack of vision as well as commitment towards containing China through bilateral cooperation. On the Indian side, the question has been whether Vietnam would be a cooperating partner or would confide with its ideological partner. On the other hand, Vietnam was not been firm on commitments in terms of engaging India; it is more a relationship of demand and supply. Both nations are economically prosperous and must chart out their strategic priorities and levels of engagements. This also depends on the political will on both sides and the rather subdued stance on the defence ties between the two nations.

NOTES

1. David Brewster, 'India's Strategic Partnership with Vietnam: The Search for a Diamond on the South China Sea?', *Asian Security*, Vol. 5(1), 2009, p. 26. For recent debates on strategic issues see Harsh V. Pant, *Contemporary Debates in Indian Foreign and Security Policy: India Negotiates its Rise in the International System*, Palgrave Macmillan, New York, 2008.
2. David Brewster, 'India's Strategic Partnership with Vietnam: The Search for a Diamond on the South China Sea?', *Asian Security*, Vol. 5(1), 2009, p. 27. Also see Kripa Sridharan, *The ASEAN Region in India as Foreign Policy*, Dartmouth, Singapore, 1996.

3. David Brewster, 'India's Strategic Partnership with Vietnam: The Search for a Diamond on the South China Sea?', *Asian Security*, Vol. 5(1), 2009, pp. 28-29.

4. David Brewster, 'India's Strategic Partnership with Vietnam: The Search for a Diamond on the South China Sea?', *Asian Security*, Vol.5(1), 2009, pp. 28-29. Also refer to Sudhir Devare, *India and Southeast Asia*, ISEAS, Capital Publishing, New Delhi, 2006.

5. Though there are varying opinions about the success of ARF. For a more positive analysis about the stature of ARF see Hiro Katsumata, *ASEAN'S Cooperative Security Enterprise: Norms and Interests in the ASEAN Regional Forum*, Palgrave Macmillan, London, 2009, pp. 16-37.

6. Vijay Sakhuja, The Indian Navy's Agenda for Maritime Security in the Indian Ocean, Terrorism Monitor, Vol. 8(8), 26 February 2010.

7. Pradeep Chauhan, Maritime Cooperation and Confidence Building in Sam Bateman and Joshua Ho eds. *Southeast Asia and the Rise of Chinese and Indian Naval Power: Between Rising Naval Powers*, Routledge, London, 2010, pp.204-205.

8. Pradeep Chauhan, Maritime Cooperation and Confidence Building in Sam Bateman and Joshua Ho eds. *Southeast Asia and the Rise of Chinese and Indian Naval power: Between Rising Naval Powers*, Routledge, London, 2010, pp.205-206.

9. C. Ravindranatha Reddy, 'India and Vietnam: Era of friendship and Cooperation 1947-1991', Emerald Publishers, Chennai, 2009, p. 36.

10. Quoted in C. Ravindranatha Reddy, 'India and Vietnam: Era of Friendship and Cooperation 1947-1991', Emerald Publishers, Chennai, 2009, p. 36.

11. Ministry of Defence Policy Paper No.1, Defence Diplomacy at http://www.mod.uk/ NR/rdonlyres/BB03F0E7-1F85-4E7B-B7EB-4F0418152932/0/polpaper1_def_ dip.pdf

12. David Brewster, 'India's Strategic Partnership with Vietnam: The Search for a Diamond on the South China Sea?', *Asian Security*, Vol. 5(1), 2009, pp. 32-33.

13. Pankaj K. Jha, 'India-Vietnam Relations: Need for Enhanced Cooperation', *Strategic Analysis*, Vol. 32 (6), 2008, p. 1089.

14. David Brewster, 'India's Strategic Partnership with Vietnam: The Search for a Diamond on the South China Sea?', *Asian Security*, Vol. 5(1), 2009, p. 30.

15. The supplies of Carbines from Pakistan to Vietnam has created concerns in India but according to the Vietnamese defence personnel India does not manufacture those weapons which were required by Vietnamese security personnel.

16. David Brewster, 'India's Strategic Partnership with Vietnam: The Search for a Diamond on the South China Sea?', *Asian Security*, Vol. 5(1), 2009, pp. 30-31.

17. Pankaj K. Jha, 'India-Vietnam Relations: Need for Enhanced Cooperation', *Strategic Analysis*, Vol. 32(6), 2008, pp. 1089-1090.

18. The India-Vietnam Partnership, #3006, 19 November 2009, http://www.ipcs.org/ article/southeast-asia/the-india-vietnam-partnership-3006.html

9

India and Vietnam in the Emerging Southeast Asian Security Complex

Binoda Kumar Mishra

In recent times, there is much talk in the Indian strategic and academic circles about possible India-Vietnam strategic (defence) cooperation. The prospects of such cooperation, it is argued, rest on the fact that both India and Vietnam are friends for long time and on the perception that both have an interest convergence in preventing China from emerging as a threatening hegemon in the region. India's increasing defence engagements with Vietnam are seen as a strategic move in the right direction.

In this context, this chapter examines Vietnam's position in the emerging Southeast Asian Security complex and the prospect of India playing a meaningful role in Vietnam's security calculation. The chapter also attempts to articulate the argument that the prospects of India-Vietnam strategic cooperation would remain predicated more upon Vietnam's strategic calculations than India's. It further argues that containment of China cannot be the base for closer strategic relationship between India and Vietnam.

Security Complex in Southeast Asia

Buzan's "Regional Security Complex" provides an analytical tool for understanding the security interactions between a pair of states within a geographical region to which both the states think they belong. India and

Vietnam, in analytical sense, belong to the extended region of Asia Pacific with Southeast Asia as the core. The security scenario in the region is described as a "regional security complex"[1] or as an evolving "security community."[2] A description of the trends of security interactions among the Southeast Asian countries would make it clear that the region is yet to qualify as a security community in the real sense of the term, at least in matters related to the traditional security concerns of most of the countries of the region.

Before going into the details of the kind of security threats that arise from inter-state tensions and the larger regional threats, one may refer to Buzan's famous security complex, more specifically heterogeneous security complex.[3] Considering the fact that the security scenario within Southeast Asia has become very complex and multi-factored, it would be useful to identify the region as a Buzanian heterogeneous security complex where various actors and sectoral determinants interact to shape the state of inter-state relations. Therefore, taking note of the complex intermingling of actors and factors, it is prudent to discuss some of the major state to state relationships to develop a broader sense of the security trend in the region.

Bilateral relations and associated tensions between Southeast Asian countries are deeply ingrained in their historical relations, past experiences and entrenched animosities. These have a strong impact on their mutual security perceptions. Bilateral tensions were pushed to the back seat during the Cold War when state to state relationship was determined solely by ideology driven political considerations. Ideology was complemented by the tussle for power and influence over the region. However within the region, the criterion for determining a friend or a foe was largely on the basis of historical experience. Else, it would be difficult to explain Thailand's eagerness to strike a chord with China during the Vietnam-Cambodia imbroglio. The Chinese on their part, not only reciprocated positively, but also gradually withdrew support from the communist insurgencies in Southeast Asia, especially in the non-communist states of Thailand and Malaysia. It definitely had a positive impact on the security perceptions of these two states. All these point to the fact that the bilateral issues between states within Southeast Asia have nothing to do with the Cold War; they emanate from regional causes and contexts. Therefore, there was only a lull in those problems during the Cold War period but re-emerged in the post-Cold War period. In addition, emerging issues have added a new texture to these problems. Thus, it is necessary to look at the state of major bilateral relations that constitute mutual threat perceptions. Issues that draw specific attention include overlapping territorial (including maritime) claims and border demarcation problems, cross-border insurgency support, economic competition, refugees, and illegal immigration.

Tensions between Thailand and Myanmar did not come to light until late 1980s and early 1990s that began with the rise of democratic and ethnic forces in Myanmar. Relations became tensed as a number of camps opened in Thailand leading to incursions by the Myanmar army. Military clashes have also occurred on the issue of border between the two countries. Maritime border problems have caused tensions regarding the question of fishing rights. Border issues also plague Thai-Malay relationship as much as Thai suspicion that Malaysia encourages the separatist movement in Southern Thailand. Malaysia on the contrary, is unhappy with the unchecked Thai infiltration into their country. Two neighbours, Indonesia and Malaysia, are not very confident about one another. Especially after loosing the two islands of Ligitan and Sipidan to Malaysia, Indonesia is unhappy. Indonesia is also suspicious that Malaysia assists anti-state forces in Aceh. Besides, there are other maritime delimitation problems between the two countries including the Ambalat area in the Celebes Sea. In the case of Malaysia and Singapore, it is a different kind of tension that is symptomatic of their historical problems that date back to the formation of the Malay Federation back in the 1960s. As if to compensate for the loss of territory to Singapore, since the day of separation, Malaysia consciously has been using water link as a foreign policy component giving itself leverage over Singapore. Though there is an International Court of Justice (ICJ) judgement on the disputed Pedra Branca Island, the judgement is incomplete leaving scope for differences between these not-so-friendly neighbours.

Territorial disputes also challenge good relations between the Philippines and Malaysia. Apart from their conflicting claims on Sabah wherein the Philippines lays a claim on the Sabah, both the countries have laid claims on Investigator's Shoal in South China Sea. Malaysians are also annoyed the way the Filipinos have crowded Sabah. Anti-social activities have increased in Sabah and the Malaysian government is irritated. The Philippines is also under the impression that Malaysia is providing sanctuary to the Moros, most of them come as refugees and operate from Sabah. Besides, these bilateral problems, a number of border disputes exist between Thailand and Cambodia, Thailand and Laos, Malaysia and Brunei, and Malaysia and Brunei. "There are several outstanding border issues between Vietnam and some of the other ASEAN member states, notably Malaysia and Indonesia, which may test intra-mural peace."[4] There exist maritime boundary dispute between Vietnam and Thailand in the Gulf of Thailand.

This synoptic description of the issues that characterise the inter-state relationship between the members of Association of South East Asian Nations (ASEAN) shows that in terms of traditional security, there exist a handful of problematic issues preventing the emergence of a security community to substantiate Amitav Acharya's claim that Southeast Asia is emerging as a security community. One may argue that ASEAN is emerging as an unit to address non-traditional security issues that affect all the states equally, but in their traditional security concerns they remain as divided as states of any other region. In the background of these numerous points of potential conflict, we see a steady increase in military spending by all the Southeast Asian countries over the years. Except Cambodia, all countries are showing interest in spending more on defence. The only pause in the post-Cold War era was the financial crisis of the 1997. In the 2000s, it is showing an upward trend through all countries buying weapons from countries outside the region.[5]

It was the proxy war between the two superpowers during the Cold War that instigated a "self-stimulating military rivalry between states, in which their efforts to defend themselves cause(d) them to enhance the threats they pose to each other."[6] During the post-Cold War period, the arms procurement can be seen as a result of a particular anxiety. The anxiety about a power namely China is slowly looming large over the strategic horizon of the region. Though China does not belong to the physical geography of Southeast Asia, in every sense, it is part of Southeast Asia. With the end of the Cold War the security complex related to it eased substantially. The initial post-Cold War period not only witnessed the absence of the Soviets in the region, but also saw the US withdrawing from its bases in the Philippines.

In terms of superpower presence, there emerged a vacuum in the region enticing players adjacent to the region to rush in to fill the vacuum or to advance their strategic interest. The prominent benefactor of this situation was China. With its rapid economic and military development, China was in the best place to take advantage of the situation. It considers Southeast Asia as part of its ancient empire and thus China reserves the right to expand its influence in the region. "With Soviet power out of picture, the longstanding military-political links between China and Southeast Asia became more important, triggering the growth of links in the military-political security dynamics of Northeast and Southeast Asia."[7]

Apart from border tensions with some of the Southeast Asian countries, the most important issue that, in a way, brought the entire Southeast Asia to an anxious position vis-à-vis China is the "South China Sea". It is to be mentioned here that the South China Sea is also an issue in between various Southeast Asian states. Lee Yong Leng, a political geographer calls it a "geopolitical lake" over which competitive claims of territory among the littoral states develops into a complex web of conflict and rivalries.[8] "The geographic core of the competition is the Spratly Island archipelago consisting of hundred islets, reefs and rocks extending into over 250,000 square miles of the central South China Sea."[9] The presumed large-scale deposit of oil and natural gas along with marine wealth is the centre of attraction for most claimants. Despite differences among the Southeast Asian states over South China Sea, there seems to be a convergence of fear regarding China. Geographically, the Spratly are closer to Vietnam, Malaysia and the Philippines than to mainland China. "But China claims sovereignty over all the islands, using historical records, maps and cultural relics to support its claim."[10]

China's creeping assertiveness over the issue of South China Sea territories looms large in the minds of Southeast Asian countries. A feeling of vulnerability vis-à-vis the rising and assertive China has brought back balance of power calculation that was supposed to have dissipated along with the Cold War. Southeast Asian countries saw sense in re-engaging the other major power particularly the US as an insurance against future Chinese aggression. It is possible to explain the creation of ASEAN Regional Forum (ARF) and the inclusion of the US, Japan and subsequently India as moves by ASEAN members as a balance of power. While analysing the security context in Asia Pacific in 1993 that led to the formation of the ARF, the need for engaging major powers was felt to maintain stability in the region. The Chairman's statement declared that "the continuing presence of the United States, Japan and China, and other states of the region would contribute to regional stability."[11] Thus, the doubt over future Chinese posture in the Southeast Asian region and in the larger region of Asia Pacific entailed that ASEAN looks for counter force that ASEAN itself was unable to present. But it must be borne in mind that it was not just a counter force strategy that led to the formation of ARF; if counter force was the only objective, China would not have been invited to be part of ARF. Thus, a better explanation of ARF and the inclusion of China, among other powers is that the ASEAN countries did not wish to antagonise China overtly. Second, considering the enormous economic potential China presents, antagonising it would not be a prudent move by any stretch of imagination. In Southeast Asia, therefore, "though all the members are confronted with China's rising power, they have differential relationships with PRC that derives from various aspects that include: contrasting historical experiences, ethnicity and economic relations as well as domestic and international conditions."[12] The security underpinning in engaging China lies in the belief that by engaging China, it would be possible to "socialise China into being a good neighbour"[13] and at the same time ARF with other powerful members would act as a balancer against China if it behaves in an irredentist manner.

Vietnam's Security Perceptions: The China Factor

One can see reduction of chances of mutual conflict among the Southeast Asian countries in the post-Cold War period and an increasing anxiety among the ASEAN countries both individually and collectively vis-à-vis China. Vietnam has been subject to direct Chinese aggression, in the past for more than once and it is Vietnam that China is also worried about as in the hands of Vietnam, China has been humiliated. Therefore, the discussion on emerging security complex in Southeast Asia involving China would remain incomplete without a specific discussion on Vietnam's security perceptions. It is also in this context that the prospects of India-Vietnam defence cooperation assume importance. After the end of the Cold War, all countries reassessed their political and security situation in the changed international settings and so did China in the year 1993. In 1993, the authoritative Chinese Central Military Commission chaired by Deng Xiaoping and Jiang Zemin published a report titled "Can the Chinese Army Win the Next War?" The report summed up the threats perceived by Chinese leadership in the coming years. It characterised India as the "longest potential threat," US as the "open adversary" and "the number one military power in the world," Japan as "a resurgent powerful adversary," Vietnam as "unpredictable super-killer," and Russia as "still powerful threatening force."[14] This shows Vietnam's presence in Chinese psyche as an adversary and not for without reasons.

Located in the southern border of China, "Vietnam came under Chinese suzerainty for a period of roughly one thousand years."[15] In the post-World War II period, Vietnam has been subjected to direct Chinese military actions twice apart from the Chinese nationalist forces occupying Northern part of Vietnam briefly at the end of World War II. The first one was in the year 1979 with a bitter conflict over land border and the second was in the year 1988, when both had a clash in the South China Sea. There have been no war or clashes between the two countries from then on, but on several occasions China has displayed enough aggressive postures to keep Vietnam on its toes. Towards the end of the Cold War and at the beginning of the 1990s, specifically between 1989 till 1992, both enjoyed a stable relationship, but the year 1992 saw renewed aggressive posturing from the Chinese side over the Spratlys. Vietnam's claims to Paracel and Spratly archipelagos are based on historical records showing its control over these islands since 17th century. Vietnam further substantiates its claim with the help of 1982 United Nations Convention on Law of the Sea.[16] It presently controls only 20 islets, cays and reefs in the Spratly archipelago. Paracel was completely taken over from Vietnam by China in 1974.

With this background, China's assertiveness in 1992 by concluding an agreement with Crestone, an American company, to explore in the disputed island in the Spratly and planting a sovereignty marker on a tiny reef in the Spratly sent signals of Chinese attempt to formalise its claim of sovereignty over the whole of Spratly. By these two events, Vietnam realised the hard fact that there cannot be any guarantee in the future about Chinese peaceful intents towards Vietnam. The unpredictability entailed a (Foreign) policy that would remain flexible to meet unexpected challenges from China.

Vietnam's Foreign Policy and Approach towards China

The *Upanishads* say that if one realises the realities of life and acts accordingly, his life will change so much that his friends would fail to recognise him. This is apt in describing Vietnam's current foreign policy philosophy in comparison to some time ago. In the entire Southeast Asia, it was the US and her ideology that was reigning when Vietnam was the only country actively acting as a forward post of the socialist ideology in the region. Thus, ideology, during the Cold War period, played a dominant role in all aspects of Vietnam's life including its foreign policy. The (sudden) collapse of the former Soviet Union created a crisis in Vietnam's international support base leading to sense of severe vulnerability. This sense of vulnerability induced Vietnam to abandon the course of ideology as a guiding principle of foreign policy. The Vietnamese realised that both their regime and the national security were jeopardised during the mid-1980s[17] due to this ideologically intoxicated foreign policy of the Cold War times. They, thus, wasted no time in revisiting their foreign policy in the light of the realities of the day, which called for pragmatism. One can mark the distinctive change in Vietnam's foreign policy approach in the post-Cold War era. The character of foreign policy of every country has undergone some change after the fall of the Soviet Bloc, but no one has made substantial changes as Vietnam has.

The Paris settlement of October 1991 brought to light the fact that Vietnam had lost the strategic advantage it enjoyed in Indochina during the Cold War. With this Vietnam's tensions also eased to some extent, but China still remained an irritant. "The relationship with China remains most problematic, however, because of the intrinsic mistrust and inequality that distinguishes it and the two countries' immutable close proximity."[18] Unlike the Cold War times, Vietnam did not contemplate an aggressive retaliatory posture towards China. Instead, Vietnam used the expanding ASEAN to shift focus from Sino-Vietnam issues to broader strategic pattern in the wider East Asia in general.[19] In its bilateral dealings with China, Vietnam also seems to be adopting a flexible approach that keeps Vietnam's options open. Thus, one can see a mixture of four kinds of prudence in Vietnam's approach towards China; they are the four paradigms: realism, asymmetry, socialist internationalism, and interdependence. "Realism corresponds to the balancing approach; the asymmetry corresponds to defence approach; socialist internationalism corresponds to solidarity approach; and interdependence corresponds to enmeshment with China. Though realism remains to be primordial, the other three rose to significance during different periods of Vietnamese history."[20] In Vuving's analysis, the contemporary Vietnamese approach towards China is marked primarily by enmeshment backed up by deference, though balance of power approach remains a preferred option if Vietnam is guaranteed of adequate support to enable Vietnam to stand up against China in any future scenario.[21]

In the absence of a regular support base for Vietnam in the post-Soviet world, it looked around for a possible counter force to deter future Chinese assertiveness against its own interests. Around the same time, India seemed eager to engage ASEAN and speculations emerged that ASEAN countries can use India as a counter weight against China in this region. Given India's long standing friendship with Vietnam, it is argued that India can provide Vietnam the required support to help her feel safer vis-à-vis China. A security convergence is discovered (rather made out) between India and Vietnam in preventing the rising China from becoming hegemonic in the region. Much of these arguments are more conjectural than based on ground positions. Therefore, before looking at the possible interest convergence between India and Vietnam, it is imperative to have a brief discussion on India's Look East Policy that brought India into Southeast Asia.

India's Look East Policy

The rise of India and China in the 21st century is of interest to the developed world that fear job loss and many other deprivations. But India and China, on the other hand, have a tough task at hand as they constitute one third of world's population and aspire to provide the people the quality of life comparable to the West. This compulsion along with an age-old saying that "great powers, either established or aspiring, even if good neighbours, do compete," makes competition between these two 'Asian giants' imminent. Nowhere will this competition have as much effect as on Southeast Asia, the immediate neighbourhood of these two countries. Larger Asia Pacific and South Asia could potentially come under the impact. Both China and India are late but near simultaneous entrants into Southeast Asia; but China, it is assumed, has integrated itself substantially with the region where as India, it is argued, to be lagging behind.

India's engagement with Southeast Asia resumed and this engagement came to be known as Look East Policy. From then on India is slowly but increasingly getting engaged with Southeast Asia. Beginning as a sectoral dialogue partner in 1992, India became a full dialogue partner in 1995, member of ARF in 1996, a summit level partner in 2002, and finally a member of the East Asia Summit in 2005. This "unusually proactive" move[22] from the Indian side has generated a debate as to what is the objective of this Look East Policy? It has been termed as a manifestation of India's assertiveness in the immediate neighbourhood and at the same time, it has also been identified as a strategic move specifically designed to contain China in China's traditional sphere of influence. Another interpretation is that it is primarily an automatic fallout of India's expansionist attitude.

India's genuine interest in Southeast Asia was evident from its desire to be part of the region in any form the members of this region wanted. While the ASEAN was in the making, the then Foreign Minister of India, M.C. Chagla, during his visit to Singapore and Malaysia in May 1967, expressed

India's support to the formation of ASEAN and wanted India to be part of this grouping in any form the members think fit.[23] Suffice to point out that China was not supportive of the formation of ASEAN and called it "Puny Counter-revolutionary Alliance."[24] In 1992, India started her formal engagement with Southeast Asia as a bloc and this long gestation is generally accounted to two factors: (a) the emergent ASEAN was primarily an association of Western Alliance; and (b) India was seen as hobnobbing with the then Soviet Union. But the reality is India had always wanted to be a part of the grouping in some capacity or the other but India was not invited at the inception of the grouping. Secondly, economically, India focused on West Asia due to the presence of oil on which India was heavily dependent and strategically Pakistan attracted most of India's foreign policy attention being seen as the most immediate threat.

Things started changing from 1980s. India's efforts to engage with Southeast Asia almost materialised in 1980, when it was about to get the status of a dialogue partner. "But India's support to Vietnam's invasion of Cambodia and her subsequent recognition of the Vietnam backed regime in Cambodia upset ASEAN."[25] Around that time, the importance of West Asia began to reduce for India due to drop in oil prices, and the Gulf war in which both the then superpowers were heavily interested and deeply involved. It was perceived to be against India's interest to remain involved in a region where both the superpowers were involved; as any action would have angered one or the other of the big powers. Secondly, India started producing two third of its own oil requirement which further reduced the primacy of West Asia for India. Thirdly, by becoming a group, Southeast Asia experienced steady economic growth which was seen as an opportunity for India's surplus skilled and semi-skilled labour force. Fourthly, ASEAN, on its part, started looking outside its original six members in order to obtain optimality in economic terms under the guiding vision of S. Rajaretnam who, in 1973, set "outward looking" as a strategy for ASEAN's steady development.[26] The above reasons were significant for India to seriously pursue ASEAN and engage fruitfully at the earliest with this emerging regional organisation in her neighbourhood.

There emerged one requirement that brought in some sense of congruity in the security and strategic interests between India and ASEAN states. It is the rise of China in both economic and military terms. This is the only factor that can be identified as common traditional security concern among most, if not all of the Southeast Asian countries. There is a general sense of anxiety among the Southeast Asian countries vis-à-vis China. It is a fact that China has tried to woo the ASEAN countries by keeping aside her territorial and other disputes, but this has done little to assuage the anxiety among the Southeast Asian countries. This certainly helped India's cause of becoming associated with ASEAN in some form as evident from the fact that India was accepted as the dialogue partner of ASEAN ahead of China. Engagement with future major players is the preferred approach for ASEAN and China, India, Japan and the US are identified as the major powers to operate in the region. The importance of India at this stage is well articulated by the former Prime Minister of Singapore, Goh Chok Tong, as the western wing of the ASEAN aircraft, while the eastern wing comprised of China, Japan and Korea.[27]

In the security sphere, it is thus clear that ASEAN as a group is interested in India for the specific congruity in security interest its members have, which is anxiety over China's long-term intentions. Other than this, there is no security or strategic convergence in the traditional sense of security. India, therefore, is engaged more bilaterally in the region than with ASEAN as a group. Though it has been a general practice among the Southeast Asian countries to resolve their disputes peacefully through dialogue, there are moments when force has been projected as a means to resolve conflict. For example, in March 2005 Indonesia sent warships to the Sulawesi Sea to protest against Malaysia's decision to award a contract to an Anglo-Dutch firm to explore and mine the Ambalat and East Ambalat oil and gas blocks. Such incidents drive home the point that each of the Southeast Asian nations need to maintain modernised military equipment and trained personnel to deal with any future eventuality. India figures prominently as a source to seek assistance for modernising armed forces and equipment. The various defence agreements between India and individual Southeast Asian states suggest that India caters to these specific needs since "compared with ASEAN countries, India's weapon systems are not only good in quality but also inexpensive."[28]

Prospects for Greater Indo-Vietnam Defence Relations

India's relations with Vietnam had remained warm during the Cold War and continue to improve further in the post-Cold War era. During the Cold War, India had opposed US military intervention in Vietnam risking Indo-US relations. India also supported Vietnam's Cambodia adventure against the wishes of China and the US. With this background, in the post-Cold War period, Vietnam treats India with strategic importance.[29] The single point where both India and Vietnam see a strategic convergence is the China factor. Both India and Vietnam have disputed territories with China and have been subjected to Chinese aggressiveness in the past and thus both distrust China. The convergence is clear that both India and Vietnam do not wish China to emerge more influential in the region.

Despite this convergence, India and Vietnam did not develop their defence relations substantially during the 1990s. Only at the turn of the century serious attempts were made by India and Vietnam to come closer in defence matters. In 2000, both countries agreed to an institutionalised framework for regular discussions between Indian and Vietnamese Defence Ministers to share strategic threat perceptions and intelligence. They further agreed to conduct joint naval exercises. The strategic relationship was strengthened in 2003 when both committed to assist each other in protecting their interests in international arena, and agreed to take gradual steps to expand cooperation in the security and defence fields.[30] In 2007, both agreed to expand their cooperation into civil nuclear cooperation and joint working on developing Vietnam's uranium ore. This comes along with India's military hardware support to make Vietnam's aging naval ships operational. In 2010, both have identified training of military personnel and dialogue on strategic affairs on both sides, as immediate areas of cooperation.[31]

The increased defence interaction between the two countries is indicative of the fact that India and Vietnam are on the path of becoming substantial strategic partners in coming times. The real prospects of such defence cooperation resulting in substantial strategic partnership would depend on two major factors, viz. the preference of ASEAN nations and Vietnam in particular as to how do they wish to manage their traditional security affairs among themselves and vis-à-vis China; and how willing is India to commit herself to the cause of ASEAN nations and particularly of Vietnam. On the first issue, it seems that ASEAN as a unit is more inclined to manage intra-regional conflicts in non-military way showing signs of a security community. As far as China threat is concerned, given the economic prospects of emerging China to all the ASEAN nations, direct confrontation is almost eliminated as an option. Multi-dimensional engagement of China and involving regional and extra-regional powers is clearly the preferred way. The involvement of Japan, South Korea, China, India and the US has resulted in a super-complex of security regimes of South Asia, Southeast Asia and Northeast Asia.[32] In this super complex, if the presumed objective is to contain emerging China from becoming more assertive, then countries having the power and will to openly stand against China are going to emerge as key players for ASEAN countries and particularly for Vietnam. In this context, India and the US are the natural choices.

The US is forthcoming in its intention to interfere in Asia Pacific matters as evident from the statement by the Secretary of State, Hillary Clinton strongly advocating US interests and US rights to protect its interest in the region, referring particularly to South China Sea, in July 2010 ARF meeting at Hanoi. This sudden move must not be seen as a statement without reason or purpose. It came in response to two very important Chinese actions in the South China Sea in 2009. In June 2009, the People's Liberation Army (PLA) advised the Chinese Central Military Commission to build an airport and a seaport on the Mischief Reef in the Spratly island.[33] Secondly, "around the same time, PLA navy conducted a large scale naval exercise in the South China Sea to demonstrate Chinese sovereignty over the islands."[34] These events suggest that "China would never waive its right to protect its core interest with military means."[35] These events called for strong counter posture which the US displayed to assuage the fear of ASEAN countries and particularly of Vietnam against China.

India, on the other hand, appears to be reluctant to commit itself to any contentious issues in the region that involves China. India's power is perceived to be limited as India, being the sole power in South Asia, has not been able to establish peace and stability in the region. Secondly, India's "no stand" on contentious issues such as Taiwan and South China Sea is seen as lacking in will to play a bigger role in the emerging strategic scenario in the Asia Pacific. Two factors limit India's ambitions to play a bigger role in the region: Engaging China; and inhibition to get too close to the US. This century is witnessing an increased economic engagement between India and China with China emerging as India's largest trading partner. India does not intend to antagonise China on issues that do not directly bother India. Secondly, committing a too close defence relationship amounting to an alliance with Vietnam would effectively draw India into the strategic alliance headed by the US. This is an uncomfortable situation for India considering India's image as a big power in her own rights. Unless India decides her strategic course of action for the Asia Pacific region, Vietnam will see India as of moderate utility for her strategic interests and would rather depend on the US for protecting her interests vis-à-vis China. The defence cooperation between India and Vietnam promises prospects only if India shows clear commitment to Vietnamese strategic interests and reconciles to the fact of working with the US may bring her in direct confrontation with China.

NOTES

1. Barry Buzan and Ole Weaver, *Regions and Powers: The Structure of International Security*, Cambridge, New York, Melbourne, Madrid, Cape Town, Singapore and Sao Paulo, Cambridge University Press, 2003.
2. Amitav Acharya, *Constructing a Security Community in Southeast Asia: ASEAN and the Problem of Regional Order 2nd Edition*, Oxon, New York: Routledge, 2009.
3. Barry Buzan introduced the word *Security Complex* where the interdependence between the states is intense enough to the extent that their security concerns cannot be analysed or their problems solved independently from the other states within the region. In *the heterogeneous security complex* model the interaction and interdependence within a region involves a number of actors from different sectors thus giving a holistic estimate of the intensity of interactions and interdependence within that particular region. See, Barry Buzan, *People States and Fear: An Agenda for International Security Studies in the Post-Cold War Era*, Boulder, Rienner and London, Harvester Wheatsheaf, 1991.
4. Amitav Acharya, *Constructing a Security Community in Southeast Asia: ASEAN and the Problem of Regional Order 2nd Edition*, Oxon, New York: Routledge, 2009, p. 151.
5. Amitav Acharya, *Constructing a Security Community in Southeast Asia: ASEAN and the Problem of Regional Order 2nd Edition*, Oxon, New York, Routledge, 2009, pp. 161-163.
6. Barry Buzan, *An Introduction to Strategic Studies: Military Technology and International Relations*, London, Macmillan, for the International Institute for Strategic Studies, 1987, p. 69.
7. Barry Buzan and Ole Weaver, *Regions and Powers: The Structure of International Security*, Cambridge, New York, Melbourne, Madrid, Cape Town, Singapore and Sao Paulo, Cambridge University Press, 2003, p. 156.
8. Lee Yong Leng, *Southeast Asia: Essays in Political Gegraphy*, Singapore, Ingapore University Press, 1982, p. 112. cited in Donald E. Weatherbee, *An International Relations in Southeast Asia: The Struggle for Autonomy*, Lantham, Boulder, New York, Toronto and Oxford, Rowman & Littlefield Publishers, INC, 2005, p. 133.
9. Donald E. Weatherbee, *An International Relations in Southeast Asia: The Struggle for Autonomy*, Lantham, Boulder, New York, Toronto and Oxford, Rowman & Littlefield Publishers, INC, 2005, p. 133.
10. Malclolm Chalmers, *Confidence-Building in South-East Asia*, University of Bradford, UK, Westview Press, 1996, p. 46.
11. Chairman's Statement, ASEAN Post-Ministerial Conference, Senior Officials Meeting, Singapore May 20-21, 1993.
12. Ralf Emmers, *Cooperative Security and the Balance of Power in ASEAN and the ARF*, London and New York, Routledge Curzon, 2003, p. 133.

13. Barry Buzan and Ole Weaver, *Regions and Powers: The Structure of International Security*, Cambridge, New York, Melbourne, Madrid, Cape Town, Singapore and Sao Paulo, Cambridge University Press, 2003, p. 161.

14. "Can the Chinese Army Win the Next War?", Beijing: Central Military Commission, 1993, cited in Ashok Kapur, "China and Proliferation: Implications for India," *China Report*, Vol. 34, Nos. 3-4, July-December 1998, pp. 403-404.

15. Keith W. Taylor, *The Birth of Vietnam*, Los Angels, University of California Press, 1983. Cited in Carlyle A. Thayer, "Vietnamese Perspectives of 'China Threat'" in Herbert Yee and Ian Storey (eds.), *The China Threat: Perceptions, Myths and Reality*, Oxon, Routledge Curzon, 2002, p. 266.

16. Nguyen Hong Thao and Ramese Amer, "Managing Vietnam's Maritime Boundary Disputes," *Ocean Development & International Law*, Vol. 38, No. 3, 2007, p. 305.

17. Excerpts from Michael Leifer, "Vietnam's Foreign Policy in the Post-Soviet Era: Coping with Vulnerability," in Chin Kin Wah and Leo Suryadinta, *Michael Leifer: Selected Works on Southeast Asia*, Singapore ISES, 2005, p. 633.

18. Excerpts from Michael Leifer, "Vietnam's Foreign Policy in the Post-Soviet Era: Coping with Vulnerability," in Chin Kin Wah and Leo Suryadinta, *Michael Leifer: Selected Works on Southeast Asia*, Singapore ISES, 2005, p. 648.

19. Barry Buzan and Ole Weaver, *Regions and Powers: The Structure of International Security*, Cambridge, New York, Melbourne, Madrid, Cape Town, Singapore and Sao Paulo, Cambridge University Press, 2003, p. 157.

20. Alexander L. Vuving, "Strategy and Evolution of Vietnam's China Policy: A Changing Mixture of Pathways," *Asian Survey*, Vol. 46, Issue 6, 2006, p. 807,

21. For a detailed discussion on the contemporary Foreign policy strategies of Vietnam, see, Ibid. pp. 805-24.

22. Scholars in India do not consider India to be generally proactive in her foreign policy.

23. K.P. Saksena, *Cooperation in Development: Problems and Prospects for India and ASEAN*, New Delhi: Sage Publications, 1986, p. 53.

24. "Meeting in Bangkok: Puny Counter-revolutionary Alliance," *Peking Review*, 18 August 1967. Cited in, M. Ayoob, p, 11.

25. Chulacheeb Chinwanno, "The Dragon, the Bull and the Ricestalks: The Roles of China and India in Southeast Asia," in Saw Swee-Hock, Sheng Lijun and Chin Kin Wah, (eds.), *ASEAN-China Relations: Realities and Prospects*, Singapore: Institute of Southeast Asian Studies, 2005, p. 159.

26. It was S. Rajaretnam, the Foreign Minister of Singapore and one of the founding fathers of ASEAN who advocated the idea that ASEAN, in order to achieve optimality in economy has to attract outside powers to be involved in the region. For more see, New themes for Asia. South-East Asia in transition. Singapore solution/by S. Rajaratnam, Reprinted from The Australian outlook, Dec. 1973, East Melbourne: Australian Institute of International Affairs, 1973, pp. 243-260.

27. Goh Chok Tong's speech at the ASEAN plus India Summit, Phnom Penh, November 2002. Cited in Sudhir Devare, *India and Southeast Asia: Towards Security Convergence*, Singapore: Institute of Southeast Asina Studies, New Delhi: Capital Publishing Company, 2006, p. 50.

28. "Hu Shisheng, "India's Approach to ASEAN and its Regional Implications," in Saw Swee-Hock, Sheng Lijun and Chin Kin Wah (eds.), *ASEAN-China Relations: realities and Prospects*, Singapore: Institute of Southeast Asian Studies, 2005, p.132.

29. The then President of Vietnam Tran Duch Luang's Statement during a meeting with then Foreign Minister of India, Jaswant Singh. During November 2000. S. Prasamrajan, "Ahoy Hanoi: With India and Vietnam reviving old bonds, the chances of a strategic tie-up become stronger," *India Today*, November 20, 2000, p. 50.

30. *Joint Declaration on Framework of Comprehensive Cooperation Between Republic of India and Socialist Republic of Vietnam*, May 2003.

31. P.S. Suryanarayana, "India, Vietnam Agree to Firm Up Defence Ties," *The Hindu*, July 28, 2010. online http://www.thehindu.com/news/article536828.ece, accessed on September 10, 2010.

32. Barry Buzan and Ole Weaver, *Regions and Powers: The Structure of International Security*, Cambridge, New York, Melbourne, Madrid, Cape Town, Singapore and Sao Paulo, Cambridge University Press, 2003, p. 164.

33. H. Khasnobis, "Stakeholder in the Sea: China and USA as Arbitrators in Sovereignty Disputes," *The Statesman*, September 27, 2010.

34. Ibid.

35. "American shadow over South China Sea," *Global Times*, July 26, 2010. http://opinion.globaltimes.cn/editorial/2010-07/555723.html, accessed on September 22, 2010.

10

India and Vietnam: Forging a Durable Strategic Partnership

P.V. Rao

India and Vietnam have a long tradition of shared perspectives and concerns in the post-colonial Asia. Any serious discussion of their mutual relations and their patterns of evolution can not ignore the colonial background and the anti-imperialist struggles of Vietnam and the Indian support to these struggles. In the words of a contemporary Vietnamese scholar, "early relations between Vietnam and India were founded upon the shared values of decolonization and nationalism. Although, hardly any material evidence was available, spiritual support was highly forthcoming during the struggle for national self-reliance."[1]

Pandit Jawaharlal Nehru was the first head of a government to visit Vietnam soon after its victory against the French in 1954 and, four years later President Ho Chi Minh of the new republic reciprocated by visiting India in February 1958.

The two independent republics formalized their nascent bilateral relations first at consular level, with India opening her consulate general office in Hanoi in 1954, followed by Vietnam's counterpart at New Delhi in 1956. It was about half a decade later in January 1972 that India and Vietnam had elevated their diplomatic relations to the ambassadorial status. Their mutual relationship, therefore, was built on a foundation of anti-colonial and nationalist ideologies. Viewed in a broader regional context, India's Southeast Asian policy in the Cold War era to an extent was shaped by her consistent support to Vietnam's nationalist war against the United States. J.N. Dixit, India's former Foreign Secretary would record that though the Southeast Asian nations made overtures to India to join the Association of South East Asian Nations (ASEAN) in 1967, they "were, however, rebuffed by New Delhi because India had structured its South-East Asia policy on the basis of its overall view of the Cold War (and) the situation in Vietnam...."[2]

Apart from the moral identification of the Nehruvian and post-Nehruvian Indian leadership with the Vietnamese anti-imperialist struggle, geo-political considerations too influenced Indian diplomacy in the Indo-China region. Sino-Indian war and the subsequent adversarial relationship between India and China for over two decades had cast its influence on India's support to the Vietnamese nationalist cause. In other words, India-Vietnam evolving relationship needs to be seen not only through an anti-imperialist ideological prism, but that there was also a concurrent regional geo-political logic which shaped the nature of mutual ties over the decades. Such geo-political dynamic continues to influence, rather in greater vigour, contemporary Delhi-Hanoi relationship.

Before a unified Vietnam emerged, India had carefully balanced her relations with the two rival regimes of South and North Vietnam. New Delhi had to needle through her declared public commitment to the Vietnamese nationalist war against the United States and her professed non-alignment. Hence, as a balancing strategy, India had recognized both the Hanoi and Saigon regimes. However, once both regimes were unified into a single republic in 1975, India could easily steer out of the dilemma of dual-recognition and hence throw her weight fully behind the Socialist Republic of Vietnam. During the following years, war-torn Vietnam had received substantial Indian assistance to help reconstruct her economy and infrastructure.

Post-unified Vietnam, as is well known, had to face serious neighbourly challenges to its territorial integrity and the pressing tasks of nation-building. The border war between Vietnam and her giant northern neighbour, China in 1979 brought into sharp focus threats to her national security from within the region. In historical perspective, the latest war between China and Vietnam was reminiscent of many such invasions from the north during the preceding centuries. Not much later, Hanoi was to fight again the Chinese backed

Khmer Rouge in Cambodia. In fact, just to recount the past, Vietnam was involved throughout the 1980s in the Cambodian war in which the Chinese-Vietnamese conflicting perspectives and interests in Indochina became more pronounced, a strategic reality which soon was to lead to a polarization of regional power equations in Asia. Thus if the rival Khmer Rouge enjoyed the Chinese military support, the Cambodian regime was backed by Vietnam and her ally the Soviet Union, the former super power. The convergence of Soviet-Vietnam interests on the Cambodian issue coupled with India's close relations with Moscow added a new geo-political dimension to India's relations with united Vietnam. All the three were united, albeit for individual reasons, in their opposition to the Chinese role in Indo-China. Vietnam almost remained isolated in Asia with not only China but also with the ASEAN group of six countries which strongly backed Cambodia.

It was during such troubled times of regional conflicts in Indochina, almost soon after the ending of the long US-led war against Vietnam, India and Vietnam had moved far closer. This time India was not acting in the symbolic manner of morally identifying with the nationalist cause of the Vietnamese people against the western powers, but New Delhi weighed down diplomatically in favour of Hanoi's wars with China. Gradually, the two republics were discovering a common strategic space created by the emerging geo-political environment in Asia.

In retrospect, the Asian strategic developments during the 1970s and 1980s carried considerably parallel implications for both India and Vietnam. Following the Indo-Pakistan war of 1971 over the liberation of Bangladesh and the defeat of Pakistan, South Asian geo-politics changed radically. India, as was widely acknowledged by the world, emerged as the preeminent regional power in South Asia. This new geo-political reality was, however, overshadowed by the Sino-American rapproachment (ping-pong diplomacy), which dramatically altered the Asian geo-politics, rather the global politics. Amidst these rapid developments in South Asia, India and Soviet Union had concretized their Cold War friendship by signing a Treaty of Peace, Friendship and Security in 1971 as war clouds were gathering over the subcontinent.

Within the Indochina, as mentioned above, regional conflicts following the unification of Vietnam compelled the latter to build strategic relations with India and the Soviet Union. India supported, as mentioned above, Vietnamese policy in Cambodia as against the Chinese backed Khmer Rouge regime. Subsequently, India was to extend formal recognition to the Hun Sen government in Cambodia and joined Vietnam in expelling Khmer Rouge from the Non-Alignment Movement (NAM). These pro-Vietnamese actions by India in Indochina had seriously annoyed the Southeast Asian countries with which India never had cordial relations during the Cold War years. As Tridib Chakraborti rightly points out, New Delhi, at this time, did not risk surrendering its close ties with Hanoi and (also) Moscow because it valued its intimate relations with these countries as much more strategically important than its standing among the ASEAN countries.[3]

Around this time, some trends were apparent in India's relations with the Southeast Asian countries so much so the six countries of the ASEAN group almost decided to invite India into their regional forum. But New Delhi's defiant diplomatic moves in favouring Vietnam in Cambodia alienated the ASEAN countries once again, leading them to keep India out of the ASEAN group. India's pro-Vietnamese actions in this context were guided by strategic considerations. India's major concern was to keep China out of Cambodia and the region in general. As well summed up by a scholar:

> Prime minister Indira Gandhi realized that if India were to become a paramount power in South Asia, it would have to prevent a Chinese advance into Southeast Asia... a strong anti-Chinese Indochina would guard the flank of the Indian sphere of influence in South Asia. There was thus a convergence of Vietnamese and Indian views. Both were concerned with checking the Southern advance of Chinese power.[4]

Such strategic logic continues to govern India's relations with Vietnam even today, though the regional environment and the strategies of pursuing it have largely altered.

Post-Cold War Regional Consensus

Both India and Vietnam had during 1990s undertaken a serious reconsideration of their involvement in the wider Asia which resulted in a fundamental change in their respective approaches to dealing with the region. The two republics, under the altered geo-political and economic environment, had shed previous prejudices about their contiguous neighbourhood and designed a fundamentally new framework of engaging their neighbours, at bilateral and multilateral levels.

India's "extended neighbourhood", a post-Cold War strategic doctrine, devised the comprehensive framework of engaging the regions to her east and west. A new set of values, ambitions, power equations, regions and countries became integral to the extended neighbourhood. It carved out a vision of power play and projection for 21st century India. To accommodate foreign policy to the above objectives, India had decided to build and improve her strategic image in Asia. India's strategic aspiration is to emerge as an Asian power and play active role in the Asian power balance. Accordingly, India is upgrading her military capabilities and projecting power in Asia. She is adopting a dual strategy which aims at bolstering the hard military power and at the same time cultivating close political, economic, energy and cultural synergies with the Asian countries. Elucidating such post-Cold War Indian strategic narrative, J.N. Dixit stated that "while aspiring to increase our own strength potentialities, we also wish to create an environment of cooperation, transparency and technological interaction with all our neighbours. This is with a view to building up stable security environment."[5] A number of bilateral and multilateral agreements are signed with the Asian countries so much so today there is hardly an Asian regional group in which India is not represented.

Vietnam too initiated a new era of forging closer relations with her Asian neighbours with whom her relations since the end of the Second World War were marked by ideological differences, political suspicions and security divide. A combination of strategic developments of serious significance to Vietnam's security, even identity, such as the Sino-Soviet rapprochement in late eighties, Soviet collapse, its eventual withdrawal from Asia and the consequent power vacuum in the region caused the Vietnamese leadership to debate the options open to the country in the rapidly changing regional strategic environment. Just as India's sense of isolation following the Soviet withdrawal grew in magnitude, Vietnam too felt similarly. Both were equally concerned over the prospect of China filling the strategic space vacated by their common friend. In this context, it has been observed that "better relations with ASEAN could from Hanoi's perspective, offset some of the vulnerabilities arising from the changing great-power relationship in the Asia-Pacific region. ASEAN was seen as a valuable political ally against China, even though it could not entirely offset the loss of the Soviet Union as a donor and security guarantee."[6]

With a slightly altered emphasis, the above statement is as much relevant to India, Vietnam's another "traditional friend". Rather the value of India to Hanoi had increased multifold, and in a lesser degree of the latter to New

Delhi too. Both, therefore, found in ASEAN a workable multilateral framework in which they could relieve part of the insecurities borne out of the huge void created by Soviet abdication from the Asia-Pacific. Vietnam of course tried to patch up differences with her northern neighbour, but despite her normalization of relations with China in 1991, Hanoi continued to worry about the long-term Chinese ambitions in the region. In particular, of more immediate concern to Vietnam were the Chinese territorial encroachment into the maritime boundaries in the South China Sea, claimed by Vietnam such as the Parcels Island. That the Chinese had even used force to assert their claims over the disputed maritime zones in the South China Sea heightened the insecurity of Vietnam, the much smaller power. To quote a Vietnamese scholar:

> In the first decade of the 21st century, bilateral tensions have eased, but distrust between the two countries remains still high.... It (Vietnam) joins ASEAN in a policy of engagement towards China, hoping to enmesh China in a regional network of interdependent relations so that the Chinese tendency to use force is restrained. In that context, India is an attractive partner to be involved into the fabric of international relations in Southeast Asia.[7]

ASEAN, therefore, has become the important regional multilateral platform for co-engagement between India and Vietnam apart from their close bilateral relationship. In recognition of India's heightened relevance to her regional security, Vietnam strongly supported every Indian move to deepen her ties with the ASEAN such as seeking its summit partnership, joining the ASEAN Regional Forum (ARF), East Asian Summit (EAS) and the Asia-Pacific Economic Cooperation (APEC). In addition, India and Vietnam are members of the six-member Mekong-Ganga Cooperation (MGC), a sub-regional cooperation group, formed to promote sectoral cooperation in such areas as transportation, tourism, human resources and culture. Cambodia, Laos, Mynammar and Thailand are the other four members of the Mekong-Ganga Cooperation formed in 2000. Interestingly, another sub-regional group pioneered by China too was concluded around the same time, without Vietnam. The MGC, however, is a virtual non-starter in comparison with its Chinese-backed counterpart. The near simultaneous formation of these two different Mekong sub-regional groups, one encouraged by India and another by neighbouring China, was seen as not a mere coincidence, but as spilling the Sino-Indian geo-political competition into the Mekong Basin.

Bilateral Defence Cooperation

Indian involvement in Vietnam's defence and security affairs began much earlier than with the Southeast Asian countries. Over the years, the two republics have been cultivating closer mutual engagement in military affairs. During and after the Sino-Vietnamese border war of 1979, senior military officials of Vietnam visited and apparently kept their Indian counterparts updated on the Chinese military actions. Indian Army Chief General Sunderjee visited Vietnam in 1987 to assess the nature of India's military assistance to resist Chinese pressure on the border. Indian military supplies, exercises, personnel training, naval port visits by Indian warships and submarines had become the regular feature. Such growing military interaction between India and Vietnam provoked speculation that Vietnam is India's answer to China's military presence in Myanmar, India's eastern neighbour.

A bilateral Memorandum of Understanding (MoU) on defence cooperation was concluded in 1994 under which India committed to service and maintain the military equipment supplied earlier by the former Soviet Union. The MoU was part of a series of such pacts signed by India with the Southeast Asian countries under the newly launched Look East policy. The MoU with Vietnam, however, did not assure direct military supplies by India to the communist republic. The scope of the MoU was subsequently enlarged in 2000 through a fresh protocol which institutionalized regular defence dialogue, naval exercises, Indian training to the Vietnamese defence personnel, repairs to the Soviet-supplied MIG aircraft and assistance to the production of small and medium arms. Striking a satisfactory note on the growing India-Vietnam defence relationship a Vietnamese scholar comments that "apart from regular visits of high-ranking military delegations, including warships, the two countries have close ties on the procurement of weaponry and military hardware.... *Vietnam has become one of the important importers of India's weaponry and military hardware since 1990.*"[8]

The successive bilateral defence pacts between India and Vietnam eventually consummated into a strategic partnership agreement. It was signed at New Delhi in July 2007 during the Vietnamese Prime Minister Nguyen Tan Dung's visit. Confining not merely to the military relationship, the strategic partnership agreement committed both the republics to strengthen bilateral relations "in the political, economic, security, defence, cultural, science and technological dimensions." (*The Hindu*, July 20, 2007) Its gamut of issues also included extensive cooperation in developing nuclear power, enhancing regional security and combating terrorism, transnational crimes and drug trafficking. In addition, the agreement also called for mutual cooperation in regional and multilateral institutions, a partnership already very evident in view of Hanoi's support to successive Indian efforts to join the ASEAN institutions.

The significance of the India-Vietnam strategic partnership lies in the fact that Vietnam is the only country among the ASEAN members with which India had signed one such so far. India fashioned out a "strategic partnership with Singapore in all but name,"[9] was a conclusive statement made by the visiting Indian Foreign Minister to the island republic in 2007. Of course, India had concluded strategic partnership agreements with about a dozen countries in the post-Cold War period including Australia, European Union, United States, Iran, Israel, Japan, Russia, Germany, France and Nigeria. Moreover, Vietnam is not the only ASEAN country with which India has been upgrading her relations in the defence sector.

A series of defence cooperation and strategic dialogue pacts were inked by India particularly with the Malacca Straits littorals like Indonesia, Malaysia, Singapore and Thailand almost immediately after launching the Look East Policy drive in 1991. An India-Malaysia Defence Committee was set up in 1992, naval exercises began with Singapore in 1993 following a bilateral defence dialogue pact. A noteworthy feature of these defence pacts with her Southeast Asian neighbours is that India followed them up immediately by initiating military exercises with the new partners. Thus in 1995 an India-sponsored multilateral naval exercise, *Milan* had involved the key Malacca littorals – Indonesia, Malaysia and Singapore – in the Andaman Sea. Vietnam was not part of this Bay of Bengal biennial naval exercise until after a decade when she was invited only recently to take part in the much enlarged *Milan*, from the original five to twelve participants including the Pacific navies of Australia and New Zealand. Nor the Vietnamese navy was part of the twenty six member multilateral Indian Ocean Naval Symposium (IONS) sponsored by the Indian Navy at New Delhi in 2008, for whatever the reasons.

Indian warships are conducting joint exercises with the Vietnamese warships in the South China Sea. Informed sources say India was in favour of seeking long-term naval facilities at Cam Rahn Bay which functioned as a naval base for the Soviet Union during the Cold War. Reports were also circulating in late 1980s that Vietnam was offering India warship facilities at her Cam Rahn Bay. Setting aside these conflicting reports, Vietnamese sources recently confirmed that Hanoi was denying not only to India, but to any other power base facilities at its Cam Rahn Bay. Briefing the press at the first meeting of the Asia-Pacific Defence Ministers held at Hanoi in October 2010, Vietnamese foreign ministry spokesperson, amidst reports that the Russian Navy was planning reentry into the base, informed that the strategic naval base would not be leased out to any foreign power for military purpose.[10]

Strategic Partnership: China Factor

Given their natural geo-political concern over the powerful immediate neighbour, China can not escape being the dominant factor in the India-Vietnam strategic partnership. Moreover, as India and China staked their active involvement in the larger Asian strategic landscape, Vietnam has rather inadvertently become integral to the Sino-Indian strategic competition in the region. Thus both New Delhi and Hanoi, given the congruence of their regional objective, consider hedging China in Asia was in their common interest. "Vietnam treats India with strategic importance" was the greeting statement by Vietnam President Tran Duch Luang to the visiting Indian Foreign Minister in 2000.

In this context, some Indian analysts are advocating a stronger Indian military relationship with Vietnam to check the Chinese role in South Asia. They are dismayed over the supposed Indian reluctance to endow her traditional friend with powerful military capabilities other than the current spares and services inputs. Vietnam's geo-political location in the Asia-pacific region, the argument runs, richly endows her with a strategic value to counter the Chinese power and assertiveness in the regions of South Asia and East Asia, provided Hanoi is richly equipped with Indian military hardware including even missile capability. According to one such analyst,

> "The major defense and security requirement of Vietnam would be to build up its conventional military deterrence. India can contribute vitally by providing Prithvi Ballistic Missiles and Brahmos Cruise Missiles.... China was never sensitive and continues to be insensitive to India's strategic sensitivities on the building of Pakistan's nuclear weapons and nuclear capable missile arsenal. Then why should India be sensitive to what China thinks when it comes to Vietnam."[11]

Commenting on the eve of Vietnam Defence Minister's visit to India in November 2009 to attend the annual bilateral defence dialogue, another Indian scholar in Southeast Asian studies finds a stronger rationale for upgrading Vietnam's military capabilities with Indian hardware. Vietnam, to quote him, should be engaged in a "more comprehensive way and the time is ripe for India to devise a specific Indochina policy, because clubbing Vietnam into the Look East policy will not yield many dividends, if India wishes to have a strategic presence and a more benign status in the region."[12]

Limits to Strategic Partnership

In view of the above debate on promoting Vietnam as India's key strategic partner in the Asia-Pacific region, it is pertinent to ask to what extent Hanoi is willing to identify itself fully with India's strategic interests in the Asia-Pacific. India no doubt is broadening her presence in the region not merely to counter the Chinese role, but to stake her claim as a key constituent in the emerging Asian power balance. Her ascendancy is all too an acknowledged reality though the level and strength of her involvement in the region is varyingly assessed. To that end India as already noted is closely cultivating and balancing her relations with all the big powers involved in the Asia-Pacific including China. Will Vietnam be a party to all the Indian moves and levels of engagement with the other powers? Simply, will Hanoi throw all her political weight behind India as the dependable ally! Some Indian observers have already noticed a sense of caution in the Vietnamese support to Indian diplomacy in the region.

Sino-Vietnamese relations have since early 1990s matured into a normalization period. Vietnam has built through a series of agreements with close political, economic, military and even cultural ties with China. The positive trend in their bilateral relations is too evident to be ignored, despite the continuing sensitivities on territorial rights and claims. As summed up by a keen observer of this normalization process,

> "the current political will in both China and Vietnam to improve and expand bilateral relations and to manage the territorial differences by peaceful means augurs well for the future development of their bilateral relationship.…The positive scenario has been outlined with stability and collaboration between the two countries. It would be a relationship in which disputed issues are managed and even resolved through bilateral talks."[13]

Against this background of Sino-Vietnam normalization, to expect Hanoi pursue an India-centric approach toward China could turn out to be a self-defeating strategy for India. In fact, as a former Indian ambassador to Vietnam had observed that Hanoi was pursuing a matured and pragmatic policy in dealing with China and would not like to provoke the latter unless directly threatened. Contradicting the commonly held belief, he noted that Vietnam had never taken the first step to back the Indian efforts to join such regional bodies as the ASEAN Regional Forum (ARF) and East Asian Summit (EAS) obviously to avoid offending China. Vietnam's overall approach is to prefer the presence of big powers in the South China Sea and maintain a balanced relationship with the key players like India in the region.

Recalling similar strain in Vietnam's regional diplomatic behaviour, a former Secretary of India's Foreign Ministry would say:

> "Vietnam and India were close friends during the Cold War years, but the residual goodwill of that period has not translated into any concrete benefits for India as Vietnam has focused on rebuilding its economy and working out stable equations with its giant neighbour China, and the US. In many respects India and Vietnam are competitors in the world market."[14]

Advocates of India's strong strategic support for Vietnam premise their thesis on China's strategy of encircling peninsular India through the so-called "string of pearls." This much quoted theory by the Indian mainstream strategic community forcefully calls for an Indian quid pro to China in its neighbourhood in South China Sea. Vietnam is seen as the best candidate to fill the job. On close scrutiny, some well informed Indian analysts discount the string's alarmist value to Indian security interests in South Asia. A former Indian Chief of Army and reputed strategic analyst finds that except the Gwader naval base built for Pakistan on the Makran coast, the stated purpose of all other Chinese developed naval complexes in India's neighbourhood – Bangladesh, Myanmar and Sri Lanka – is "purely commercial." Given India's formidable maritime dominance in the Indian Ocean, "dispassionately and without hysteria and paranoia as 'maritime encirclement' (by China) of a country of India's dimensions and capabilities is just not possible."[15] Substantiating this line of argument another analyst would conclude that "it shouldn't be possible for China or any other power superpower to encircle a country like India. The only thing that encircles is our fear that they will."[16]

Should India opt for choosing Vietnam as her strategic ally by raising heavily the latter's conventional and missile capabilities, New Delhi cannot afford to ignore the neighbours' sensitivities in the region. Southeast Asian countries do not want a big power competition in the region to disturb their regional order. In the best tradition of their ASEAN Way, they would try to ensure a stable regional political and military balance by engaging the big powers through constant dialogue and persuasion. ASEAN countries over the decades have succeeded in carefully managing the competitive interests of big powers in their own way, without a matching military strength of their own. Nor they allowed any single power to dominate the regional affairs, as best illustrated by denying China central role in the EAS and retaining its driver's seat for themselves. Intra-regionally too, ASEAN members have not allowed their regional boat to weigh heavily in favour of any single power, Indonesia or Singapore, despite their many and recurring intra-regional disputes over borders, trade, water and migrants.

Conclusion

India and Vietnam over the decades have evolved a politico-diplomatic tradition of their own to serve the mutual ideological and geo-political commonalities. The systemic changes caused by the withdrawal of Soviet Union from Asia and the advent of a new geo-political equation due to the interplay of new forces in the Asia-Pacific, including India, has affected an otherwise stronger Cold War bilateral bond between India and Vietnam. Both have, goaded by individual interests, shed their past regional mindsets to seek membership in the regional multilateral arrangements like the ASEAN, ARF and EAS. Given this altered context, both the republics have to accept certain operative norms set by these groupings, which means they can not continue to define and deepen their bilateral relations with the ease and flexibility of the Cold War era. Plainly put, India and Vietnam have to honour the regional political and security sensitivities in deepening their bilateral relations, including the military field.

Writing on India's approach to Asian regional and naval security, Dixit would counsel as follows:

> "The expansion of our own strategic potentialities as well as the patterns of cooperation and interaction that we seek to engineer has to be a measured and gradual process. The enthusiasm and anxiety syndrome should be avoided at all costs, as proved by the negative response that we got recently when we expressed our wish to join the ASEAN Regional Forum."[17]

The above caution should no less govern the current anxiety for a heightened strategic equation with Vietnam by India.

NOTES

1. Nguyen Nam Duong, in, "Engaging the 'Traditional Friend': Vietnam's Approach to India in the ASEAN Context," in P.V. Rao, ed. *India and ASEAN, Partners at Summit,* Knowledge World, New Delhi, 2008, p. 339.
2. J.N. Dixit, *India's Foreign Policy, 1947-2003,* Picus Books, New Delhi, 2003, p. 93.
3. Tridib Chakraborti, "Disparate Priorities: Explaining the Penumbra of India's Look East Policy," in K. Raja Reddy, *India and Asean, Foreign Policy Dimensions for the 21st Century,* New Century Publications, New Delhi, 2005, p. 53.
4. John W. Garver, quoted in, Prakash Nanda, *Rediscovering Asia, Evolution of India's Look East Policy,* Lancer Publishers & Distributors, New Delhi, 2003, p. 225.
5. J.N. Dixit, "Role of Navies in Asia's Regional Security," *Journal of Indian Ocean Studies,* Vol. 9, No. 2, August 2001, p. 19.
6. Amitav Acharya, "China and South-East Asia: Security Aspects," in K.Santhanam and Srikant Kondapalli, *Asian Security and China, 2000-2010,* Shirpa, New Delhi, 2004, p. 246.
7. Nguyen Nam Duong, in P.V. Rao, op. cit., p. 345.
8. Nguyen Nam Duong, Ibid., p. 346 (Italics added.)
9. P.V. Rao, ed. *India and ASEAN, Partners at Summit,* op. cit., p. 36.
10. P.S. Suryanarayana, "Cam Bay not for Lease: Vietnam," *The Hindu,* October 13, 2010.
11. Subash Kapila, "India-Vietnam Strategic Partnership: the convergence of Interests," *South Asia Analysis Group,* Paper no.177, January 2001.
12. Pankaj Jha, http://www.ipcs.org/article/southeast-asia/the-india-vietnam-partnership-3006.html (visited on January 15, 2011)
13. Ramses Amer, "Sino-Vietnamese Relations," in K. Santhanam and Srikant Kondapalli, op.cit, p. 275.
14. Rajiv Sikri, *Challenge and Strategy, Rethinking India's Foreign Policy,* Sage, 2009, 198.
15. Shankar Roychowdhury, "Noose or Necklace," *Deccan Chronicle,* January 11, 2011.
16. Suhasini Haider, "Only our fears can encircle us," *The Hindu,* September 27, 2010.
17. J.N. Dixit, "Role of Navies in Asia's Regional Security," *Journal of Indian Ocean Studies,* op. cit, p. 19.

11

India and Vietnam: A Time-tested Friendship in the New Global Order

Tridib Chakraborti

"India is wholeheartedly supporting and assisting us in many ways in the fields of agriculture, animal husbandry, communication and transport, science and technology. We consider these as valuable contributions to healing the wounds of war and national construction in Vietnam. Our feelings for you are crystallized as a cloudless sky". This was explicitly expressed by the then Prime Minister of Vietnam, Pham Van Dong, when he visited India in February 1978. Similarly, before his three day visit to India from 4-6 July 2007, the Vietnamese Prime Minister, Nguyen Tan Dung, in an interview, said: "Despite strong historical and cultural linkages, India and Vietnam have not lived up to the potential of their ties. The developments in bilateral cooperation have neither met the aspirations of the two peoples nor fully tapped the existing potential of the two countries. There are greater opportunities for deepening the cooperation between our economies. This is the question, which we keep asking ourselves. Why have we not lived up to our potential?" These two statements of the Vietnamese leadership have clearly raised a mixture of confidence and doubts regarding India, from Cold War to post-Cold War years. What are the reasons behind the "cloudless sky" being shaded with mild clouds as lamented and signaled through the comment of the Vietnamese Prime Minister in 2007? Does this mean that India has lost its Cold War mindset towards Vietnam in the post-Cold War years? Obviously not; but if we compare this with China, it is clear that the space that New Delhi had gained in the Cold War period, lost its rhythm in the post-Cold War years.

India and Vietnam have long entertained traditional, close and reliable relations and multi-faceted cooperation with each other. Both these countries shared certain obvious similarities in their modes and orientations in the decolonized context of the post-Second World War period. Both countries shared quite similar historical experiences of protracted imperial subjugation and anti-colonial resistance against their respective colonial masters, were forced into comparable problems of economic underdevelopment and impoverishment, and had set before themselves the goal of self-sufficient national development, though, admittedly, their nuances of state-building had varied considerably, primarily due to the indeterminacy of the social order in India and the vicissitudes of a Marxist orientation in Vietnam. In spite of these obvious differences in their social contexts and ideological beliefs, these two newly independent Third World countries did not find it difficult to follow a policy of cooperation with each other.

During the Cold War years, India's relations with Vietnam remained extremely cordial, except for minor bitterness in the early years. Both India and Vietnam enjoyed a convergence of strategic interests, which largely provided the basis for building and reinforcing mutual association between them. India, in the past, had stood by Vietnam in opposing US military intervention at the cost of embittering Indo-US relations. At that time, the Indian mindset was totally in favour of Vietnam, and this was vindicated when Kolkata City and its streets echoed the slogan of "My name is Vietnam, Your name is Vietnam, Our name is Vietnam", and thereby confirmed its solidarity and support to the Vietnamese people in their struggle for national salvation and reunification. Moreover, India's growing understanding with the former Soviet Union due to strategic and circumstantial reasons, and Hanoi's development of close and warm relations with Moscow at the cost of friendship with the People's Republic of China (PRC) brought India and Vietnam closer to each other. Thus, in the post-Vietnam War period, (since 1975) New Delhi's friendly ties with Hanoi improved briskly. India, during these years, stood up in the United Nations against US and China on the Cambodian issue and its recognition of the pro-Vietnamese Heng Samrin government in Cambodia in July 1980 eventually dissatisfied the US and

Chinese leadership, as well as isolated New Delhi from the orbit of Association of South East Asian Nations (ASEAN) economic and political spheres. This proximity was followed by a steady progress in economic, commercial, scientific and technological cooperation between India and Vietnam. India, with its limited capacity, substantially contributed credit and other resource assistance to Vietnam to restructure its war-ravaged economy. The Indian help may be termed as a chapter in an individualistic 'Look East Vietnam' priority in its foreign policy domain solely equated on the basis of humanitarian and strategic calculations, at the cost of alienating the ASEAN countries. In other words, in the last two decades of the Cold War era, India's political and economic strategies compromised her image and de-linked her relations with the ASEAN countries on the one hand, and graduated her stance in the Indochina peninsula on the other.

In the post-Cold War years, the emergence of a New Global Order following the disintegration of the former Soviet Union severely altered the dimension of India's overall foreign policy strategy towards the Southeast Asian region. In the context of the given world environment, India drastically changed its paradigm of domestic economic and foreign policy, based on economic imperatives rather than political and strategic rhetoric. In the initial phase of the post-Cold War years, India, under the banner of its New Economic Policy, identified ASEAN as a major focus of interest, which is otherwise known as the 'Look East Policy'. This new 'Look East' outlook of New Delhi coincided with ASEAN's 'Look West' policy and regionalization thrust, and thereby, inaugurated a new phase of re-discovery and a revival in the relationship between India and ASEAN. It largely generated confidence among the leaders of India and ASEAN, who believed that this integration would provide useful outcome for each other politically, economically and strategically. Thus, in the initial years of the post-Cold War period, New Delhi was mostly engaged in establishing institutional linkages with the regional organization of Southeast Asia and attempted to generate a more confident, coordinated and dependable image among the economically developed countries of ASEAN. This endeavour of New Delhi naturally debilitated her past (Cold War) 'natural friend' image to Vietnam temporarily, setting in, no doubt, a minor slow-down phase in the hitherto ever-growing Indo-Vietnam relations. However, the expansion of ASEAN with the induction of Vietnam in 1995 restored bilateral relations between India and Vietnam. In fact, except for a few years, India, in the post-Cold War years, has again given priority to Vietnam. However, this whiff of better understanding has not been sufficient, if we compare Vietnam's present state of relations with China. India, through its emerging economic clout and strategic potential, needs to execute its 'Look East' Vietnam policy in such a manner, which might ultimately impel Vietnam not to look towards the West. New Delhi must proactively re-accelerate its past mindset towards Vietnam in the context of the changing global order, and thereby spawn greater space to contrive and rebuild the old historical, cultural, political and economic linkages in the years to come. The purpose of this paper is to analyze the emerging issues and identify areas of cooperation between India and Vietnam in the context of the global, political and security environment.

Vietnam in the Mirror of India: From the Annals of History to Cold War Years

India's friendship knots with Vietnam dates back to the beginning of the Christian era. By the end of the 2nd Century B.C., the Indian merchants first sailed across the Ocean to the shores of Southeast Asia. Their voyages in those ancient times unbolted a glorious chapter of shared exchanges leading to the growth of a civilization and culture that has endured the passage of centuries. Increasingly, their culture spread into other parts of Southeast Asia including the northern part of Vietnam. Today, Indian influence may be seen in Vietnamese folklore, religion and philosophy, art and architecture, and the Champa temple substantially exhibit this fact. The spread of Chinese influence in Vietnam was an offshoot of political rout and consequent sanitization of that country. On the contrary, Indian influences spread into the region in a peaceful way.[1] However, with the arrival of the Western colonial powers in Asia, the cultural intercourse between India and Vietnam came to a rapid end. Yet, it is significant that all through her struggle for independence against the colonial power, India remained conscious of the interests of her suffering neighbour. It was the national liberation movements of the two countries, which brought India and Vietnam closer.[2] During the Second World War, the leaders of both the countries came close to each other and laid the solid foundation of mutual relations of friendship, cooperation and understanding, and it was due to their initiatives based on the principles of anti-colonialism, anti-imperialism and non-alignment that India and Vietnam had always maintained their relations on the best friendly and fraternal terms. India extended both moral and political support to Vietnam during her liberation struggle against foreign powers. In India's view, the struggle for Indochina (mainly Vietnam) was essentially a nationalist struggle and its solution could best be accomplished by direct negotiation between the disputing parties. The mindset of India's solidarity towards Vietnam's struggle against the foreign power (i.e. against French government) during that time was clearly exhibited when on 21 January 1947, a large number of rallies and protests were organized by the students in India to observe the Vietnam Day. But, the colonial rulers in India used their guns to stop the observation and two students namely, Sri Dhiranjan Sen and Sri Amalendu Ghosh were shot dead at the University of Calcutta. This sacrifice remained a historic event in Indo-Vietnam relations in the succeeding years. In later years, the bonds of solidarity further strengthened this tie. The people of Kolkata (Calcutta) always expressed heartfelt solidarity towards Vietnam, when the latter was fighting relentlessly against the most powerful nation of the world. It was the Calcutta youth and the common people who expressed their heartfelt displeasure on the streets of Calcutta for the cause of Vietnam and chanted the famous slogan "Amar Nam, Tomar Naam, Vietnam, Vietnam" (My name is Vietnam, Your name is Vietnam, All of our name is Vietnam). This slogan during the 1960s rose in a resounding chorus from the soil of Calcutta till it became a rising crescendo, reaching even remote parts of India. They also sent blood plasma for the cause of the Vietnamese people. Thus, the solidarity mindset between India and Vietnam has always been reflected in the pages of history.

India and Vietnam in the Cold War Years

During the Cold War years, India's relations with Vietnam remained extremely cordial, barring episodes of minor unease in the early years.[3] Both enjoyed a convergence of strategic interests, which largely provided the boulevard for building a reinforcing mutual cooperation between the two countries. India, in the past, has stood for Vietnam in opposing US military intervention at the cost of embittering Indo-US relations, and that moral and humanitarian support was initiated when in June 1966, Indira Gandhi openly called for an immediate cessation of bombings and the resolution of the Vietnam conflict within the framework of the Geneva accords. Indira Gandhi also voiced her concerns in the Communiqué together with her Soviet counterpart, Aleksey Kosygin, when she visited Moscow on 16 July 1966. Besides this, New Delhi's continuity of moral support for Vietnamese struggle was time and again reflected when on 2 October 1970, at the United Nations, the

Indian government demanded a firm timetable for the withdrawal of American troops from Vietnam. Moreover, India gave the Vietnam issue an emphatic thrust in its foreign policy domain, which was clearly exhibited when the then Foreign Minister, Swaran Singh, in his statement in the Indian Parliament's lower house, the Lok Sabha, on 26 April 1972, declared that "the liberation of Bangladesh was a great heroic event and the liberation of Vietnam will be equally heroic and great." Subsequently, the Government of India expressed its happiness with the Paris Accords of 1973 that led to the American withdrawal from Indochina States.[4] Subsequently, with the rise of the Sino-Indian conflict and the Sino-Soviet dispute, India preferred to remain closer to the former Soviet Union in the context of Cold War. As long as Vietnam preferred Beijing to Moscow, New Delhi's Hanoi ties remained quite strained. The relation regained its earlier warmth when Vietnam came closer to the Soviet Union. Thus, India-Vietnam ties in the post-Vietnam unification years (i.e. since 1975) have improved briskly and remained extremely affable, gracious and based on mutual faith. In fact, till the end of the Cold War, these ties had culminated in a qualitatively new stage of development, with a steady progress in economic, commercial, scientific and technological cooperation between them.

In the post-Vietnam War period, mainly in the 1970s and 1980s, India's stand of supporting the military action of the Vietnamese army, backed by Soviet Union during the Cambodian crisis in January 1979, where installation of Heng Samrin as the Head of the State of Kampuchea by removing Pol Pot was emphasized, once again widen the then relationship between Washington, Beijing and the ASEAN nations on the one hand and India, on the other. Actually, this action of Vietnam in the Kampuchean episode, within a short period of time was converted into a major international problem and got inextricably intertwined with international power politics. Realistically speaking, when this crisis took place, the Janata government was in power in India. This government kept itself aloof in the matter of recognition of the Heng Samrin regime, owing to its principle of 'genuine non-alignment'. However, in 1980, Indira Gandhi's Congress Party again came to power, and on 7 July 1980, New Delhi recognized the Heng Samrin government and thereby endorsed Vietnam's military action in Kampuchea. The Congress (I) government preferred the Heng Samrin government to the Pol Pot regime from a moral and humanitarian point of view,[5] and thought it was strategically rewarding to adopt an identical stand with that of the then Soviet Union.[6]

The basic difference between Janata and Congress governments were that Mrs. Gandhi's Congress government judged almost all issues of international significance mainly from the view point of the Indo-Soviet alliance. Her major objective was to consolidate and promote this alliance and she judged other issues in the light of this objective.[7] This stand of India gave the Vietnamese government a major 'security relief' from the perspective of its own national interests on the one hand, but on the other, was not favourably looked upon by the ASEAN countries,[8] and isolated New Delhi from the orbit of ASEAN's economic and political sphere. In fact, this pro-Soviet political stand of India largely compromised New Delhi's hitherto non-aligned image and immensely hindered her chances of improving economic and political relations with the ASEAN countries in its entirety. This decision of India naturally acted as a bridge of further better understanding between New Delhi and Hanoi, which resulted in the steady and sustained progress in economic, commercial, scientific and technological cooperation between them.

While tracing the evolution of better economic linkages between India and Vietnam, in the context of the then regional political scenario, the moot thing which evolved in the mindset of Vietnamese leaders originated owing to India's spirit of self-reliant development programme initiated by Jawaharlal Nehru. It was discreetly thought by the Vietnamese leaders that Indian technology, especially those related to the small-scale industries, would be more relevant in developing their moribund economy, rather than banking on the advanced industrial technology. It was against this backdrop, that India, with its limited capacity, contributed substantial credit and other resource assistance to Vietnam to restructure its war-shattered economy.[9] During these years, both India and Vietnam signed a series of agreements, such as the Cultural Cooperation Agreement (1976); the Trade Agreement and the Agreement of Scientific-Technological Cooperation (1978); the Agreement on Encouraging and Protecting Investment; Agreement on Avoiding Double Taxation; and Agreement on Cooperation in the fields of Mining, Health Care and Environment. Besides, the Government of India, under the patronage of the Indian Technical and Economic Cooperation (ITEC) Programme, had not only set up the O'Mon Water Rice Research Centre and the Song Be Milk Buffalo Forage Research Centre, but had shared its experience in crossbreeding of a number of animals (milk buffalo, milk goat, fish and shrimp) and supplied Vietnam with a number of highly productive breeds and seeds, such as maize, cotton etc.[10] Vietnam also remained one of India's largest aid beneficiaries for restructuring its dilapidated economy and received Indian credit assistance of Rs 141.15 crores on soft term, with repayment being spread over 15 years, at a modest 5 per cent rate of interest, to import railway, telecommunication and sugar production equipment.[11]

Furthermore, up to 1985, Vietnam received 5 lakh tons of wheat and rice as commodity loan from India during her acute food crisis in the late 1970s. Treating her as a 'Most Favoured Nation' (MFN), on 18 December 1982, India signed an agreement with Vietnam for setting up a 'Joint Economic, Scientific and Technical Commission', which it had not done with any other country of the Southeast Asian region during the period under review. Besides Council of Mutual Economic Assistance (COMECON) countries, India's economic assistance to Vietnam figured prominently in her national reconstruction process. These promising economic relations between New Delhi and Hanoi during the Cold War years (i.e. between 1977 and 1990) were not shaped by their Soviet linkages, but developed primarily as a self-styled, coordinated bilateral approach on the basis of mutual confidence and deep understanding. Furthermore, although Indian economic assistance to Vietnam was meager in comparison to that of the COMECON (before it was dissolved in early 1990s) members, New Delhi figured prominently in Vietnam's national reconstruction process. Thus, India's economic aid to Vietnam has remained a classic illustration of a developing country helping another waning developing economy and creating close interdependence, which has been often referred to as "an ideal model for South-South economic cooperation for the developing world."[12] This Indian response can be interpreted as the first individualistic 'Look East' policy towards Vietnam, against the backdrop of the then closer security and political relations with the former Soviet Union. This 'Look East' Vietnam policy may not be the archetype of what India follows in the post-Cold War period. Nevertheless, one cannot ignore India's overall foreign policy priority in the 1970s and 1980s (unlike 1950s and 1960s) favouring the Indochina States (mainly Vietnam) rather than the ASEAN members. Thus, in the last two decades of the Cold War epoch, India's political and economic strategies had compromised her regional image in two ways. While on the one hand, it had de-linked her relations with the ASEAN countries, New Delhi's image had graduated her niche in the psyche of the Indochina States, on the other.

The Downfall of the Soviet Union:
Budges in Foreign Policy Domain

With the abrupt crumble of the Soviet Union at the end of the Cold War, coupled with the onset of globalization, nations began to realize that the means of survival were by the securing of international trade and encouragement of foreign investments. To cope up with this new global order, in July 1991, India under the leadership of P.V. Narasimha Rao announced its New Economic Policy, which was guided more by economic imperatives and expediency than by ideological rhetoric. During that time, rapid economic development and growth of Asian countries, especially the Southeast Asian region, was witnessed. This region has a vast economic potential and is virtually an untapped market, which is up for grabs by major regional economic entities such as China, Japan, Europe or the USA. India, in the context of this New Global Order awoke to the possibility of improving relations with Southeast Asia, a region with which it had historical as well as cultural links through the past. As a result, the Government of India, for the first time since independence, turned her special attention towards the ASEAN region with economic links in mind, through its 'Look East 'policy, because of the ASEAN's success "as a regional grouping of countries". Thus, the economic exigency of the changed world system provided the ground for further cooperation, while the geo-strategic scenario not only helped in removing the basic irritants between them, but also provided scope for long-term strategic partnership between India and Southeast Asia. Like India, the ASEAN countries also in the post-Cold War years considered India a reliable economic partner and took various measures to promote trade links with New Delhi. These countries were also convinced of the seriousness of India in her liberalization policy, particularly when New Delhi took a number of initiatives under its banner of its 'Look East' policy to suit the conditions of such cooperation, which might prove to be beneficial for both of them politically, economically and strategically. Thus, this 'Look East' economic gesture of New Delhi, which coincided with ASEAN's 'Look West' and regionalization, thrust, inaugurated a new phase of re-discovery and a revival in the relationship between India and ASEAN. However, the initial years of New Delhi's 'Look East' policy has followed a three-pronged approach towards this region. These premises are first, for renewing political contacts through exchange of visits; secondly, establishing economic linkages with the countries of this region, especially ASEAN, to strengthen its economic capabilities in the post-Cold

War era; and thirdly, putting the thrust on developing strategic partnerships through various confidence-building measures and bilateral defence cooperation to work towards common security needs.[13] This three-pronged approach of New Delhi led her to establish institutional linkages with the regional organization of Southeast Asia and attempted to generate a more confident and dependable image among the members of ASEAN. But this improvement of relations with the ASEAN countries did not mean any setback in India's political and economic ties with Vietnam.

Meanwhile, between the years from 1997 and 2002, certain important events took place in Southeast Asia, which ultimately led New Delhi to re-shape its 'Look East' policy in its entirety. The re-momentum of India's 'Look East' policy from its dilatory motion actually gathered its momentum after Vietnam joined ASEAN in 1995, followed by Myanmar and Laos in 1997 and Cambodia in 1999. With the joining of Myanmar within ASEAN, New Delhi could share a common land border of more than 1,600 kilometers with an ASEAN member state. This process was further augmented with the establishment of two sub-regional organizations, namely Bay of Bengal Initiative of Multisectoral Technical and Economic Cooperation (BIMSTEC) in June 1997 and the Mekong-Ganga Cooperation (MGC) on 10 November 2000 at Vientiane, with Cambodia, Laos, India, Myanmar, Thailand and Vietnam as its members. These initiatives were mainly designed to define regions in the new global economy, while keeping their native identity and character intact. It also aimed at broadening and intensification of joint efforts at economic cooperation between India and ASEAN in the Mekong Basin. Another major goal of these sub-regional initiatives was to augment the transport reticulum that spans India, Myanmar, Thailand, Cambodia and Vietnam, and thereby to establish the Delhi-Hanoi road and railway link in the near future, and also develop transportation networks including the East-West Corridor project and the Trans-Asian highway from Singapore to Istanbul. Following these events, India's ties with Indochina States (mainly Vietnam) were recuperated and its overall 'Look East' policy vis-à-vis the entire expanse of Southeast Asia reached a new milestone when the First ASEAN-India Summit took place in Phnom Penh, on 5 November 2002. The recognition of India as a new actor in the compass of ASEAN's economic, political and strategic processes was a product of the consummation of history spanning more than one decade. Another important point should be noted in this connection that New Delhi's priority towards Vietnam during this time was greatly hindered owing to slow adjustment of this country with reference to its socialist-oriented economy in the context of globalization. Hence, India's 'Look East' Vietnam policy guideline during the first phase was evidently feeble, although without any setback on priority in her foreign policy realm, and has to be estimated from a new perspective, taking, of course, the relations of the past into consideration.

New Dynamics of India-Vietnam Relations in the post-Cold War Domain

India's re-looked, re-activated and re-accelerated 'Look East' policy has clearly highlighted the principles and engineered the future road map of ASEAN-India cooperation. This drastic improvement of ties had a consequent spillover effect on the overall India-Vietnam ties. In the post-Cold War period, both India and Vietnam have faced number of important challenges, which impeded both countries from enhancing their strategic partnership immediately. Among the most important factors which led both of them to drift apart from each other was the weak economic structure owing to their past individual economic plans and thereby the need to adjust themselves in the context of New Global Order, based on the process of market integration and liberalization. Besides this, other issues included ethnic unrest and communal violence, terrorism and transnational crimes, human rights violations, rising religious fundamentalism, increasing intra-state and inter-state conflicts, problems of arms race and arms trade, etc. However, slowly and steadily, within a decade, both India and Vietnam have trounced these internal threats and economic distress to gradually appear as emerging regional actors in global politics. This resulted in that bilateral relations between them strengthened their ties on a strong foothold based on certain manifestations. Nonetheless, in the course of growing linkages there are certain areas where better coordination and strong understanding would be essential in its entirety.

The China Factor in India-Vietnam Strategic Calculus and Understanding

China in the post-Cold War years tries to follow a dual role towards the countries of South and Southeast Asia. In the Southeast Asian region, since 1988, it has followed a policy, which was cordial in nature and thereby created a benign image. Actually, the end of Cold War envisaged the normalization of Sino-Soviet relations on the one hand, and the sudden dismantling of US military presence in the region, on the other. All these unbelievable events naturally gave China political and economic space to interact with the Southeast Asian region. It was felt by the Chinese leadership given that vacuity of space, multilateralism would be much safer and better way to expand its influence and protect its national interest in Southeast and other parts of the Asia-Pacific region. This resulted in that China pragmatically decided to adhere to a peaceful foreign policy, on the basis of the Five Principles of Peaceful Coexistence. In response to these principles, the ASEAN members welcomed China's participation in regional economic cooperation, in spite of their past bitter political and economic experiences. It was also felt by them that the exchange of a long range of goods – from primary to Hi-tech products, transfer of technologies etc. – was complementary to the development of enhanced interaction between the two sides. After establishing diplomatic relations with Singapore on 3 October 1990, China pushed for official ties with the ASEAN grouping. On 19 July 1991, Chinese Foreign Minister, Qian Qichen participated in the opening session of the 24th ASEAN Foreign Ministers Meeting in Kuala Lumpur as an invited guest of the Malaysian government and where the Chinese leadership expressed its willingness to develop better ties with these countries. This willingness on the part of China bore fruit within a short span of time and China joined a number of multilateral dialogue processes since the 1990s, including ASEAN+3, ARF, EAS and Full Dialogue Partnership of ASEAN. Besides this, in December 1997, Chinese President, Jiang Zemin and the ASEAN leaders had their first informal summit and issued a joint statement of establishing partnership of good neighborliness and mutual trust oriented towards the 21st Century, thus putting into place the framework and charting the course for all round growth of their relations. Since then, China and ASEAN linkages have evolved rapidly, highlighted by frequent exchange of visits by top leaders of the respective countries. An important event in the development of China-ASEAN relations was Beijing's accession to the Treaty of Amity and Cooperation, signed in November 2003 which ensures that the security issues would be settled peacefully.[14] This growing cordiality between China and ASEAN was further deepened when the Framework Agreement on ASEAN-China Comprehensive Economic Cooperation was signed in October 2003 at Bali, to establish China-ASEAN Free Trade Area (CAFTA). This agreement was essentially an outcome of the positive role that China played after the East Asian Financial

Crisis of 1997 and the global meltdown of 2008-09. This role of China in helping the ASEAN members to combat the financial crisis and promote trade facilitation improved its image and generated confidence among them. Thus, within a short span of time, trade between ASEAN and China increased in a rapid way, though their apprehension that China might dominate the region in future did not wither away.

This positive attitude of China towards the countries of Southeast Asia was not at all reflected equally for the region. Although, China has initiated to resolve its boundary problem with Vietnam, its claims in the Spratly islands with Vietnam and other ASEAN partners were just temporarily resolved. The recent Chinese display of strength in the South China Sea once again exhibited clearly its hegemonic mindset with reference to this issue. Besides this, Vietnam has been situated in such a premeditated position of the Southeast Asian region, that it is of mammoth strategic significance not only to India, but also to the US and Japan, since all these countries harbour suspicions about the rise of China and perceive it as a potential strategic and economic threat. In fact, China through its various modes like 'soft power' diplomacy has tried to win the minds of many Southeast Asian countries. Like the 1997 financial meltdown, in April 2009, it announced a new investment fund and loan package to help assuage the shock of the global financial crisis for ASEAN, thus representing the latest approach of China's "soft power" campaign towards the region. Many believe the aid package unveiled by Beijing was strategically announced to steal a commercial and diplomatic march over the economically ailing United States. The aid package includes a US$ 10 billion investment fund, geared for cooperation in infrastructure construction, energy and natural resources development, and improvements in information and communications.[15] Therefore, anticipating this outlook, the US, Japan and others countries of the Asia-Pacific region opted for a policy of rapprochement with Vietnam after a long period of isolation, because to them due to its critical geo-strategic location in the neighborhood of China, Vietnam holds the key to any future strategy to contain Beijing's hegemonic rise. Moreover, China in the post-Cold War period, through its Official Development Assistance (ODA) to the weak economic members of ASEAN (mainly to Cambodia, Laos, Myanmar, etc.), has attempted to re-establish a new space in the socio-economic structure of these countries. This economic assistance, especially to Cambodia and Laos, naturally gave Beijing a better foothold, which it had lost in the past years and thereby, has highly worried the Vietnamese leadership, with which it had precedent fraternal linkages.

Similarly, for India, China remains the major natural geo-strategic rival in the South Asian region. The Sino-Indian relations have always been ambivalent. China had occupied a large chunk of India's northeastern frontier. India's bitter memories with China through the 1962 war experience and the latter's incessant military and other support to Pakistan against the former confirmed New Delhi's thinking that China was bent on keeping India disturbed in South Asia, in order to fulfill its ultimate strategico-hegemonic state of mind. So, India since the end of the Cold War has regarded China's overall military and economic growth to be a four-fold threats. First, from the perspective of military means, India has expressed deep concern over China's drive to modernize its defences, and construed China's cooperation with Pakistan, Myanmar and other neighbouring states as moves towards isolating and encircling the subcontinent. Secondly, from the economic point of view India regards the economic threat of China consisting in its economic strength being transfigured into military strength; also in the context of its stiff competition with Indian commodities, Chinese goods are flooding domestic and foreign markets.[16] Thirdly, India's definition of national security strategy, since the fall of former Soviet Union evinces a thorough geopolitical logic whose primary focuses are on guarding against and containing Pakistan and China – its territorial rivals-and thereby establish and safeguard rights of control in the Indian Ocean,[17] through development of various means in order to protect its own national interest. Moreover, New Delhi has borrowed its strength, by developing better relations with the US, to compensate its weak position relating to China in the balance of power politics, towards its unfriendly neighbours. Thus, India's decision to display its 1998 nuclear tests as a response to the primary threat it faced from China and its allies caused great displeasure for Beijing, but is entirely unswerving with the outlook of most Indian strategic thinkers. Against this background, India began to receive more attention and was entrusted with the important new role of acting as a 'swing state in the global balance of power'.[18] In other words, the major powers compete to have India on their sides in the process of the construction of a New World Order. As Prime Minister, Manmohan Singh said in August 2007, while celebrating the 60th anniversary of Indian independence, "the world today wants India to do well. The world community wishes us well. Our external situation is benign and favourable."[19] Fourthly, China in the post-

Cold War years considers the Asia-Pacific region as vital to its security interest and any Indian attempt to intrude into this region will not please Beijing. However, New Delhi had made it unadorned that it perceives its strategic interests stretching from the Gulf of Aden to the South China Sea. The Straits of Malacca, which connect the South China Sea to the Indian Ocean and which have Singapore, Malaysia and Indonesia as their major littoral countries, are critical to maritime trade. The sea line of communication that passes through the Straits remains one of the busiest ocean highways in the world. It is estimated that more than 41,000 ships pass through the South China Sea each year – more than double the number that crosses the Suez Canal – and the Malacca Straits handle up to 600 ships in two ways per day. Also 20 per cent of the world's oil passes through this sea-lane regularly. So, any kind of problem in this sea-lane might generate a massive enhancement in freight rates and could be a nightmare to the littoral countries of this region. So, India's willingness to this strategic interest was clearly spelt out, when in February 1999 the Indian Prime Minister's Security Advisor, Brajesh Mishra, while speaking at the Munich Security Conference hinted New Delhi's long-term strategic ambitions by predicting that "in the 21st century, a new security order is likely to arise in the Asia-Pacific region in which India would be granted as much respect by the US and others as China (enjoys) today." This speech from the Indian side further reaffirmed New Delhi's mindset, when in April 2000, the Naval Operations Directorate announced its unilateral naval exercise plans in the South China Sea, and thereby propound its signal to expand operations from the north of the Arabian Sea through the South China Sea and to establish an expeditionary – capable force which will not only threaten China's areas of operation, but also alter the balance of naval power in the Asia-Pacific region. India's naval interest in the Asia-Pacific region was once again reverberated when Defence Minister, George Fernandes said in a statement that Indian naval interest stretched from the Arabian Sea to the South China Sea and that Japan and Vietnam were emerging as Delhi's strategic partners in countering piracy at sea. Actually, India's plans stem from several important reasons – counter-piracy, protection of trade routes, balancing China and establishing itself as a new regional power in the Asia-Pacific region.[20] Furthermore, India, through its 'Look East' policy has led to an increasing engagement with Southeast Asia and the sea lanes to further East are growing in significance for its energy security as New Delhi is looking for oil and gas supplies from Myanmar, Vietnam and Indonesia. The idea of upgrading the security structure of the Andaman and Nicobar Islands and the surrounding areas by deciding (in August 1988) to establish a 'Far Eastern Maritime Command' at Port Blair (independent of the operational control of Eastern Naval Command at Visakhapatnam), under the "unified command" of the three Services in October 2001, signals India's seriousness about its maritime policy in the post-Cold War era. Its importance has increased due to growing Chinese presence in the waters close to India. Indian official reports show concern over the Chinese-aided radar facility on Myanmar's Coco islands, capable of overseeing Indian missile test programme on its eastern seaboard.[21] The current joint naval exercises, regularly held with Japan, Singapore, Malaysia, Vietnam and other countries of Southeast Asia, and joint patrolling between India and US in the sea lanes along the Straits of Malacca, based on the new naval doctrine represents not only a new high in cooperation among these countries, but also signals India's emergence as key player in the region.

Thus, convergence of strategic interests and past friendly ties coincided with New Delhi's 'Look East' policy brought India and Vietnam closer. The Vietnamese leadership, through its past experience looks at India as "a friend and neighbour," which does not force her views or prescribe solutions, but is ready to work together and address the common problems. Besides, India's entry in the ARF, a platform of regional security dialogue, brought New Delhi closer to Hanoi together in a multilateral security framework. While explaining the relevance of ARF in India's security architecture, the Minister of External Affair of India, Jaswant Singh, in reply to a question raised in the Rajya Sabha on 2 August 2001, said that, "India's involvement with ASEAN strengthens our relations with Southeast Asia – a region of commercial, political and strategic interest to us. India's association with the ARF is consistent without 'Look East Policy' and the stronger relations we are attempting with Southeast Asian countries. ASEAN is a part of our extended neighbourhood and India both gains from and contributes to the peace, security and stability in the region."[22] Therefore, in the given milieu, both India and Vietnam enjoy convergence of strategic interests, which could provide the basis for building and reinforcing strategic cooperation between the two countries. China's perceived strategic concerns regarding India and Vietnam have diplomatically forced her to create continuous external pressure on these two countries to a large extent. In the case of India, China created the Pakistani threat (missile and nuclear threat) and in the case of Vietnam, it has continuously posed proxy military challenges through Cambodia, besides direct military force on both land and sea borders. Thus, both New Delhi and Hanoi have a natural strategic congruence on ways to contain Beijing from its aggressive actions in future and keeping it absorbed diplomatically and strategically. In a report entitled "ASEAN Regional Forum's Annual Security Outlook", published in 2001, the Government of India has argued that its security concerns in the post-Cold War years extend beyond the conventional geographical definition of South Asia. New Delhi made it clear that "given its size, geographical location and trade links, security environment ranges from the Persian Gulf to the Straits of Malacca across the Indian Ocean including the Central Asian region in the north-west, China in the north-east and Southeast Asia."[23] So, based on this geo-strategic mindset, the 'Strategic Partnership' agreement signed between India and Vietnam in July 2007, has been sufficient enough for both the countries regarding China and may be considered as an opportunity to thwart the latter's ambition of a hegemonic role in the coming years. The main theme of this Agreement is the establishment of a Strategic Dialogue, a Joint Working Group on countering terrorism, and closer defence cooperation as a prelude to establishing an Asian Community. The frequent visits of the Indian Defence Minister to Hanoi and vice-versa could be equated as a step in the execution of agreements on strategic partnerships signed between New Delhi and Hanoi. Thus, converging interests are compelling both countries to construct a strong edifice of strategic partnership. The 'China factor' plays a major role in the strategic equations of both countries, since they feel that the growing Chinese influence in the region is a threat to the existing power structure in Asia and it is necessary to counterbalance Beijing's military prowess in the region. As against such background, India's relations with Vietnam have developed quite rapidly and exhibited its excellence, thereby opening a novel chapter in the personal chemistry between them in certain areas, as discussed below.

Areas of Collaboration between India and Vietnam

Defence Assistance and Relationship

Geographically and geopolitically, India's connection with the Southeast Asian region has been always governed by two important links – land and sea. The peninsular Southeast Asia consisting of Myanmar, Laos, Cambodia, Thailand, Malaysia and Vietnam form geographically a contiguous region with India connected by land routes. Their common adversary, i.e., China, has always governed India's relations with Vietnam. Given such a common outlook, New Delhi's military ties with Hanoi developed slowly but steadily. Defence cooperation between India and Vietnam has taken place over the years in a limited manner with exchange of some military delegations and visits of naval ships. However, that situation gathered greater momentum in the post-Cold War period, following the defence agreement signed by New Delhi and Hanoi, during the Indian Prime Minister, Narasimha Rao's visit to Vietnam in September 1994. The main focus of this agreement was to promote cooperation between the defence establishments of the two countries, centred on the maintenance and upkeep of military equipment mostly supplied to Vietnam by the erstwhile Soviet Union, and the agreement was not aimed against any third country.[24] Meanwhile, in August 1997, the eighth India-Vietnam Joint Commission meeting took place in Hanoi. In this meeting, India offered to supply Vietnam spare parts and service the Soviet-origin defence equipment on a commercial basis. The document, which was finalized after the meeting, clearly stated that, "cooperation in defence is an important aspect of bilateral relations between India and Vietnam."[25] It was also agreed that New Delhi and Hanoi would take necessary steps to implement the provisions of the "Protocol on Defence Cooperation" signed during the visit to Vietnam by the then Indian Prime Minister, P.V. Narasimha Rao in 1994. It was also stated that periodic exchange of visits of defence personnel, exchange of information, transfer of relevant technologies and repair, maintenance and upgradation of defence equipment were all "important elements" of Indo-Vietnamese defence cooperation. But the most significant defence agreement was signed in March 2000, during India's Defence Minister, George Fernandes' visit to Hanoi, the first ever by an Indian Defence Minister to Vietnam. During this visit, a 15 point Defence Protocol was signed between the two countries, which promised to provide Vietnam with assistance in the modernization of its armed forces and to intensify the latter's defence strength. The major issues highlighted in this agreement were on joint naval training to combat piracy, jungle warfare and counter-insurgency training, repair of Mig aircraft, pilot training and assistance on small and medium arms production.[26] At the end of this agreement, the Indian Defence Minister hailed Vietnam as India's "most trusted friend and ally", and clearly mentioned that Hanoi "stood by us after the nuclear tests, because they understand that if [India] went nuclear there were good security reasons for it", and thereby implied the China threat was unmistakable. Finally, the Indian Defence

Minister described this cooperation as the beginning of a "periodical security dialogue", and agreed to assist Vietnam in the process of setting up its defence industry and opened its doors to the research done by the Defence Research and Development Organization (DRDO). So, these were welcome steps towards achievement of India's strategic aim to assist in building Vietnam's armed forces to be militarily strong and self-reliant, and thereby institutionalized regular meetings between the Defence Ministers of the two sides to discuss matters relating to shared threat perceptions, apart from paving the way for visit of the Indian ships to Vietnamese ports and more collaborations in naval exercises.[27]

It is a fact that historically, Vietnam had adverse relations with China. It fought its last war with China in 1979. Although Vietnam has been able to peacefully resolve its land border dispute with China, the mutual confidence between the two countries has not been fully restored. Presently, India and the US are primarily considering Vietnam's importance vis-à-vis their anti-China stance, as a result of Hanoi's past bitter relations with Beijing and its geo-strategic location, in terms of its proximity to the Sea Line of Communication (SLOC) area and to China. Axiomatically, the imperative of India's strategic endeavour to assist in building Vietnam's armed forces to be militarily strong and self-reliant has been vindicated. In 2007, two Indian naval ships, INS Mysore and INS Rajput, visited Vietnam and India provided free equipment to the Vietnamese navy, besides helping in the repair of their facilities. Furthermore, during Nguyen Tan Dung's visit to India on 6 July 2007, both countries signed a Joint Declaration on establishing a bilateral Strategic Partnership and out of seven areas of cooperation signed in the document, the two countries decided to play an important role in the promotion of regional security, by pledging to strengthen cooperation in defence supplies, joint projects, training and intelligence exchanges. They also converged on working closely on defence and security establishments; to enhance cooperation in capacity building, technical assistance and information-sharing between their respective relevant agencies for ensuring security of sea-lanes, including combating piracy, preventing pollution and conducting search and rescue.[28]

This strategic partnership is neither pertinent in the corporate sense nor in terms of defence pact, but impinges more upon the convergence of views on strategic issues, on account of a new strategic realignment in Asia. Following this visit, India and Vietnam agreed on a plethora of measures to further expand their relations in defence cooperation and 'take it to new heights', when the Indian Defence Minister, A.K. Antony paid a three-day official visit to Vietnam in December 2007. During his meeting with his Vietnamese counterpart, Gen. Phung Quang Thanh in Hanoi, Antony agreed to transfer 5,000 items of naval spares belonging to Petya class of ships to Vietnam to infuse life into many of the ageing vessels. The Indian leader also suggested an increase in the frequency of goodwill visits by naval ships, application of information technology in defence and e-technology and technical support to the Vietnamese navy. Additionally, India agreed to dispatch a four-member army team to Vietnam during the first half of 2008 to conduct training on UN peacekeeping operations. Finally, the two sides agreed to set up a Joint Working Group to facilitate the signing of a Memorandum of Understanding (MoU) on defence cooperation (including cooperation in national defence, navy, air defence and personnel training). The Indian delegation also visited defence industries in Ho Chi Minh City. The Vietnamese Defence Minister sought Indian assistance in training of defence personnel, enhancing the exchanges of delegations, expanding training cooperation, cooperation between national defence industries, an increase in the frequency of goodwill visits by naval ships, application of information technology and e-technology, and technical support for the Vietnamese navy. So far, 49 officers have attended various army and navy courses in India and 64 officers have attended English language courses. Furthermore, at the 3rd India-Vietnam Security Dialogue meeting held in New Delhi in November 2007, both the countries converged upon a number of important decisions, like the exchange of visits for better appreciation of requirements and problems, greater cooperation in the field of training of Service personnel – particularly involving junior level officers, security dialogue at least once a year, sharing of expertise on issues of common concerns such as maritime security, border management and counter-insurgency, conduct of training for Vietnamese officers in the field of UN Peacekeeping operations, invitation to Vietnamese officers to Indian military exercises as observers etc, which were aimed at providing greater impetus to their relationship.[29] The growing cordiality of defence and naval cooperation between New Delhi and Hanoi displayed its strength, when the Flag Officer Commanding-in-Chief of the Indian Eastern Naval Command visited Hanoi with two naval ships, INS Kora and INS Kirpan, on 21 April 2008, and thereby reiterated India's desire to fortify bilateral mutual understanding, friendship and cooperation between the two naval forces.

Following this event, in the succeeding years, a number of visits and counter-visits took place between India and Vietnam related to the ongoing defence collaboration between them. Among these visits, the Indian Army Chief, General V.K. Singh's July 2010 visit remained quite significant in nature. This was the first in a decade by an Indian Army Chief, who went to Vietnam to implement the roadmap of the 2009 MoU between the two Ministries of Defence. Before this visit took place, the defence collaboration and strategic convergence between India and Vietnam reached its height when the Fifth Vietnamese-Indian strategic defence talks were held in New Delhi from 23-25 June 2010, and where the Vietnamese delegation was headed by Deputy Defence Minister, Lieutenant General Nguyen Chi Vinh. At the time of this talk, the two countries discussed further cooperation on matters of defence and proposed various measures to strengthen links in the future.[30] The most significant event, which took place in 2010, was the First ASEAN Plus Eight Defence Ministers' Meeting (ADMM) held in Hanoi in October 2010. This ADMM+8 is a newly-formed gathering of ASEAN Defence Ministers and their counterparts beyond the region including Australia, China, India, Japan, New Zealand, South Korea, Russia and the US and thereby, provides an inclusive and focused configuration, bringing together the key players in the region, to collectively handle security issues such as terrorism, piracy, disaster relief and transnational crime. It was agreed by the ADMM+8 partners that this meeting would be held every three years subsequently.[31] In this meeting, the Indian Defence Minister, A.K. Antony played a very constructive role in defining the scope and objectives of this Forum, and announced a slew of measures to expand defence cooperation with Vietnam. While elaborating the measures, which were in the mindset of New Delhi, A.K. Antony mentioned to the top Vietnamese leadership, including the Prime Minister, Nguyen Tan Dung and the Defence Minister, General Phung Quang Thanh in a bilateral discussion, that India would provide support to Vietnam to enhance and upgrade the capabilities of Defence Services in general and Navy in particular.[32] He also said India would help Vietnam in its capacity building for repair and maintenance of its platforms. The armies of the two countries will also cooperate in areas like IT and English Training of Vietnamese Army personnel. Both the armies will also have a joint training in mountain and jungle warfare in India next year. While expressing deep satisfaction regarding India's commitment to modernize Vietnam's defence and other strategic areas, the Vietnamese Prime Minister, Dung said, "The

Vietnam-India strategic partnership is a good model. Our traditional and friendly co-operation has always been consolidated by generations of the two sides' leadership." The satisfaction of the Vietnamese side was once again reflected when the Defence Minister, Gen. Thanh thanked India for its valuable contribution to make the ASEAN Defence Ministers' Meeting a great success and said, "India occupies a special position in Hanoi's foreign policy framework and we are indeed moved by your support". He also welcomed more port calls by the Indian Navy to Vietnam and offered maintenance and repair facilities at Vietnamese ports.[33]

Thus, all these growing defence linkages between India and Vietnam were centred on a number of important factors, which are as follows: First, the long-pending territorial disputes with China, in which India and Vietnam are the common sufferers. Secondly, China's disputable mindset and recent muscle flexing with reference to the South China Sea problem. It was felt by the Indian policy makers that Vietnam's location is ideal to prevent China's expansion and thereby, to deny Beijing's total supremacy in the South China Sea. Both feel that growing Chinese influence is a threat for existing power structure in Asia and to counterbalance Beijing's fledging military prowess in the region, it is imperative to work together as well as lend a helping hand to major powers involved in the region's security dynamics. Finally, a number of emerging non-traditional security threats, evolved in the Straits of Malacca and the Indian Ocean Region, provided India an opportunity to upgrade its naval strength through its Naval Doctrine announced in 2004. Presently, like Vietnam, India has also started dialogue with Japan, South Korea and US in order to safeguard the SLOC as well as China's so-called 'String of Pearls' encirclement. A point to be mentioned in this connection of India's growing naval deployment in the Asia Pacific region is the recent month-long deployment of a flotilla of Indian warships, which visited Australia, Indonesia, Singapore and Vietnam and thereby sounded a frequent alarm over China's increasing forays into the Indian Ocean region, since this region is poised to become the new playground for the 21st century version of the Great Game in the coming years.[34]

Assistance in Peaceful Uses of Atomic Energy

In the 21st Century, procurement of energy remains one of the most vital components for any country in the world. In the Asia Pacific region, the procurement and preservation of energy is the key factor of a country's present national interest. Based on such a necessity, like India and China, Vietnam also joined this race and it was mainly confined to the South China Sea, since it is preparing for nuclear power electricity generation, to reduce its dependence on hydro and fossil fuel resources. From the late 1980's onwards, Vietnam has paid attention to building the strategy and policy for national energy development, and the peaceful use of nuclear energy is an important objective of the nation. Vietnam is a signatory to both the International Atomic Energy Agency (IAEA), Regional Cooperation Agreement (RCA) and South Asian Frameworks for Environmental Data-Sharing. Although Vietnam's strive to procure energy is a recent phenomenon, its mindset about the utility of this resource occurred back in the 1980s, when it wanted to upgrade its Da Lat Nuclear Reactor with the help of erstwhile Soviet Union, which was disbanded by US before it left Vietnam in 1975. Therefore, since the mid-1980s, besides the former Soviet Union, Vietnam took help from many other countries (including India) in order to develop its nuclear power plants for scientific research. India, owing to its cordial historical ties, substantially helped Vietnam in this scientific endeavour. The process of assistance started in August 1988, when a delegation of the Indian Atomic Energy Commission led by its Chairman, M.R. Srinivasan, paid an official visit to Vietnam and on 15 August, signed an accord on peaceful use of atomic energy, described as a "memo of cooperation in the use of atomic energy for peaceful purposes."[35] As per the Protocol and Work Plans signed under this agreement, a number of Vietnamese scientists and experts have received training in India. Interestingly enough, Prime Minister, Morarji Desai during Pham Van Dong's visit to India in February 1978, had offered to help Vietnam with her programme of developing peaceful uses of nuclear energy. The kind of nuclear technical aid New Delhi agreed to provide Hanoi was not initially known to the public. However, the Vietnamese said that they planned to bring the Da Lat nuclear research reactor back into operation with technical assistance both from India and the former USSR. From March 1982, with erstwhile Soviet assistance, restoration and expansion of this nuclear reactor had begun.[36] Unfortunately, this agreement failed to accelerate its mobility owing to the sudden fall of the former Soviet Union and the adjustment of the economies of both India and Vietnam in the context of the New Global Order. Meanwhile, on 23 April 1999, the Indian Atomic Energy Commission (a part of the IDAE) and the Vietnam Atomic Energy Commission (VAEC) signed another agreement for cooperation in the field of nuclear power, exchange of scientists and assistance in setting up a training centre in Vietnam. Under this agreement, around 25 Vietnamese scientists have received training at the Bhabha Atomic Research Centre (BARC) in Mumbai and few Indian scientists have visited Da Lat as yet, in order to complete Vietnam's nuclear energy programme by 2015. Furthermore, in January 2001, the Indian Prime Minister, Atal Behari Vajpayee paid an official visit to Vietnam. During his stay in Hanoi, the two countries signed a MoU between Department of Atomic Energy and Ministry of Science, Technology and Environment of Vietnam. The basis of this MoU has been the agreement between the two governments for the cooperation for Utilization of Atomic Energy for Peaceful Purposes signed in 1988, which was valid till May 2002. It also accorded for continued cooperation in the fields of human resource development and exchange of expertise.[37] This agreement was an extension of the earlier MoU signed by New Delhi and Hanoi on 23 April 1999. Thus, this issue has been no doubt a major event in the bilateral ties between New Delhi and Hanoi and a clear demonstration of a major thrust in India's 'Look East Vietnam Policy' in the post-Cold War era.

Bracing the Sub-Regional Initiative of Mekong-Ganga Project

In the post-Cold War years, especially in the context of the increasing inter-dependent global economy, many developing countries in the Third World are using connectivity as a major diplomatic tool to increase their economic, political and strategic linkages with other countries of the world. To them, venture of connectivity drive would open up freedom to travel and communicate across borders and thereby open new vistas for trade, investment and flow of ideas. India, since 1990s through its 'Look East' policy has initiated several connectivity mechanisms in order to reinforce her vision to be an integral part of the East Asian economic integration process. To advance its 'Look East' policy, New Delhi has shown great interest in entering into development and cooperation process of Southeast and East Asia and used multilateralism as a primary tool in its geo-strategic perception, since regional cooperation in South Asia lags behind owing to political and economic exigencies. The strategic emergence of the Bay of Bengal – South China Sea region in the geo-strategic space of global politics, has pragmatically changed the hitherto mindset of the Indian policy-makers and connectivity drive, through seaways, open skies, road ways and railways appears to New Delhi, as a new diplomatic technique and the cornerstone of its extended neighbourhood policy, in order to accelerate its 'Look East' policy from Phases I and II, during that time. The establishment of BIMSTEC in 1997 was the first sub-regional vehicle to promote trade and tourism in the Bay of Bengal region, and has allowed the synthetic political barriers between South and Southeast Asia to recede. Likewise, on 10 November 2000 at Vientiane, India initiated the MGC scheme with five of its eastern neighbours – Myanmar, Thailand, Cambodia, Laos and Vietnam. This initiative was actually initiated after the insertion of Myanmar within the orbit of ASEAN in 1997. The concept of MGC originally came from Thailand, which wanted to enlarge the scope of the earlier *Suwannaphum* (Swarnabhumi in Sanskrit, meaning the 'Land of Gold') comprising five Buddhist countries of Southeast Asia sharing the Mekong river – Thailand, Myanmar, Vietnam, Laos and Cambodia – to promote cultural tourism. This sub-regional initiative, as envisioned in the Hanoi Programme of Action, was designed to keep this region's native identity and character intact. It also aimed at broadening and intensifying joint efforts at economic cooperation between India and ASEAN in the Mekong region. One of the major goals of this sub-regional initiative is to enhance the transport links that span India, Myanmar, Thailand, Cambodia and Vietnam, and thereby to establish road and railway links in the near future. These important schemes are viewed important for easing the cross-border movement of goods and services across these nations, and in the process, to facilitate the operation of the ASEAN-India FTA. Further, the linkages between India and these countries of Indochina over land might give New Delhi an opportunity to expedite economic development with the Northeastern region and its integration into the Eurasian land bridge system. Thus, after partially neglecting the Indochina States for nearly a decade of 'Look East' Phase I, India relocated and re-activated its historical Mekong delta friends for future promotion of economic cooperation. Therefore, the formation of sub-regional organizations allowed New Delhi to break out of the astringent confines of the sub-continent that it had long abraded at. It also provides the potential for New Delhi and Hanoi to work closely for regional development in a multilateral framework.[38] Regrettably, as a sub-regional organization, the MGC is on the verge of idleness and so far failed to display its potentiality. The major reasons for its failure are the lack of government funding and initiatives among the members, absence of regular review mechanism of its performance, Thailand's lost interest following the formation of the Ayeyarwaddy-Chao Phraya-Mekong Economic Cooperation

(ACMECS) which brings together the same group of countries, minus India and its present ongoing domestic turmoil and New Delhi's re-active, rather than pro-active 'Look East' policy. Thus, India must play a more responsible role for further acceleration of the sub-regional initiatives.

India-Vietnam: Economics as a Strategic Parameter

The acceptance of market reforms by India and Vietnam in the post-Cold War years to a great extent hastened the economic interaction between them. Comparing the past decades, in terms of value, India's exports and imports with Vietnam increased very dramatically since mid-1990s. India's trade with Hanoi during the year 2009-10 was in the tune of Rs. 11133.10 crore, an amount much higher than the year 1991-92. However, the Balance of Trade except in initial years has always tilted in favour of India (Table 1). This increase in bilateral trade clearly reveals that both New Delhi and Hanoi are coming closer to each other. However, India's total trade figures with Vietnam have always been less than 10 per cent of its overall trade stature with the entire Southeast Asian region, not only due to Vietnam's weakness in economic structure and basket of exports, but the lack of mutual understanding of their individual domestic markets as well. Besides this, in recent times while comparing with its total world trade percentage, New Delhi's export figure with Vietnam from 2005-06 to 2009-10 increased from 0.67 to 1.03 and import percentage for the same period 0.09 to 0.18. Thus, the total trade percentages for the same tenure have been from 0.33 to 0.50. (Table 2). This dismal trade figure between India and Vietnam clearly exhibits the lack of economic mindset between the two countries to each other, since both of them producing the same products. Besides this, owing to low-cost skilled labour in Vietnam, in recent years China, the United States and Japan have invested more in the Vietnamese economy and this has naturally affected the investment flows into India in certain ways. Further, Indian companies and vice-versa failed to compete with the other foreign companies in investment to each other's domain. There was a profound feeling in Vietnamese mindset regarding New Delhi's refusal of Vietnam's proposal for a Vietnam-India Free Trade Agreement (VIFTA) in 2007, which India had signed with some other countries of ASEAN. This position of India has taken owing to huge protests from some of the southern countries like Kerala, Karnataka etc, whose agricultural and other products would suffer, both in productivity and cost of cultivation. The economic pragmatism of New Delhi through its 'Look

Table 1: India's Trade with the Socialist Republic of Vietnam: Post-Cold War Years

(Value in Rs. Crore)

Year (April-March)	Exports	Imports	Total Trade	Balance of Trade
1991-92	31.82	94.31	126.13	−62.49
1992-93	50.28	175.54	225.82	−125.26
1993-94	87.87	137.50	225.37	−49.63
1994-95	183.79	138.37	322.16	+45.42
1995-96	412.12	51.75	463.87	+360.37
1996-97	419.16	6.02	425.18	+413.14
1997-98	470.52	32.46	502.98	+438.06
1998-99	526.13	37.31	563.26	+488.82
1999-2000	668.88	49.94	718.82	+618.94
2000-01	1026.03	56.35	1082.38	+969.68
2001-02	1035.72	90.19	1125.91	+945.53
2002-03	1631.63	140.89	1772.52	+1235.56
2003-04	1876.20	175.60	2051.80	+1235.56
2004-05	2365.36	364.27	2729.63	+2001.09
2005-06	3057.86	581.69	3639.55	+2476.17
2006-07	4446.24	758.61	5204.85	3687.63
2007-08	6451.28	698.07	7149.35	5753.21
2008-09	7949.48	1862.26	9811.74	6087.22
2009-10	8673.98	2459.12	11133.10	6214.86
2010-11 (April-June)	3285.11	949.44	4234.55	2335.67

Source: Prepared by the author from various tables and pages based on *Monthly Statistics of the Foreign Trade of India*, Directorate General of Commercial Intelligence and Statistics, Ministry of Commerce, Government of India, Calcutta, Vols. I and II, Exports and Imports, Annual Numbers, April-1990 to June 2011.

East' policy, has finally put up a realistic performance in its development of relations with some economically advanced countries of Southeast Asian region (including Vietnam), when on 13 August 2009 at Bangkok, after six years of negotiations, the India-ASEAN Free Trade Agreement (FTA), as part of the Comprehensive Economic Cooperation Agreement (CECA), was finally signed. The agreement was only for trade-in-goods and did not include software and information technology. This FTA Agreement in goods will integrate the two globally important economic blocks for mutually beneficial economic gains. Under the ASEAN-India FTA, the ASEAN member countries and India would eliminate tariffs for about 4,000 products (which include

Table 2: India's Trade with Vietnam: Recent Trends

(Values in Rs. Crore)

S. No.	Year →	2005-06	2006-07	2007-08	2008-09	2009-10
1.	**Export**	3057.86	4446.24	6451.28	7949.48	8673.98
2.	% Growth		45.40	45.10	23.22	9.11
3.	India's Total Export	456417.86	571779.28	655863.52	840755.06	845533.64
4.	% Growth		25.28	14.71	28.19	0.57
5.	% Share	0.67	0.78	0.98	0.95	1.03
6.	**Import**	581.69	758.61	698.07	1862.26	2459.12
7.	% Growth		30.42	-7.98	166.77	32.05
8.	India's Total Import	660408.90	840506.31	1012311.70	1374435.55	1363735.55
9.	% Growth		27.27	20.44	35.77	-0.78
10.	% Share	0.09	0.09	0.07	0.14	0.18
11.	**Total Trade**	3639.55	5204.85	7149.35	9811.74	11133.10
12.	% Growth		43.01	37.36	37.24	13.47
13.	India's Total Trade	1116826.76	1412285.60	1668175.22	2215190.61	2209269.19
14.	% Growth		26.46	18.12	32.79	-0.27
15.	% Share	0.33	0.37	0.43	0.44	0.50
16.	**Trade Balance**	2476.17	3687.63	5753.21	6087.22	6214.86
17.	India's Trade Balance	-203991.04	-268727.03	-356448.18	-533680.50	-518201.90

Note: The country's total imports (S.No.6) since 2000-01 does not include import of Petroleum Products (27100093) and Crude Oil (27090000).

Source: http://commerce.nic.in/eidb/iecnt.asp (accessed on 24 October, 2010).

electronics, chemicals, machinery and textiles) out of which duties for 3,200 products will be reduced by December 2013, while duties on the remaining 800 products will be brought down to zero or near zero levels by December 2016 and plans to create a free-trade area with Brunei, Indonesia and Malaysia by 2011 and with the remaining ASEAN countries – the Philippines, Cambodia, Laos, Myanmar and Vietnam – by 2016, besides the pacts, agreements and FTAs already signed with Thailand and Singapore earlier. As against such background, the Government of Vietnam's earlier request to India was finally endorsed on 25 October 2009, when New Delhi granted the 'Market Economy' status to Vietnam,[39] following the Indo-ASEAN Free Trade Agreement, signed earlier the same year. Moreover, India on many occasions provided considerable assistance to Vietnam by means of commodity loans through inter-Government credit transfer to overcome the shortage of foreign exchange and the general lack of external financing which had hampered their mutual trade.

Over the years, the two-way trade between Vietnam and India is steadily on the rise, of which agricultural trade makes up a significant portion. India mainly exports to Vietnam cattle feed, mobile phones, pharmaceutical products and materials, steel and iron, textile and apparel materials and pesticides. It imports from Vietnam coal, pepper, electronic spare parts, rubber, cinnamon, machinery and equipment, bark and spices, garments and textile products and footwear. The key areas where Indian exports could make an impact in the Vietnamese market include information technology (IT) and IT training, agro and food processing, railways, energy and alternate energy, veterinary manufacturing plant, tea processing machinery, textile machinery, and power transmission and generation. The two countries have signed a number of agreements on trade cooperation, double-taxation avoidance, investment protection, consular affairs, culture, aviation and tourism, together with various other deals on mining and geology, environment and traditional medicine. So far, around 70 Indian companies in pharmaceuticals, machinery and equipment, chemicals, and agricultural materials have opened representative offices in Vietnam. As of 2010, India has 45 valid investment projects in Vietnam with a total registered capital of more than US$ 206 million, and thereby ranking 29 out of 89 countries and territories investing in Vietnam. Focuses of Indian investments are in oil and gas exploitation, mineral exploitation and processing, Sugar manufacturing, agro-chemicals, IT, and agricultural processing. TATA Group of India inked a memorandum with Vietnam Steel General Corporation to do research for the building of Ha Tinh Conjugate Steel Company and exploit Thach Khe iron mine with an output capacity of 4.5 million tons per year. It is expected to invest more than US$ 4.5 billion in the next few years. With this investment, India has become top 10 investors in Vietnam. From Vietnamese side, a Vietnamese company, FPT, has made an investment of US$ 150,000 in an Indian technology development and investment project.[40]

Besides this, like the past mindset where India had played a genuine important role for the national reconstruction of Vietnam, New Delhi since 1976 aided Vietnam through Lines of Credit extended by Department of Economic Affairs (DEA), Ministry of Finance of the Government of India. From 1976, development assistance of India to Vietnam has extended 14 Lines of Credit totaling Rs.3, 610 million. In the 1980s, Vietnam received relatively large amounts of assistance though these programmes were reduced during the 1990s. India announced another credit line of US$ 27 million to Vietnam an agreement for which was signed in August 2004 between Exim Bank of India and Ministry of Finance of Vietnam. Most recent credit line of US$ 45 million is being implemented for Nam Chien Hydropower projects in Vietnam. During the same time, India has announced an aid of Rs. 100 million to Vietnam for setting up of an Advanced Resource Centre in IT in Hanoi. Another grant of Rs. 122.07 million has also been given to Vietnam for assisting human resource development in the field of IT in six educational institutions in Vietnam, and identified areas for cooperation such as biotechnology in agriculture and healthcare, technology for new materials, IT and electronics, super-computing, nuclear energy for peaceful uses, science and technology policy making, remote sensing, non-traditional energy and so on for future cooperation.[41]

Meanwhile, both India and Vietnam agreed to strengthen cooperation in the fields of trade, investment and agricultural production, and this was approved when the Indian Minister for Food Processing Subodh Kant Sahai visited Vietnam in May 2010. During the meting with Vietnam's Minister for Agriculture and Rural Development, Cao Duc Phat, the Indian Minister expressed firm willingness to increase cooperation with Vietnam in food processing and cattle feed, saying India is capable of providing a huge resource of materials. He also called on Vietnamese enterprises to invest in food processing technology in India. This willingness from both the countries took place due to two-way trade between Vietnam and India that has been steadily on the rise owing to increase of agricultural trade in recent times. Besides, Sahai pledged favourable policies for Vietnamese investors and said India can help Vietnam by imparting training to its professionals in IT and foreign languages. The Vietnamese Minister also agreed to encourage enterprises of both sides to explore each other's markets, set up joint ventures in manufacturing and food processing industries, organize forums and trade fairs for agricultural produce and seafood in each other's markets.[42]

Another significant event, which took place in global politics in recent years, is the procurement and preservation of energy. Like China and India, Vietnam, as a leading producer of oil and gas, also has a vital place in India's quest to diversify its energy supply sources. India has been investigating overseas exploration rights and Vietnam has been a success story in this regard.[43] The ONGC Videsh Ltd. (OVL) was selected as the successful bidder in the global competitive bidding for nine offshore exploration blocks in Vietnam's 2004, and involved in exploration projects in Vietnam and signed a petroleum sharing contract with Petro-Vietnam for three blocks – 06, 12E and 19 in Nam Con Son basin, about 370 km offshore. Moreover, it also signed an MOU with Petro-Vietnam Investment and Development Company (PIDC) on 9 January 2001 for collaboration between OVL and PIDC in the exploration and production of hydrocarbons in Vietnam.[44] However, in recent years there have been diplomatic rows between the two countries on the issue of gas exploration by Petro-Vietnam and British Petroleum (BP) in the planned US$ 2-billion gas field and pipeline venture southeast of Vung Tau on the southern coast, 16 which is close to the Lan lay-Lan Do project in which ONGC is a partner. China has not been entirely contented with the presence of ONGC in the South China Sea and trying to entice Vietnamese oil companies into joint exploration so Indian companies may face stiff competition in coming years.[45] Furthermore, recently BP, which is raising capital to cover the cleanup costs of its oil spill in the Gulf of Mexico, has put many of its global assets up for sale, including an investment in the Nam Con Son basin off the southern coast of Vietnam. The Vietnam government has given approval to a consortium of state-owned Indian energy firms and Petro Vietnam to buy out BP's stake. Significantly, this large-scale natural gas project is located in an area of the Nam Con Son basin where BP announced in March 2009 that it would cease exploration in response to pressure from China.[46] However, India's Petroleum Minister, Murli Deora, in October 2010 agreed to buy BP's 35 per cent stake in the $1.3 billion Nam Con Son gas project in Vietnam.

Thus, in spite of these above-mentioned economic ties between India and Vietnam developed so far, the spiraling trade figures between them are no match to India's overall trade figures with the Southeast Asian countries. It is regrettable that despite such deep-rooted friendship, cooperation and good understanding at political and cultural levels, the economic linkages between India and Vietnam are still nominal and lack proper balance. There is a surprising lack of awareness in Vietnam on the potential of and developments made by Indian industry. The Vietnamese enterprises have failed to correctly assess the Indian markets and economic potential, while the Indian businessmen are still affected by the style of work that prevailed in the subsidy-based period and thus, show no great flair for competition in an open market system. India, which is a huge market, has been gradually opened up and liberalized, naturally demanding immense capital. But Indian investors unfortunately have concentrated mainly on the internal projects, neglecting the opportunities in foreign markets, due to a variety of reasons, of which, the most important are the similarity in their underdeveloped economic structures and silos of exports. In spite of long years of cordial bilateral relations, Vietnam believes that economic and trade cooperation with India has not matched the political and cultural links that exist between the two countries. To promote cooperation, enterprises on both sides need to reach out and approach one another for exchanging information, surveying markets and assessing cooperation possibilities between them. Thus, a concrete policy mechanism has to be evolved and perfected to encourage businessmen to increase further cooperation and trade exchanges.[47] India is a large market and is expected to be one of the most powerful economies with numerous comparative advantages, and scientific and technological prowess, particularly in IT. Likewise, Vietnam possesses abundant natural resources, industrious, dynamic and well-educated labour force and is also a promising market. The potential for bilateral cooperation is still vast and in need of further exploitation. Vietnam's current process of integration into the world economy and reforms in India are creating new opportunities to strengthen bilateral ties. To implement this process, both the countries should provide deeper insight, based on rational pragmatism, prevailing against the deadweight of bureaucratic inertia. Therefore, economics as a strategic parameter in India's 'Look East' Vietnam policy has not been properly tapped and utilized in the visage of challenges posed by globalization, the menace of international terrorism and a realm of other significant disorders of the international system.

Bridging the Development Gap among Old and New ASEAN Members

One of the important initiatives that India has taken with reference of its 'Look East' policy has been its active participation in the Initiative for ASEAN Integration (IAI) programme – a regional framework for development of integration and cooperation – aimed at narrowing the development gap mainly with the Cambodia, Laos, Myanmar and Vietnam (CLMV) countries within ASEAN and enhancing regional integration. While respecting the Singapore Prime Minister, Goh Chok Tong's proposal of IAI taken in the Fourth Informal Summit in November 2000, at Singapore, India, being a responsible 'Dialogue Partner' of ASEAN, actively played a very constructive role in the process. India has successfully completed the "Railway Training Programmes" for 48 trainers from CLMV countries in India. In addition, New Delhi is presently implementing a project, namely "India-Singapore Joint

Training Programme for CLMV in English Language Training" and has been involved in an Entrepreneurial Development project in each of the CLMV countries. The objective of this project is for India to provide technical and advisory services to these countries for the establishment of Entrepreneurial Development Institutes in each of these countries, as part of efforts to train entrepreneurs and prepare small enterprises that face the challenges of globalization. So far, New Delhi has already established Entrepreneurship Development Centres in Cambodia, Laos and Vietnam, and in Myanmar it will be set up very soon.[48] Moreover, through this IAI programme, India has set up English Language Teaching Centres in Da Nang province in central Vietnam. Under the framework of India-Vietnam Protocol on IT, Vietnam receives Indian assistance for training its manpower in the area of IT and other enabled services. However, to make the bilateral cooperation in the field of human resources development more effective, in February 2007, the Vietnam-India Action Plan for 2007-09 was concluded between Vietnam's Deputy Prime Minister and Foreign Minister, Pham Gia Khiem and his Indian counterpart, Pranab Mukherjee.[49] The ASEAN countries have looked upon this active focus of New Delhi on the IAI programme as a sign of India's commitment to play a positive role in ASEAN's regional initiatives and its processes.

India-Vietnam Ties: South China as the Motivating Vigor

In recent times, a new confrontation has once again evolved between China and Vietnam over the Spratly Islands in the South China Sea. Both China and Vietnam are making claims over the strategically as well as economically important 200 islands of Spartly. There have been several brief naval skirmishes in the past 30 years between them and that has been temporarily eased following the signing of ASEAN initiated Code of Conduct by the disputing parties with reference to these Islands. The rivalry with China has manifested in similar ways for New Delhi, with implications for India's strategic and economic interests in Vietnam. Recently, China raised strong objections to Indian OVL exploration activities in two Vietnamese oil blocks in the South China Sea. China has said that unless its permission is taken for the exploration in blocks 127 and 128, the activity is illegal. The reason for China's objection seems to be more than dispute with Vietnam as China itself is engaged with the Philippines and Vietnam for joint exploitation of petroleum resources in the said disputed area. India and China have been close competitors for oil blocks all over the globe though they also have some joint collaboration in oil exploration activities in Russia, Sudan, and some other countries of the world. With such competition for energy resources and regional power pie in the background, the India-Vietnamese relationship would inevitably be driven by the need for a common hedge against China. Furthermore, the recent movements of Indian Navy in the South China Sea and New Delhi's assistance in shoring up of Vietnam's naval and air capabilities in an attempt to deny China total supremacy in the region have highly dissatisfied the Chinese leadership. The origin of this Chinese dissatisfaction was mainly mooted owing to Indian armed forces' frequent help in order to overcome Vietnam's operational difficulties by supplying it with spare parts to upgrade the 125 MIG-21 planes of the Vietnamese Air Force, with enhanced avionics and radar systems. Besides this, the Indian Air Force pilots have also trained Vietnamese fighter pilots, and in 2005, the Indian Navy dispatched more than 150 tonnes of spares to Hanoi for its Russian Petya and OSA-11 class missile boats, in addition to the engagement in joint patrols of the Indian and Vietnamese coast guards and continuing joint exercises of the two navies have further added fuel to fire.[50] This fire was further augmented when a flotilla of Indian warships completed its month-long visit to the Pacific, mainly to Australia, Indonesia, Singapore and Vietnam in recent times, and thereby has largely alarmed China and quietly put in place India's own counter measures to woo and bolster China's neighbours as a long-term strategy.[51] Thus, New Delhi's naval deployment, based on its policy of 'Look East' and the Quadrilateral grouping naturally dissatisfied the Chinese hegemonic naval mindset in the region and for that, strategic partnership between India and Vietnam would remain the main cornerstone of the present phase of Indo-Vietnam relations.

Points of Discord between India and Vietnam

If you go through India's relation with Vietnam in the post-Cold War years, it is clearly reflected that most of the times, the relations have been sweet in nature. But this does not mean that the bilateral ties were smooth in its entirety. Following the Vietnamese Prime Minister, Nguyen Tan Dung's visit to India in July 2007, both the countries signed a Joint Declaration on establishing a bilateral strategic partnership. Since then, in many spheres, India has given Vietnam prime importance in its overall 'Look East' policy. But, the Vietnamese government expressed its dissatisfaction about India's lack of occasional commitment to supply some of the missile systems as agreed by the BJP government to modernize Vietnam's military. It was committed by

New Delhi during the BJP government's tenure that it would gift Vietnam with the Prithvi and BrahMos missile systems, in order to counter Chinese naval dominance in the South China Sea and greatly aid Vietnam in its strategy of sea denial and coastal defence. Unfortunately, India failed to maintain its commitment based on two important reasons and they were: first, the Congress government has increasingly focused on economic rather than military cooperation with Vietnam, and thereby, has tried not to antagonize its immediate neighbour, China, with which New Delhi is evolving better ties. Secondly, some felt that the BrahMos must first be fully inducted into the Indian Armed Forces before a surplus can be generated for friendly states such as Vietnam. As against such reasons, Vietnam had procured 100 SMG-PK 9 mm submachine guns and 50 sniper rifles from the state-run Pakistan Ordnance Factories (POF) in Rawalpindi in 2007, in a veiled but nevertheless significant expression of its displeasure to New Delhi.[52] This action of Vietnam, to some extent, frustrated the Indian leadership but was finally erased from the Indian mindset on the perception that Vietnam has procured these arms in the context of the growing Chinese presence in the South China Sea.

Conclusion

Having discussed the trajectory of Indo-Vietnam relations from the Cold War to the post-Cold War years, it is evident that India's ties with Vietnam during the Cold War years were exclusively determined by contemporary politics. However, in the post-Cold War years, the sudden fall of the former Soviet Union, led to the entire global strategic, political and economic centre of gravity to shift from the Euro-Atlantic region to Asia with special reference to Southeast and East Asia. India, in the context of the new-fangled worldwide arrangement, radically altered its foreign policy design from political rhetoric to economic imperative, based on the New Economic and 'Look East' policies and extended its strategic lash both with East and West. In the East, no other countries are more deserving for nurturing strategic partnership than Vietnam, which has the potential of being a regional power on the eastern fringes of Asia with a long sea board on the South China Sea, besides having extensive convergence of strategic interests with India. Along with Myanmar, in Southeast Asia, India should build up a strategic partnership with Vietnam, since both have ample areas of communion of geo-strategic configuration. New Delhi, through it 'Look East' policy has quietly developed institutional and economic linkages with the developed ASEAN members and had temporarily soft-pedaled its historical links and Cold War 'Look East' Vietnam friend. However, this lack of initiative was short-lived. Presently, both have pragmatically realized the essentiality of geo-strategic importance of the Asia Pacific region, due to the galloping economic development and increasing strategic presence of China in the region. In such a tactical environment, while making all efforts towards keeping China peacefully engaged in the Asia Pacific region, India and Vietnam realistically comprehended to work towards building a bilateral strategic partnership based on the convergence of interests and expediency. In thinking so, India has again given paramount importance as much to its economic interests as well as national security and strategic imperatives towards Vietnam, which according to Atal Behari Vajpayee, "[It] is not Look East. It is re-look East."[53] From New Delhi's point of view, India's politico-strategic partnership with Vietnam seems more than what is recognized as desirable at present. Among other things, it would balance the Sino-Pakistan strategic linkages, for which Vietnam, according to Atal Behari Vajpayee, was a "critical element" in India's plans to forge stronger ties with ASEAN. "It is pivotal for our 'Look East' policy", he said.[54] Similarly, Vietnam's present outlook in the context of the New World Order is to strengthen its economic position at the internal level on the one hand, and evolve better ties with those countries, with which its strategic interests have been tagged, on the other. As against such background, Hanoi has already recognized New Delhi as a global player and believes that increased synchronization with India will be strategically important in this New Global Order. This doable strategic partnership needs to be unwarily nurtured and sustained on a long-term basis, rather than on tactical expediency.

India and Vietnam, after a decade of economic, political and diplomatic investments towards the developed countries of Southeast Asia have learnt a lesson that they still have not yet spouted the enormous potential of open markets of one another for mutual benefits. India has no territorial problems with Vietnam. The Indo-Vietnam relations are a product of historical understanding, quite independent of time and any government cannot invert that subjective realism; whatever may be its ideological view in the changing world order. They must plan on keeping things in such a way that more vigorous trade and commercial links with each other are pragmatically implemented. India, through its emerging economic clout and strategic potential in the Asian region, needs to execute its 'Look East' Vietnam policy in such a manner, which might ultimately impel Vietnam not to look towards the West. India, in spite of its decade of various diplomatic interactions towards the developed countries of Southeast and East Asia, has suffered from a partial corneal cataract towards the emerging Vietnamese market, which has been tapped by many countries, rather than being harnessed by India for its strategic-economic benefit. Needless to say, this optimistic attitude and initiative needs to be sustained without losing track of the core objectives. In doing so, New Delhi should follow a more pragmatic, premeditated and vision-oriented 'Look East' Vietnam policy, in order to spawn greater space to contrive and rebuild the old historical, cultural, political and economic linkages in the years to come.

NOTES

1. Tridib Chakraborti, "India-Vietnam Relations: A Time Tested Look East Friendship," *Jadavpur Journal of International Relations*, Vol. 6, 2001-02, Jadavpur University, Kolkata, pp. 239-240.
2. *Vietnam Courier* (Hanoi), No. 1, January 1986, p. 4.
3. Tridib Chakraborti, n.1, pp. 240-42.
4. Tridib Chakraborti, "Strategic Convergence between India and Vietnam in the Twenty-first Century: 'Look East' as a Parameter", *India Foreign Affairs Journal*, (New Delhi), Vol. 3, No.4, October-December 2008, p. 40.
5. Tridib Chakraborti, *India and Kampuchea: A Phase in Their Relations—1978-81*, Minerva Associates, Calcutta, 1985, p. 89.
6. Tridib Chakraborti, "From National Reconstruction to Market Economy: Space and Time Analysis of India's Look East Vietnam Policy" *in P.V. Rao (ed), India and ASEAN:* Partners at Summit, *Knowledge* World Publishers, New Delhi, 2008, p. 321
7. Tridib Chakraborti, n. 5, p. 127.
8. Tridib Chakraborti, "India's Southeast Asia Policy in the 1980s and 1990s: Contrasting Shades in Foreign Policy Priorities", *Jadavpur Journal of International Relations*, Vol. I, 1995, Jadavpur University, Calcutta, p. 147.
9. Tridib Chakraborti, n.1, p. 243.
10. Tridib Chakraborti, "India's Economic Support to Socialist Vietnam: An Aspect of India's Foreign Policy", in A. Lakshmana Chetty (ed.), *The States of Indochina: Stability, Development and Foreign Relations*, Centre for Studies on Indochina, Sri Venkateswara University, Tirupati, Andhra Pradesh, 1997, p. 45.
11. Tridib Chakraborti, n. 8, p. 155.
12. Tridib Chakraborti, "India and Vietnam: A New Dimension in South-South Economic Cooperation", *Asian Studies* (Calcutta), Vol. 8, April-June 1990, pp. 55-56.
13. G.V.C. Naidu, "India and ASEAN", *Strategic Analysis*, Vol. 19, No. 1, IDSA, April 1996, pp. 69-72.
14. For details see http://www.aseansec.org/15268htm (accessed on December 16, 2010).

15. For details see Brian McCartan, "A helping Chinese hand", April 30, 2009, http://www.atimes.com/atimes/Southeast_Asia/KD30Ae01.html (accessed on 26/10/2010).

16. Lan Jianxue, "Post-Cold War Sino-Indian Relations: Normalization and Strategic Harmony", *South Asian Studies*, No. 2, 2005, pp. 9-10.

17. Wei Ling, "On Indian Security Strategy and Sino-Indian Security Relations', *Journal of People's University of China*, No. 6, 2005, pp. 95–105.

18. C. Raja Mohan, 'India and the Balance of Power', *Foreign Affairs*, July/August 2006.

19. For detailed speech of Manmohan Singh, 'Prime Minister's Speech on the Occasion of 60th Anniversary of India's Independence', 15 August 2007, New Delhi, see http://pmindia.nic.in/speeches.htm

20. Tridib Chakraborti, n. 6, p. 327.

21. Ibid., pp. 326-27.

22. For detail speech see 28. See, meadev.nic.in/govt/part-qu/rajyasabha/aug2-163.htm (accessed on 22 November, 2010).

23. *The Dawn*, 18 June 2001.

24. *The Pioneer* (New Delhi), 8 September 1994; also see *The Hindu*, 8 September 1994.

25. *The Times of India*, 3 August 1997.

26. Man Mohan, "India Vietnam Expand Defense Cooperation", *The Times of India*, 29 March 2000.

27. Tridib Chakraborti, n. 4, p.45.

28. *Nhan Dan*, 7 July 2007.

29. http://www.india-defence.com/reports-3652 (accessed on 22 October, 2010)

30. *Nhan Dan*, 26 June 2010.

31. For details see Sitanshu Kar, "Bilateral Defence Cooperation between India and Vietnam" http://www.indiastrategic.in/topstories776.htm (accessed on 22 October, 2010).

32. For details see http://indiadefenceonline.com/2256/india-to-boost-ties-with-vietnam/ (accessed on 22 October, 2010).

33. For details, see http://www.defence.pk/forums/india-defence/76430-india-vietnam-expand-defence-cooperation-covering-all-three-services.html (accessed on 22 October 2010).

34. For details see news.rediff.com/column/2010/oct/07/co (accessed on 22 October 2010).

35. *The Indian Express*, 17 August 1988.

36. Tridib Chakraborti, n. 6, pp. 328-329.

37. For details, see http://www.pib.nic.in/archive/pm_visit_iv/indoiv.html (accessed on 22 October 2010).

38. Tridib Chakraborti, n. 6, p. 329.

39. For details see http://www.thaindian.com/newsportal/world-news/india-grants-market-economy status-to-vietnam_100265515.html (accessed on 22 October 2010).

40. For details see www.commodityonline.com/news/India-Vi...(accessed on 22 October 2010).

41. For details see http://www.indembassy.com.vn/tabid/72/default.aspx...(accessed on 25 October 2010).
42. For details see www.commodityonline.com/news/India-Vi...(accessed on 22 October 2010).
43. For details see http://www.ongcvidesh.com/op_vietnam.asp (Accessed October 25, 2010). Also see http://www.mofa.gov.vn/en/nr040807104143/nr040807105001/ns050413105103/view (Accessed 25 October 2010).
44. Tridib Chakraborti, n. 4, p. 51.
45. For details see Pankaj K. Jha, 'India-Vietnam Relations: Need for Enhanced Cooperation', *Strategic Analysis,* Vol. 32, Issue 6, November 2008 , pp. 1085-1099.
46. For details see http://thehanoist.wordpress.com/2010/07/29/vietnam-hedges-its-china-risk/ (Accessed 25 October, 2010).
47. Bui Cong Quac, "Some Thoughts on India-Vietnam Relations", *Vietnam*, New Delhi, 2000, pp. 6-7.
48. Tridib Chakraborti, "The Distance-Proximity Paradox: Unravelling India's ASEAN Policy over Three Decades", in Anjali Ghosh, Tridib Chakraborti, Anindyo J. Majumdar, and Shibashis Chatterjee (eds.), *India's Foreign Policy*, Pearson, New Delhi, 2009, p. 294.
49. Tridib Chakraborti, n. 4, p. 52.
50. For details see FN http://www.defencetalk.com/forums/military-strategy-tactics/india-vietnamstrategic-partnership-9559... (accessed on 12 December 2010).
51. For details, see S.N. Sachdeva, "Undoing China's String of Pearls", 22 October 2010, http://www.navhindtimes.in/opinion/undoing-china-s-string-pearls (accessed on 24 November 2010).
52. For details see http://www.defencetalk.com/forums/military-strategy-tactics/india-vietnam-strategic-partnership-9559 (accessed on 24 November 2010).
53. *The Week*, 28 January 2001.
54. *The Hindu*, 10 January 2001.

Index